Economic Conversion

Economic Conversion

REVITALIZING AMERICA'S ECONOMY

Edited by
Suzanne Gordon and Dave McFadden

Ballinger Publishing Company • Cambridge, Massachusetts
A Subsidiary of Harper & Row, Publishers, Inc.

International Standard Book Number: 0–88730–012–X (CL)
0–88410–967–4 (PB)

Library of Congress Catalog Card Number: 84–12300

Printed in the United States of America

Library of Congress Cataloging in Publication Data

Main entry under title:

Economic conversion.

Bibliography: p. 241
Includes index.
1. Disarmament—Economic aspects—United States—
Addresses, essays, lectures. 2. Disarmament—Economic
aspects—Addresses, essays, lectures. I. Gordon,
Suzanne, 1945-   . II. McFadden, Dave.
HC110.D4E385   1984   338.973   84–12300
ISBN 0–88410–967–4

For
Alexandra and Alexander

Contents

List of Tables

Acknowledgments

We would like to thank our colleagues for their fine contributions to this book, and to express our gratitude to all those conversion campaigners around the world whose energy and courage have produced an exciting movement for real social and economic change. Finally, we would like to thank Sidney Shapiro and the Max and Anna Levinson Foundation for the moral and financial support that has helped make this book possible.

Introduction

Suzanne Gordon and Dave McFadden

Most Americans are unfamiliar with the concept of economic conversion. Mention it and the standard response is, "Conversion? What's that?" Even many social change activists who are aware of the concept of conversion planning tend to view it as peripheral to their main political concerns. For example, when a prominent liberal advocate of the National Nuclear Weapons Freeze campaign spoke recently to a well-heeled gathering of freeze supporters in Cambridge, Massachusetts, he was asked what he thought about efforts to find jobs for defense workers who might lose theirs if the arms race were halted or military spending reduced. Any job losses resulting from the implementation of a nuclear freeze, he responded, will be "insignificant" when compared with the "major unemployment problem" created by a nuclear war.

Although there are some exceptions, a great many peace activists share this point of view. When compared with the immediate need to prevent a nuclear holocaust, working to convert military production facilities to socially useful forms of production seems to be a rather secondary or long-term strategy. And so, at best, conversion is considered something someone else should be concerned about—a matter better left, for example, to activists in the labor movement.

Ironically, when conversion is discussed in labor circles, it is frequently seen as a peace issue. "It's hard to bring up conversion," said one progressive labor leader recently, "because people think it means being soft on the Russians. It's just too hot for some unions to handle." Because conversion has been so closely associated with attempts to alleviate unemployment among defense workers, even many sympathetic union activists feel it has little relevance to other segments of the labor movement. "Why should I bother with conversion?" one female president of a service sector local union asked, when invited to attend a labor meeting on conversion. "I represent mostly blacks, and women workers in hospitals, not highly skilled, white, male military workers."

If labor groups think conversion is a peace issue and peace groups consider conversion a labor issue, many industrial policy planners tend not to think about conversion at all. They document and bemoan the distorting effects of military spending on the U.S. economy and recommend cuts in the excessive Pentagon budget. But few industrial policy planners understand that conversion is a job-creating strategy that can help transform industries involved in civilian as well as military production. Similarly, those policy planners who argue for a "democratic" industrial policy often fail to grasp that conversion is a means of insuring that the democratic planning they advocate actually involves working people themselves, rather than just technocrats of a more liberal persuasion.

Finally, conversion is sadly unrecognized as a strategy that can also address the needs of those active in groups working for economic justice and a clean environment for all. More than any others, perhaps, activists who campaign for minority rights, better housing, social welfare programs, and environmental protection are unaware of the promise and richness of economic conversion.

In short, the key groups that should be most involved in the conversion debate and in the movement to enact conversion legislation—organized labor, the peace movement, left-liberal industrial policy planners, and the economic justice communities—are often the least involved.

That this should be true is particularly unfortunate when one considers the problems that both the United States and other industrialized economies confront today. In all the countries in the West, basic industry is in decline. Despite a modest economic recovery in 1984, factories continue to close, unemployment levels remain high, and the general quality of life and standard of living erodes further. As Seymour Melman points out in his contribution to this collection, the consequences for ordinary citizens and the economy as a whole are devastating.

Unfortunately, the solution many countries offer to these economic problems is an escalation in military production and military spending. Although, as Robert DeGrasse, Jr., explains, the notion that this will benefit, rather than harm, society is no more than a myth, the military continues to consume an increasing share of the research and development and productive capital and federal budget dollars of governments in the West. With the United States leading in military spending, the most recent Reagan administration proposals for fiscal year 1985 include a requested 13 percent increase in the military budget, bringing the amount spent on the military to $305 billion for the year beginning October 1984. This kind of military escalation, Lance Compa persuasively demonstrates in his essay on the military and labor, is all too often supported by precisely those people whom it hurts the most—working people and the unions that represent them.

It is because the problems of both economic decline and military expansion are so urgent that it is necessary to demonstrate the relevance of conversion planning to all those interested in creating a more just economic order and in eliminating the threat of total planetary destruction. This means not only working for conversion but also defining conversion in a compelling and convincing way.

✓   Conversion, as it has been classically defined, describes the process through which military production facilities are transformed into civilian production facilities. Because of the link between job creation and military spending, it is a critical strategy for those interested in reducing defense dependency and working for disarmament. As Philip Webre and Doyle Niemann have written:

> There have been a variety of efforts in recent years to transfer money from the military budget to the civilian budget. While these efforts have much to recommend them, it is important to note that the mere transference of funds from military to civilian production is not an adequate conversion strategy. Dollar for dollar, civilian spending generally creates more jobs than a comparable amount of military spending, but there is no guarantee these jobs will go to workers displaced by military spending reductions. . . . Without a guarantee of new production in place of present military production, defense contractors, their employees, and the communities dependent upon them will have little choice but to continue to resist, with every resource at their command, any cutback in spending, regardless of whether that spending is consistent with national security needs.

Thus, conversion attempts to reemploy workers in the same industries and, wherever possible, factories in which they previously worked. By initiating a thorough survey of workers' skills, existing plant and equipment, and conducting an equally extensive exploration of new and existing markets—locally, regionally, nationally, and internationally—management, workers and their unions, and community groups can identify profitable civilian product lines that, optimally, require a minimal amount of retooling and retraining. The most well-publicized conversion effort in recent memory took place both in the United States and Great Britain after World War II. When massive numbers of soldiers were demobilized and demand for military products slackened, large and small companies in both countries either *reconverted* from wartime production or branched out into new manufacturing areas. Conversion is the term commonly used to describe this process of immediate postwar corporate diversification.

Because the *reconversion* of industry after the war took place in an entirely different technological context, as Lloyd Dumas explains in his essay on conversion legislation, the kind of conversion activity underway today cannot use the immediate postwar conversion as its guide. Instead, conversion efforts in the United States draw their inspiration from more recent conversion experiments. In this country, the most widespread conversion efforts were undertaken by the Pentagon's Office of Economic Adjustment (OEA), established in the early 1960s. This office was mandated to assist communities faced with military base closings to plan and develop economic projects that would provide jobs for displaced workers. Over twenty years, nearly one and a half times as many jobs have been created as were lost due to the OEA's successful advance conversion planning.

Perhaps the most important and well-known conversion campaign, however, originated not in the United States but in Great Britain. Developed in the mid-seventies, the Lucas Corporate Plan – described by Hilary Wainwright and Dave Elliott in Chapter Seven – resulted from a campaign conducted by workers at Lucas Aerospace, Europe's largest aerospace manufacturer, to avert the firm's planned layoffs of thousands of employees. Representing workers at seventeen plants who belonged to thirteen different unions, the Lucas Shop Stewards Combine Committee drew up a comprehensive 1,200-page plan for the alternate use of their job skills and plant equipment in the production of 150 different socially useful products that would keep the entire work force fully employed.

Because postwar conversion efforts, the Lucas Plan, and the OEA have centered around military production facilities, conversion has become linked almost exclusively with the transformation of military industries. Conversion is, however, far more than a solution to the problem of overdependence on military production. It is a model that can be enormously effective when applied to any production facility whose product is no longer in demand, or competitive on national or international markets. When management decides to discontinue a particular product line or shut down an entire factory – laying off hundreds or thousands of workers in the process – the same skill auditing, product researching, designing and production planning techniques used in the development of the Lucas Plan can be employed to propose production alternatives to management and thus maintain or even create jobs. This broad definition of conversion, as the chapter on European conversion activity elaborates, presents conversion as a job-creating strategy that unions and workers can use to fight the kind of structural unemployment that is increasingly common in Western industrialized societies. It can also, as Clyde Sanger argues in "The West and the Rest," help free up financial resources for developing countries that are adversely affected by the skewed budgetary priorities of the industrialized world.

Conversion, thus defined, might seem to be no more than another form of corporate diversification. While economic conversion can result in new or more varied product lines, it is dramatically different from the kind of diversification corporations themselves routinely initiate. Conversion, as we define it, is initiated and influenced by workers and communities rather than by management alone. In many instances, conversion planning has become the primary tool used to wean employers away from their dependence on highly profitable, risk-free military production, or to force nonmilitary manufacturers to consider making new products and thus keep factories open and workers and communities thriving.

Unlike traditional corporate diversification, moreover, conversion is not merely a strategy that prevents job loss. Conversion advocates are as concerned with what is produced and how goods are produced as they are in job creation and maintenance. These concerns are reflected in the concept of socially useful production: What products does a community really need? What kind of production options will enhance quality—not just quantity—of life? How can governments be induced to spend money researching, developing, and then purchasing products that are useful to a wide range of community groups and that serve a wide range of community needs? How can workers begin to feel that they are creating and producing useful goods, not simply wasteful goods?

These are the questions workers at Lucas Aerospace asked; and they are, Joel Yudken explains, the questions thousands of other workers in the United States—like those at McDonnell-Douglas—are increasingly posing. Their answer is an unequivocal rejection of the current options available to many industrial workers who are forced to choose between unemployment and military employment, or between alienating jobs and underemployment. Conversion advocates therefore recognize that the conversion process must help working people and their communities frame a new series of choices and that these must be centered around the concept of socially useful production, rather than production that merely serves the profit requirements of corporate managers.

To insure that decent employment serving a broad range of community interests is the result of conversion experiments requires a great deal of planning. As the essay on technology excerpted from the International Association of Machinists book *Let's Rebuild America* suggests, conversion schemes will never succeed in eradicating unemployment or producing nonalienating work if workers do not seriously reflect upon the technical ramifications of their work. This means doing more than seeking out sympathetic technical experts who will explain that a particular plant can produce a new line of products: It means examining the very production processes to be used in any new alternative production scheme. For if new technologies are not to further increase unemployment or rob workers of vital skills, great attention must be paid to the kind of technology utilized in the production of any alternative products. Similarly, as Lloyd Dumas, Kenneth Geiser and David Gold explain, conversion will necessitate far greater acceptance of the concept of national planning. In both "The Military Economy" and "Undoing the Iron Triangle," Robert DeGrasse and Gordon Adams convincingly demonstrate the extent to which planning is already an established part of America's economic system. The problem, of course, is that some of the most active economic planners in the country are Pentagon officials and the constituency they serve is an elite of military contractors. To institute truly democratic planning requires a radical change in the country's economic decisionmaking process and greater participation of the communities' economic planning affects.

All the essays in this book argue that conversion is a way to encourage this change. It is, moreover, a unique strategy. While many current left-liberal critiques focus on what is wrong with our nation's economy and offer theoretical solutions, conversion stresses the positive and the possible. Instead of merely complaining about plant closings and unemployment, conversion advocates can propose workable plans for creating jobs and keeping plants open. Instead of working to protect a dwindling pool of jobs, labor/conversion campaigners can propose ways to create new jobs. Instead of lamenting the fact that arms factories produce only "weapons of death," conversion advocates can develop concrete production alternatives that meet real human needs. The chapters on the Lucas Plan, McDonnell Douglas, and European conversion activity describe some of the production alternatives available. "One of the least problems we face," Seymour Melman has said, "is discovering what useful work is to be done."

Why then is conversion planning not more widespread? What will it take to make the conversion movement a more potent force for real change?

What it will take, argue the chapters on strategies for change, is people—alliances of the key groups most affected by current economic policies and increases in military spending. Past conversion proposals, for example, faltered because they were almost exclusively the theoretical constructs of economists, academicians, or politicians and had little or no support within labor or the community. Beginning in 1973, Senator George McGovern introduced conversion legislation in nearly every session of Congress, but this legislation failed, in great part, because it lacked support from trade unions and community organizations. Only the McKinney-Dodd conversion amendments to the Public Works Bill of 1979 began to attract broader support because they were developed in conjunction with the International Association of Machinists and five other national unions.

Fortunately, conversion initiatives today are coming from those hardest hit by current economic and military policies. Inspired by the Lucas Model, the Machinists union has begun to help shop stewards plan the future formation of alternative use committees in a number of factories, as Gene Carroll reports in his chapter on "Getting Labor Involved." The United Electrical Workers Union is promoting conversion plans in plants where its members are threatened by closings and layoffs, and a large United Auto Workers local in California is actively working with the community-based Mid-Peninsula Conversion Project to influence military-contracting policies of the McDonnell Douglas Corporation. The national nuclear weapons freeze campaign has voted to support conversion and is lobbying for a new conversion bill introduced by Congressman Nicholas Mavroules (D–MA). Similarly, more environmental and community activists, says Kenneth Geiser, now recognize the value of integrating conversion strategies into their work and, John Ullmann counsels, even some businessmen and women can be persuaded to consider the wisdom of conversion planning.

While all these developments are encouraging, they are only a beginning. Despite some labor support for conversion and some plans to begin creating alternative use committees, it is only now that national labor unions are founding alternative use committees in the United States. And although some members of the peace movement are valiantly working to promote conversion, as we have seen, the peace movement as a whole has yet to appreciate the importance of conversion or the need to link peace activity to labor struggles for jobs and job security.

In order to succeed in its goals, the conversion movement must attempt to forge a new alliance of groups that have worked together only infrequently in the past. Organized labor is central to any successful conversion alliance, just as it is central to the success of any disarmament campaign. This is true because the union movement—in spite of its weaknesses—has a high level of organization and great strength in certain areas of the country, and has great political power. Because of this, labor played a key role in past successful coalitions for civil rights and social legislation. While labor has not always taken the lead in these struggles, no victory was possible without its participation.

Just as campaigns for conversion legislation have foundered because labor has not been sufficiently involved, so too local conversion and disarmament campaigns have not been successful when their advocates have neglected issues of employment security vital to the workers affected. During the campaign against the B-1 bomber in the early seventies, for example, activists talked about conversion, job security, and alternative production. Nonetheless, the legislation introduced in Congress as part of an anti–B-1 effort would have cut off money for the fighter-plane without making any provision for the workers whose jobs would have been eliminated as a result. Military contractors, not surprisingly, were able to point to this weakness to convince unions and their members to lobby for B-1 appropriations and were thus able to overcome all opposition to this costly and questionable weapons program.

This past year, military contractors were able to conduct a similar lobbying campaign that seriously undercut the goals of the disarmament movement. After many legislators voted for a nuclear freeze, for example, they also approved funding for the MX missile program. In and around Boston and New York, the same congressmen and senators who supported the freeze also joined competing local coalitions formed to convince the Navy to base the battleship *Iowa*—armed with nuclear-tipped cruise missiles—in their respective harbors. Much support for the Navy on this issue was not based on defense needs, but on the need for jobs. The port that got the *Iowa* was, supposedly, guaranteed thousands of them.

If conversion plans or conversion legislation had already been in place, politicians and labor unions might have taken very different positions on the "military questions" involved in the battleship *Iowa* siting decision and funding for the MX missile. But such plans and legislation must be pushed by a peace movement that takes economic justice issues seriously and a labor movement that takes peace issues equally seriously. Do we, as Gene Carroll suggests, place a higher priority on full employment issues and job security protections? Or do we, as some freeze advocates seem to imply, leave it to someone else? For their part, as Christopher Allen asks in his comparative essay on trade union attitudes toward social change and the state, do labor unions in this country begin to take peace issues seriously as well? Or will the labor movement continue to work merely to protect its dwindling ranks and contribute very little to building a broad movement for fundamental social change?

The answers to these and other questions are not simple. Indeed, as the essays in this book argue, the debate and political struggle about them must be waged on many different fronts. National legislation is clearly necessary, but actual conversion of military industries will, most likely, only result from a truly mass movement that forces legislators to curb the kind of waste and profiteering that so clearly pervades the military procurement process. While disarmament, conversion, and labor activists generate grass roots pressure for such a national shift in economic policy, conversion experiments can and must be carried out at local levels. Many of these local experiments will do no more than slow the process of reverse conversion—the abandonment of civilian product lines in favor of military production; others may facilitate factory conversion in nonmilitary situations, thus providing persuasive evidence that workers and communities can develop the capability to formulate their own investment and production plans.

The movement, we have said, is just beginning, but its promise is great. In producing concrete proposals for alternative production, and an alternative role for the majority of Americans, it can produce the goods that help create not only jobs but — more importantly — a model of a society that values peace and justice as well.

PART I

The Scope of the Problem

1

The Military Economy

Robert W. DeGrasse, Jr.

The economic aspects of arms spending have often dominated questions of national security. Considering the amount of public funds spent on the military, this is hardly surprising. In fiscal year 1983, the national defense budget will be $214.8 billion, which is 26.7 percent of the total federal budget and 6.7 percent of the expected gross national product (GNP).[1] Expenditures of this magnitude can have substantial impacts. For example, cuts in military procurement as the Vietnam War wound down left many people unemployed in heavily defense-dependent areas such as Seattle, Santa Clara County in California, and the Route 128 area around Boston. Yet during the war, rapidly increasing arms spending produced an inflationary surge that hurt the entire nation.

Decisions regarding which weapon to build or where to locate a military base should be determined by our security needs. Very often, however, these choices are strongly influenced by economics. Four recent occurrences illustrate this point. Item one: During a campaign trip to Columbus, Ohio, last fall, President Reagan warned that support for the nuclear freeze could hurt the local economy because it would mean cancelling the B-1B bomber, which is partly manufactured in that area.[2] Item two: At the same time, highly visible Democratic Congressional candidates were calling for cuts in the military budget because they believed that rapid growth in Pentagon spending hurts the economy. Item three: Not long before the 1982 elections, Congress was the scene of a pitched battle over who should supply the Air Force with new transport planes. Members of Congress from Washington state fought to have Seattle's Boeing Company awarded the contract, while members from Georgia worked to keep the project in their state at Lockheed.[3] Item four: During the December 1982 Congressional debate over cutting one of the two nuclear aircraft carriers from the Pentagon's budget, numerous members defended the program because it would create employment in America's

Excerpted from Robert W. DeGrasse, Jr., *Military Expansion, Economic Decline* (New York: The Council on Economic Priorities, 1983).

3

industrial heartland. One member went so far as to call the aircraft carrier program a "jobs bill."[4]

Before World War II, the notion that economic benefits sprang from military spending had little currency. To the contrary, most people saw military spending as an impediment to economic growth, justified only in wartime. Arms production during World War II began to change that perception as it helped propel the United States out of the Great Depression. Military spending, financed by massive federal deficits, solved the double-digit unemployment that plagued the economy throughout the 1930s.

Keynesian economics provided a theoretical basis for claims that military spending can be good for the economy. It explained how the war helped end the depression. "Keynesian" economic logic was often employed during key debates over military policy in the cold war, affirming not only its intellectual but also its political power.

An internal administration document, written during 1949, developed the rationale for the initial cold war buildup. National Security Council Memorandum (NSC) 68, produced by an ad hoc committee of State and Defense Department officials under the leadership of Paul Nitze, called for a massive military buildup to "contain" the Soviet Union. The memorandum also challenged the traditional view that military spending was harmful to the economy:

> From the point of view of the economy as a whole, the [military build-up] might not result in a real decrease in the standard of living, for the economic effects of the program might be to increase the gross national product by more than the amount being absorbed for additional military and foreign assistance purposes.[5]

While the economic benefits were not the central justification for the buildup, Nitze thoroughly discussed the contents with the administration's leading Keynesian economist, Leon Keyserling, who expressed "full agreement" with the economics of NSC 68.[6] During the post-Sputnik debate over the "missile gap" in the late 1950s, Keynesian economics was again invoked to counter traditional economic logic.

While the economic problems of the Vietnam War years eroded the public perception that military spending is good for the economy, the World War II experience has still not been forgotten. Nor have most Americans forgotten that the nation prospered through much of the cold war when military budgets were high. Thus, when President Reagan took office in 1981 promising to revitalize the economy and rearm America, many people viewed these two goals as complementary.

Administration officials, most prominently Secretary of Defense Weinberger, have nurtured this notion among numerous audiences.[7] The

Reagan administration, which promised to curtail the Keynesian role of government, has drawn heavily from Keynes to help justify their military buildup. Secretary Weinberger has claimed that military spending is a better way to stimulate the economy than transfer payments. He has also asserted that cutting the military budget during a recession will cost the economy 35,000 jobs per billion dollars of reductions.[8]

In making those claims, however, the Reagan administration has ignored the short- and long-term "opportunity cost" of a massive peacetime military buildup. Will increased arms production create more jobs than other forms of spending? On balance, will it help or hinder efforts to revitalize our lagging economy?

THE MILITARY BUDGET, THE ECONOMY, AND JOBS

The employment created by military spending has a powerful influence on our defense policy. Despite the fact that numerous members of Congress were calling for deep cuts in the administration's military build-up during the fall of 1982, the proposed FY 1983 Department of Defense budget was cut by only a token amount. Analysts for Prudential-Bache Securities suggest that two economic factors prevented deeper cuts. First, they believe that the broad geographic distribution of Pentagon spending gives even the Congressional doves good reason for voting for arms increases. Second, they note that pressure to vote for military programs is greater during a period of high unemployment. Therefore, these Wall Street analysts predict that military spending will continue to grow rapidly and recommend that investors purchase defense stocks.[9]

It is hard to argue with their logic. The pervasive influence of military contracting makes it difficult for our elected representatives to vote against major weapons systems, even when the weapons are of questionable military value.

Throughout the recent recession, Reagan administration officials have reminded the American people of the economic benefits of higher arms spending.[10] Yet thorough examination of its immediate impact shows that the benefits are dwarfed by the opportunity costs. Moreover, as we discuss later, the real question Congress should be asking is whether the military value of a given program is greater than its long-term economic costs.

The Pentagon is the largest single purchaser of goods and services in the economy. During 1981, national defense purchases by the federal government totalled $153.3 billion.[11] In comparison, the business expenses of Exxon, the largest corporation in America, were 33 percent less during the same year. The cost of operating the nation's second largest corporation, Mobil, was 60 percent less.[12]

The military has been the largest single source of demand in the economy throughout the last three decades. After adjusting for inflation, there has been little variation in the substantial size of the Defense Department's budget since the early 1950s. Excluding the dramatic increases during the Korean and Vietnam wars, military spending has remained high at about $170 billion (in 1983 dollars).

Although Pentagon spending has been a major factor in the economy, the military's proportionate share has declined as the overall economy has grown. While the military budget stayed the same, the gross national product (GNP) has almost tripled in real terms during the past three decades. As a result, the military's share of the GNP dropped from an average of 10 percent during the 1950s to an average of 6 percent during the 1970s.

The military's share of government spending has also fallen, but by a smaller amount. Of the goods and services directly purchased by the federal government during the 1970s, the military consumed 70 percent. In the 1950s, the Pentagon's share averaged 85 percent. The military's portion stayed so high because much of the growth in civilian government spending has been in transfer payments, which are not direct government purchases.

While transfer payments do affect the economy, their impact is usually more geographically diffuse than direct purchases. For example, unemployment benefits are paid to anyone who qualifies, no matter where they live. On the other hand, contracting for a tank or building a hydroelectric dam directly affects a specific area. The difference is politically important. Members of Congress can demonstrate their political effectiveness back home by steering federal purchases into their states. The responsibility that any one senator or representative can claim for additional transfer payments is usually less clear.

Since military spending is by far the largest category of federal purchases, it is an extremely important source of political power. Two examples illustrate this point. First, as chairman of the Senate Subcommittee on Defense Preparedness during the 1950s, Lyndon Johnson built his political career calling for a larger Air Force and helping direct aircraft contracts into his home state.[13] Second, in 1969, toward the end of Mendel Rivers's (D–SC) long tenure as chairman of the House Armed Services Committee, there were nine military installations located in his district. A Lockheed plant was located there because, as Representative Rivers explained, "I asked them to put a li'l old plant here."[14]

Just as with any other form of spending—whether it be that of an individual, a corporation, or the government—military spending also creates jobs. The Defense Department alone directly employed more than three million people in fiscal year 1981—over two million on active duty in the armed forces and another million in civil service jobs. At least two million more people were employed in FY 1981 by private corporations with military contracts and by other institutions, such as universities.[15]

While military spending clearly creates jobs, a meaningful assessment of the Pentagon's employment impact must include an accounting of the jobs forgone by using resources to produce weapons. Any form of spending creates jobs, but the key question is: How does military spending compare with other uses of the same money? Does it create as many jobs per dollar spent as do other options? Does it provide employment in the occupational categories with high unemployment?

The comparison between the number of jobs created by military purchases from the private sector and the number created by other forms of private spending is quite different. Most industries selling to the Pentagon create fewer jobs per dollar spent than the average industry in the American economy. Seven of the eleven manufacturing industries selling the greatest volume of goods to the military create fewer jobs per dollar than the median manufacturing industry. Seven of the nine largest military suppliers create fewer jobs per dollar than the median nonmanufacturing industry. More importantly, the three largest manufacturing industries—those accounting for over 40 percent of the Pentagon's total purchases from the private sector—create fewer jobs per dollar than the median manufacturing industry.

Those comparisons, based on data from the Labor Department's employment requirements table, include both direct and indirect employment. Direct jobs are those created in the industry that provides the final product to the Defense Department. Indirect jobs are those created by the final producer's requirements for goods and services. For example, the aircraft industry requires structural forgings, communications equipment, titanium, and numerous other intermediate goods to produce jet fighters. Aircraft firms also use outside services such as air transportation and accountants. Such purchases indirectly create employment.

One factor that the lower job-creating manufacturing industries that serve the Pentagon share is a high level of technical sophistication. The aircraft, communications equipment, missile, and computer industries all produce very specialized, highly complex products. In each case, the production process requires particularly expensive skilled labor, raw materials, and intermediate products. The other three manufacturing industries that create fewer jobs than the average—automobiles, chemicals, and petroleum products—produce more general goods; however, the production process in each of these industries requires a larger amount of sophisticated capital equipment than is used by the average manufacturing firm.

In both cases, the technical sophistication of the industries limits the number and types of jobs created.

The concentration of military purchases in a small number of lower job-yielding industries helps explain why various economic analyses have found that transferring military expenditures to other sectors of the economy creates more jobs. Three econometric simulations of a compensated reduction in military spending done during the 1970s all show that the alternatives—whether greater civilian government spending or a tax cut—create higher employment.[16] More recently, the Employment Research Associates used the Labor Department's employment requirements table to test the impact of shifting $62.9 billion in 1981 from military purchases to personal consumption expenditures.[17] This scenario showed a net gain of some 1.5 million jobs after the shift. The funds created a total of 3.3 million jobs if spent on private consumption, but only 1.8 million jobs if spent on military purchases.

The Employment Research Associates' study indicates that military contracting creates roughly 28,000 jobs per billion dollars of spending (in 1981 dollars). This is slightly less than the 30,000 jobs created by the median industry in the Bureau of Labor Statistics' input-output model. Military contracting also provides fewer jobs than public works projects such as new transit construction. It creates significantly fewer jobs than personal consumption and educational services. However, military contracting does create more jobs than industries such as oil refining and car manufacturing.

While military purchases create fewer jobs than most alternative expenditures, they still represent a significant source of demand in the economy for goods and services. The importance of providing an alternative source of demand when arms expenditures are reduced is underscored by the results of econometric simulations that do not compensate for lower levels of military spending by either cutting taxes or increasing other types of spending. For example, a recent simulation by Data Resources, Inc., comparing the Reagan administration's arms buildup to a much slower one, found that the smaller buildup resulted in almost one percentage point more unemployment.[18]

Military purchases also create a very different mix of jobs than other expenditures.[19] Military contractors generally employ a larger portion of technically skilled workers than does the average manufacturing firm. In eleven of the top fifteen manufacturing industries producing output for the Pentagon, the percentage of the industry's work force accounted for by production workers is lower than the average for all manufacturing.

The high cost of technically skilled labor is also a major reason why the manufacturing industries receiving most of the Pentagon's contracts create fewer jobs than the median. While some have speculated that military spending creates fewer jobs because the production process is capital-intensive,[20] this speculation is only true for a small number of industries serving the Pentagon, such as oil refining. In the major suppliers, including the aircraft, communications equipment, and missile industries, large parts of the assembly process are often performed by skilled technicians and engineers. Moreover, much of the capital equipment used by large defense firms is very old because there is little incentive to make new investments.

Normally, a firm invests to increase production efficiency and reduce costs in order to increase sales and profits. In the defense sector, however, lower cost seldom increases the market for a product, and cost overruns are regularly reimbursed.[21] Capital purchases by military contractors are not ordinarily subsidized by the Defense Department. Therefore, there is little incentive to invest. Indeed, numerous reports identify lower productivity growth, resulting from less investment, as a major reason for cost overruns in the defense sector.[22]

On the other hand, Pentagon procurement practices encourage greater use of highly skilled workers. Defense Department officials value high performance above cost.[23] Thus, to gain the edge in selling to the Pentagon, military contractors often hire additional engineers. Moreover, the highly demanding specifications of military components often cannot be met by off-the-shelf items. As a result, many parts must be produced in small batches by subcontracting firms like machine shops and specialty semi-conductor producers. These firms use much more skilled labor than firms that mass-produce standard components.

The specialized nature of military employment reduces its economic usefulness. Much of the new employment generated by a military buildup goes to people who need it least. Professional and technical workers have the lowest unemployment rate of any occupational category in the economy. Even during December 1982, when overall unemployment was 10.8 percent, unemployment for professional and technical workers was only 3.7 percent. Demand for engineers was so great during the 1980 recession that salaries continued to rise dramatically. Indeed, during that recession, increased military spending fueled inflationary pressures in the high technology sector while the rest of the economy faltered.[24]

At the other end of the spectrum, military spending creates very few jobs for those most in need of work. Meanwhile, unemployment among laborers and machine operators was above 20 percent in December 1982. And, although the present buildup will increase the need for skilled workers, programs to help train the groups with the highest unemployment rates—young people and minorities—have been cut severely.

MILITARY SPENDING: STIMULANT OR IMPEDIMENT?

Although a great many Reagan administration officials contend that military spending helps the economy, there is a good deal of evidence that suggests the contrary. In the historical mainstream of economic thought, military spending has been generally viewed as an impediment to economic progress. Since soldiers and arms producers do not create goods and services that can be consumed by others, many economists see arms spending as subtracting from a nation's total resources. If the "dead weight" of military spending becomes too great, it is assumed that an economy will suffer.

Since World War II, Americans have come to expect that our standard of living would increase indefinitely. During the 1950s and especially the 1960s, the future promised greater opportunity and prosperity, even though we already enjoyed the world's highest per capita income. In the 1970s, however, the "American dream" began to crumble under the weight of an economy plagued by inflation, unemployment, and slow growth.

Stagflation during the 1970s eroded the yearly increase in real income that Americans had come to expect. From 1960 to 1973, the yearly increase in per capita disposable personal income averaged 2.8 percent after accounting for inflation. Between 1973 and 1981, however, the average increase was only 1.6 percent. Production and nonsupervisory workers fared worse. Instead of increasing, their hourly earnings actually fell 1.6 percent a year, between 1973 and 1980, after rising 1.5 percent a year from 1960 to 1973.[25]

During the past decade, unemployment has continued its post-World War II trend—remaining at a higher level after each recession than it was prior to the downturn. In December 1982, unemployment reached a level unmatched since the Great Depression: 10.8 percent.[26] Few economists expect it to fall below 10 percent until late in 1983. Even though employment in other industrial nations also rose after the oil crisis, America's unemployment rate remained higher than most.

Economic growth in the United States has also been sluggish. America's average inflation-adjusted rate of growth in gross domestic product (GDP) since 1960 ranks thirteenth among seventeen major non-Communist nations. As a result of stronger economic growth, eight European nations surpassed America's standard of living by 1980, as measured by the level of GDP per capita.[27] Throughout most of the 1970s, Switzerland,

Denmark, and Sweden all enjoyed a higher level of GDP per capita. By the end of the decade Germany, Norway, Belgium, the Netherlands, and France also passed the United States.

A growing number of economists place a large measure of blame for our economic problems on the declining competitiveness of U.S. manufactured goods in both foreign and domestic markets. "U.S. industry's loss of competitiveness over the past two decades has been nothing short of an economic disaster and goes a long way toward explaining the shrinking standard of living," explained *Business Week* in a special issue entitled "The Reindustrialization of America."[28] During the past decade, American manufacturers have lost almost a quarter of their share of the international market and about 3 percent of their share of domestic manufacturing sales. These declines cost the American economy some $125 billion in lost production and at least two million industrial jobs. The nation's reduced manufacturing competitiveness occurred even after a 40 percent devaluation of the dollar during the 1970s that made foreign goods more expensive, and American goods cheaper, in the international market.[29]

A variety of other factors has been cited to explain the declining competitiveness of U.S. manufacturers. Some observers believe that increased social spending and expanded government regulations have reduced the amount of new investments made by American firms.[30] Others have argued that lower labor costs have provided our competitors with a key advantage.[31] More recently, some analysts have pointed to shortsighted management techniques employed by major American firms as a reason for our decline.[32] Still others have suggested that industrialization in the United States has proceeded sufficiently to exhaust most of the profitable opportunities in old-line industries, such as automobiles and steel.[33] Only a few analysts have examined the possibility that military spending has been a major contributor to declining fortunes in the manufacturing sector.[34]

Although not the only reason for our economic woes, arms expenditures robbed the civilian sector of key resources, such as engineers and investment capital, that might have been used to modernize U.S. manufacturing industries. While America's manufacturing firms were becoming less competitive, the United States spent more on arms than all of our NATO (North Atlantic Treaty Organization) allies combined. Even after adjusting for the relative size of each economy, America's military burden was by far the heaviest among major industrialized nations. Over the past two decades, America spent 35 percent more of its gross domestic product on the military than did the United Kingdom, which had the second largest military burden. At the other extreme, in relative terms, Japan spent only about one-seventh as much as did the United States.

THE TECHNOLOGICAL IMPACT OF MILITARY SPENDING

Moreover, the oft-cited argument that military spending encourages technological progress resulting in civilian spin-offs that could enhance productivity and competition does not seem valid. The military's substantial funding for advanced weapons systems and research and development has certainly yielded some benefits. To be seen in perspective, however, positive effects must be weighed against any negative influences arms programs may have on technological advancement. At least three broad areas should be considered.

First, military-oriented research and production diverts scientists and engineers from civilian pursuits. As a result, we are left with fewer people to develop civilian technologies such as consumer electronics, fuel-efficient cars, alternative energy systems, and mass transit. This drawback is particularly worrisome when high technology resources are limited, as they are today. Competition between the Pentagon and private industry for highly skilled labor, key subcomponents, and raw materials can drive up the price of American high technology products, making them less competitive in the world market.

Second, military-oriented programs can distort a new technology by encouraging applications that are too sophisticated to be marketed commercially. British and French experience with the Super-Sonic Transport (SST) program is one example of this problem. While the United States wisely chose not to develop a civilian SST, our European allies proved that the military's pioneering research on flying at supersonic speeds did not have widespread commercial application. Nuclear power, with its unsolved safety problems and excessive cost, is another example. Military-sponsored programs designed to spur development of faster integrated circuits and more automated machine tools may also distort their development for commercial markets.

Third, at the political level, we must assess the implications of according the military significant control over science and technology policy. While many of our politicians, including President Reagan, extol the virtues of the free market, they still allow the Pentagon to control about a third of all public and private research and development funds and to purchase over 10 percent of the durable manufactured goods produced in our economy.

Between 1960 and 1973, Defense Department contracts for hardware averaged 16.9 percent of the durable manufactured goods sold in the United States. Since then, hardware contracts have averaged 10.9 percent of durable manufactured goods production. Of the major hard goods purchased by the Pentagon over the past three decades, at least 70 percent have been components of high technology systems such as aircraft, missiles, and space systems, and electronics and communications equipment.[35] As a result, the military's share of industry output in sectors such as aerospace, electronics, and communications is considerably higher than for durable manufactured goods as a whole. Although the military's share of industry output was declining during the 1970s, the Defense Department's purchases have significantly influenced the direction of the high technology industries.

The Pentagon further influenced technological development by funding 38.1 percent of all public and private research and development between 1960 and 1973. In the post-Vietnam period, this figure fell to 25.6 percent. Space-related R&D, at least 20 percent of which had direct military applications (Appendix C), averaged another 11.8 percent of all R&D between 1960 and 1973. Since then, the space program has accounted for 7.2 percent of all public and private R&D.

Military R&D has been the federal government's largest mechanism for influencing technological growth. Defense Department R&D averaged 61.4 percent of all federal R&D between 1960 and 1973. Since then it has accounted for 52.7 percent. Space research accounted for another 16.7 percent before 1973 and 14.3 percent since then.

Between weapons procurement and R&D, the Pentagon employs a substantial share of our nation's technical personnel. Estimates of the percentage of scientists and engineers engaged in Defense Department-sponsored projects range from 15 to 50 percent.[36] While the higher estimates might have applied to the research and development during the 1950s and 1960s, they could not have covered all production personnel as well.

If the economic benefits of devoting these technological resources to the military outweighed the costs, we would expect to find that the technological superiority enjoyed by American industry during the 1960s would have been maintained or expanded. Since the Pentagon has "seeded" our research laboratories and purchased new products when they were too costly for civilian applications, American industry should have been in an excellent position to commercialize high technology goods. We would also expect that technological advancements resulting from our military effort would have enhanced the efficiency of our factories, leading to increases in manufacturing productivity. Indeed, since America's support for military technology was only part of the largest R&D effort undertaken by a major industrial nation (except the Soviet Union) over the past two decades, there is every reason to expect these results. Unfortunately, neither spin-off has occurred. Since 1960, American high technology industries have lost ground to the Japanese and the Western Europeans in the competition for shares of both the U.S.

domestic and worldwide markets. Growth in the productivity of American manufacturers has also fallen substantially.

American firms have experienced some of their largest market-share reductions in industries that are heavily engaged in military contracting including aircraft, electronics, and machine tools.

America's declining productivity growth also suggests that our technological progress has slowed. Many factors influence productivity growth; two of the more important paths to greater manufacturing efficiency are improving production technology and creating more attractive products. Funding for research and development should thus have a positive impact on productivity growth because new tools and new products are nurtured in our research labs. While traditionally the relationship between R&D and productivity growth has been found by economists to be quite significant, recent evidence suggests that the relationship has changed.[37]

Cross-national data comparing R&D expenditures are indicative of this change. While American investment in R&D has been substantial, productivity growth has been weak. The United States has maintained the greatest number of R&D scientists and engineers and the highest proportion of these researchers in the total labor force of any country except the Soviet Union. We spend more on R&D than France, West Germany, and Japan combined.[38] In addition, U.S. expenditures on R&D as a proportion of the gross national product were higher than four of the five other industrial countries for which data can be obtained—the United Kingdom, France, West Germany and Japan. The Soviet Union was again the exception. Yet in spite of this enormous R&D effort, U.S. productivity growth during the 1970s ranked second to last among those six nations.

If we chart the share of national resources that the six nations devoted to military and space R&D, we find that as that factor increases productivity growth tends to decline. The Soviet Union, the United States, and the United Kingdom are at the top of the list in military-related R&D expenditures and at the bottom in productivity growth. It seems that while those nations have been locked in a technological arms race, Japan, West Germany, and France have been concentrating on developing civilian technology that increases manufacturing efficiency.

The reason that military spending has probably slowed our technological progress seems clear: Using scientific and engineering talent to solve military problems is an inefficient means of stimulating scientific or commercial advancement. Growth in our base of scientific knowledge comes most readily from basic research without the constraint of specific applications. The development of new products—fuel-efficient automobiles, alternative energy systems, and computer-controlled machine tools, for example—is most quickly accomplished by applying R&D talent directly. While military programs sometimes provide a market for new products and occasionally result in a civilian spin-off, much of the effort expended to develop weapons systems like laser-guided missiles and electronic jamming devices does not help the civilian economy. Moreover, military requirements can distort engineering practices by placing greater emphasis on high-performance capabilities than on reducing cost. Evidence of this problem can be found in the difficulties that military contractors have experienced attempting to develop civilian products. For example, attempts to enter the mass transit market by Boeing Vertol (trolley cars), Rohr (subway cars), and Grumman (buses) all failed in part because their products were too complex and unreliable.

Clearly, military spending is a limited countercyclical aid. It creates fewer jobs than most other industries. It employs highly skilled people who would have relatively little trouble finding jobs elsewhere. Military expenditures are concentrated in only a few regions and industries. Moreover, even though military spending creates a substantial demand for goods and services, cutting military spending would not make us more prone to depression. Increasing civilian government programs and/or reducing taxes could replace the purchasing power lost by cutting the arms budget. While large reductions in the current level of military spending would create adjustment problems in selected regions and industries, many of these difficulties could be overcome with planning and specific assistance programs.

When the economy requires federal assistance, programs should be developed to fill the nation's greatest needs, not simply the most convenient pork barrel. The construction industry, hard hit during the recent recession, will receive a shot in the arm from the recently approved government program to rebuild the nation's deteriorating roads and bridges. Yet the sad state of America's infrastructure leaves us with many other public works options. Instead of creating greater competition for skilled labor by increasing military spending, the federal government might also institute training programs to help those currently unemployed to develop technical skills that will be heavily in demand during the 1980s. If the federal government were to develop a comprehensive mass transit program, we could revive an industry that would employ production workers laid off by the auto makers and create a hedge against future increases in energy prices. These options clearly indicate that we should not spend money on the military just because it creates jobs.

Some might still wonder if it is possible to create enough public support for civilian government programs to replace military spending as a source of demand. However, we would rephrase the question: Can the U.S. government afford to continue relying on the military budget as the largest public mechanism for economic stimulation when military expenditures draw such wealth from the civilian economy? While we might have been able to "afford" a substantial military burden during the 1950s and 1960s, the loss of skilled labor and investment from the private economy during the 1980s could cost us dearly in export potential. Many American industries could continue to lose markets to foreign producers if U.S. firms do not modernize their factories, and America's technological leadership could continue to slip away if we ask too many of our brightest engineers and scientists to solve military-related problems instead of creating better civilian products. These considerations indicate that, instead of relying on military spending as a source of jobs, we should avoid any military expenditure that is not necessary for our security.

NOTES

1.   *Budget of the United States Government, FY 1984* (Washington, D.C.: U.S. GPO, 1983), pp. 9–53.
2.   Herbert Denton, "Reagan Cooly Received on Midwest Swing," *Washington Post*, 5 October 1982.
3.   Richard Halloran, "Expansion of Military Air Transport Fleet is Stalled by Dispute in Congress," *The New York Times*, 20 June 1982.
4.   U.S. Congress, House of Representatives, *Congressional Record*, 8 December 1982, pp. H 9123–H 9129.
5.   Thomas Etzold and John Lewis Gaddis, eds., *Containment: Documents on American Policy and Strategy, 1945–1950* (New York: Columbia University Press, 1978), p. 426.
6.   John Lewis Gaddis, *Strategies of Containment* (New York: Oxford University Press, 1982), p. 94.
7.   "Cutting Defense Won't Solve Job Problem, Weinberger Says," *The Washington Post*, 9 November 1982; Peter Meredith, "Shipyard Jobs Tied to Defense Votes," *The Baltimore Sun*, 6 March 1982.
8.   George Wilson, "Senators Urge Defense Spending Cut," *The Washington Post*, 2 February 1983.
9.   Paul H. Nisbet and Richard L. Whittington, "Defense: Increase Spending or Cut Jobs," *Industry Outlook: Aerospace/Defense* (Prudential-Bache Securities, Inc., 8 December 1982).
10.   Denton, "Reagan Cooly Received"; Wilson, "Senators Urge Defense Spending Cut"; "Cutting Defense Won't Solve Job Problem, Weinberger Says"; Caspar Weinberger, "Address to the National Press Club," *News Release*, Office of the Assistant Secretary of Defense (Public Affairs), 8 March 1982, p. 3; "Weinberger Says Military Spending Rise Won't Spur Inflation or Disrupt Economy," *Wall Street Journal*, 29 July 1981; Meredith, "Shipyard Jobs Tied to Defense Votes."
11.   *Economic Report of the President* (Washington, D.C.: U.S. GPO, February 1983), p. 163.
12.   "Fortune 500," *Fortune Magazine*, 3 May 1982, 260.
13.   Richard Kaufman, *War Profiteers* (New York: Doubleday, 1972), pp. 32–36.
14.   Peter H. Prugh, "The War Business, Mendel Rivers' Defense of Armed Forces Helps His Hometown Prosper," *Wall Street Journal*, 17 June 1969.

15. U.S. Department of Defense, Office of the Assistant Secretary of Defense (Comptroller), "National Defense Estimates, Fiscal Year 1983," p. 82. This publication estimates that Pentagon contracts with private industry employed 2,230,000 people in 1981. This figure is probably overstated, given the results of input-output analysis performed by Marion Anderson, Jeb Brugmann, and George Erickcek, "The Price of the Pentagon: The Industrial and Commercial Impact of the 1981 Military Budget" (Lansing, Mich.: Employment Research Associates, 1982).

16. Roger H. Bezdek, "The 1980 Impact – Regional and Occupational – of Compensated Shifts in Defense Spending," *Journal of Regional Science*, (February 1965); Ronald P. Smith, "Military Expenditure and Investment in OECD Countries, 1954–1973," *Journal of Comparative Economics* 4 (1980): pp. 19–32; R.P. Smith, "Military Expenditure and Capitalism," *Cambridge Journal of Economics* 1 (1977): 61–76; Chase Econometrics Associates, *Economic Impact of the B-1 Program on the U.S. Economy and Comparative Case Studies* (Cynwyd, Pennsylvania: Chase Econometric Associates, 1975); Norman J. Glickman, *Econometric Analysis of Regional Systems* (New York: Academic Press, 1977). Each of the above is discussed in Michael Edelstein, "The Economic Impact of Military Spending" (New York: Council on Economic Priorities, 1977).

17. Anderson, Brugmann, and Erickcek, "Price of the Pentagon."

18. Data Resources, Inc., *Defense Economics Research Report* (August 1982); 5.

19. Bezdek, "1980 Impact of Compensated Shifts," 195.

20. Anderson, Brugmann, and Erickcek, "Price of the Pentagon."

21. Jacques S. Gansler, *The Defense Industry* (Cambridge, MA: The MIT Press, 1980), ch. 3.

22. U.S. General Accounting Office, Comptroller General, "Appendix I – General Accounting Office Draft Report on Defense Industry Profit Study, Dated December 22, 1970" (Washington, D.C.: U.S. GAO, January 1971), p. 51; U.S. General Accounting Office, Comptroller General, "Impediments to Reducing the Costs of Weapons Systems, Report to Congress" (Washington, D.C.: U.S. GAO, 8 November 1979), p. 31. (Hereafter, "Impediments"); U.S. Congress, Senate Committee on Banking, Housing and Urban Affairs, jointly with the Subcommittee on Priorities and Economy in Government of the Joint Economic Committee, "Department of Defense Contract Profit Policy" (Washington, D.C.: U.S. GPO, 21 March 1979), pp. 1–2.

23. Gansler, *The Defense Industry*, p. 83; U.S. General Accounting Office, "Impediments," p. 23; Morton J. Peck and Frederic M. Scherer, *The Weapons Acquisition Process: An Economic Analysis* (Boston: Harvard Graduate School of Business Administration, 1962), p. 594.

24. U.S. Congress, House Committee on Armed Services, "The Ailing Defense Industrial Base: Unready for Crisis," a report of the Defense Industrial Base Panel (Washington, D.C.: U.S. GPO, 31 December 1980), p. 13.

25. *Economic Report of the President* (Washington, D.C.: U.S. GPO, February 1982), Tables B-24 & 29.

26. U.S. Department of Labor, Bureau of Labor Statistics, "The Unemployment Situation: December 1982," *News*, 7 January 1983, Table C.

27. *National Accounts of Organisation of Economic Cooperation and Development Countries, 1950–1980, Volume I* (Paris: O.E.C.D., 1982), p. 88.

28. The Business Week Team, *The Reindustrialization of America* (New York: McGraw-Hill Book Co., 1982), p. 10.

29. The Business Week Team, p. 11.

30. N.Y. Stock Exchange, Office of Economic Research, "U.S. Economic Performance in a Global Perspective," February 1981.

31. Peter Drucker, "The Danger of Excessive Labor Income," *The Wall Street Journal,* 6 January 1981.
32. Robert H. Hayes and William J. Abernathy, "Managing Our Way to Economic Decline," *Harvard Business Review* (July–August 1980); Leslie Wayne, "Management Gospel Gone Wrong," *The New York Times,* 20 May 1982.
33. Nathaniel J. Mass and Peter M. Senge, "Reindustrialization: Aiming for the Right Targets," *Technology Review* 83: 8 (August/September 1981).
34. Seymour Melman, *The Permanent War Economy: American Capitalism in Decline* (New York: Simon & Schuster, 1974), chs. 4–5; Lloyd J. Dumas, ed., *The Political Economy of Arms Reduction* (Boulder, CO: 1982), ch. 1; Mary Kaldor, *The Baroque Arsenal* (New York: Hill and Wang, 1981), chs. 2–3.
35. U.S. Department of Defense, Washington Headquarters Service, *Prime Contract Awards, FY 1981,* February 1982, Table 6.
36. Jacques S. Gansler, *The Defense Industry* (Cambridge, Mass.: MIT Press, 1980), p. 54 (estimates that 20 to 30 percent of all scientists and engineers work on military projects); Richard Dempsey and Douglas Schmude, "Occupational Impact of Defense Expenditures," *Monthly Labor Review* (December 1971): 12 (estimates 20 percent); Murray L. Weidenbaum, *Economics of Peacetime Defense* (New York: Praeger, 1974), p. 27 (estimates 50 percent); Ramo, p. 80 (estimates 50 percent).
37. Eleanor Thomas, "Recent Research on R&D and Productivity Growth: A Changing Relationship Between Input & Impact Indicators?" (Washington, D.C.: NSF, September 1980).
38. National Science Board, *Science Indicators 1980* (Washington, D.C.: National Science Foundation, 1981), p. 2.

2

Profits without Production: Deterioration in the Industrial System

Seymour Melman

For a decade after World War II, the automobile industry in the United States not only paid the highest wages in the world to its industrial workers but also produced the lowest priced cars in the world. Detroit pay scales were two to three times those of auto workers in Western Europe, but the average productivity of labor in the U.S. auto industry—thanks to greater mechanization and more refined organization of work—was about three times that of Western Europe. As a result, the Detroit product was so attractively priced that it not only dominated the U.S. market but was also exported to markets around the world.

By 1980, twenty-five years later, the situation had been transformed. The U.S. automobile industry was able to sell only 73 percent of the cars appearing on the roads of America. The remaining 27 percent were imported from Western Europe and, especially, from Japan.

The automobile industry has been the flagship enterprise of the mass-producing, high-productivity economy. During the twentieth century its methods have been the model for other industries worldwide. Therefore, the loss to this industry of one customer out of four within the U.S. home market is proof of a massive industrial breakdown.

The air has been full of recriminations about who is at fault. Everyone knows, of course, that the automobile industry's "Big Three" firms clung far too long to the production and selling of big cars for big profits; but the main issue here is competence in production. The top managers of the Big Three have singled out the high wages of U.S. auto workers as the prime cause of their noncompetitiveness in the marketplace. In fact, however, in 1980 the average hourly payment to U.S. auto workers ($15.02)

Excerpted from Seymour Melman, *Profits Without Production* (New York: Alfred A. Knopf, 1983).

was less than the earnings of their German ($15.46) and Belgian ($15.30) counterparts.[1] To be sure, average hourly earnings of U.S. auto workers in that year were more than twice those of Japanese workers ($7.16), but it is important to recall that during the 1950s, when the wages of U.S. auto workers were two to three times those of Western European workers, that proved no barrier to the U.S. industry's holding its domestic market as well as sizable markets abroad. At that time, Detroit offset the wage differential with high productivity of labor and capital. What, then, happened to the productivity of labor and capital in the 1980s? Why is the U.S. automobile industry unable today to compensate, as it once did so effectively, for differences in labor and other costs? The place to begin is with the quality of the means of production and then the methods of production organization.

Machine tools are the basic production equipment of the automobile industry. In 1978, 76 percent of the machine tools used in the U.S. automobile industry were ten years old or older. Its production equipment was older than the average for all U.S. manufacturing (69 percent ten years old and older).[2] The managers of the Big Three failed to modernize and upgrade their basic production equipment. Many production divisions were treated as "cash cows," being milked of their assets. The failure to upgrade production methods is also reflected in large productivity differences among the various factories. When automobile factories were ranked by productivity per employee during the late 1960s, the top quarter was two and a half times as productive as the lowest quarter. This signalled a pattern of neglected maintenance and withholding of fresh investment in important parts of the industry.[3]

But the development of major differences in the organization of production between the U.S. and the Japanese automobile industries has probably had the major effect on productivity. The core of the matter is this: Major Japanese automobile firms have discovered the connection between stabilization of production rates and increased productivity of labor and capital, as well as the wide range of cost savings that are made possible when a production system is operated in a sustained, stable pattern.

Two ideas are crucial here. Stable operation of a single machine means working at rates within predictable and acceptable limits. The average output (productivity) of the machine improves automatically as it approaches stability. For example, when a power plant is operated in a stable manner, more electricity is produced for each ton of fuel that is consumed. The rolls in steel rolling mills last longer when they are used at more even speeds.[4]

The second underlying idea is that stabilization of output rate in an entire factory raises the productivity of the system as a whole. This results from the ramified effects caused by the removal of interferences with the steady operation of single machines and with the flow of work through many operations.

As must be obvious, more is involved here than a simple statistical harmony between machines and materials. Stabilization of output in an entire production system requires a method of organization of work, of decisionmaking about production, that encourages sustained cooperation among workers, technicians, engineers, and administrators. Such cooperation is the vital element that permits a production system to respond to the requirements of stable operation. And there is little evidence to support the prevailing idea that a managerially imposed supervisory system can produce, in an automobile factory, the fine integration of operations made possible by a cooperating work force.

The stabilized production system comprises, together with a congruent mode of work organization that induces cooperation in production, the optimum productivity system for any given degree of mechanization of work. Yet in American automobile firms like Ford, supervision rather than cooperation prevails. Ford has twelve layers of organization, "from the factory floor to the chairman's office, compared with only seven layers at Toyota. At Toyota a foreman reports directly to the plant manager. In a typical Ford plant the foreman must struggle through three layers of in-plant management to get to the plant manager."[5] The same Ford official estimates that halving the white-collar staff "in Ford's North American automotive operations alone would lower Ford's costs from $4 billion to $2 billion per year."

In sum: as the U.S. automobile industry managers have stressed their goals of short-term profits/power, they have operated production facilities by methods that are the obverse of those required for a stable production system, thus debasing the productivity of both labor and capital. The product quality, cost, and price noncompetitiveness of U.S. automobile firms are derived effects of these conditions.

For a century after the Civil War, the manufacture of steel occupied a central position in the industry and economy of the United States. The prices set by steel's managements became costs for the rest of the industrial system. Similarly, the pay scales prevailing in the steel industry, including those negotiated with the United Steelworkers of America after the 1930s, became a standard for wages in the rest of the industrial work force. With easy access to abundant and cheap coal and iron ore, and sitting in the middle of the world's largest market for steel, U.S. producers held key advantages over steelmakers in Western Europe and Japan.

Soon after World War II, new technologies made possible a revolution in steelmaking. The basic oxygen furnace superceded the open-

hearth furnace. Continuous casting of steel shapes replaced the traditional rolling mill. These new production methods, plus ever more refined control systems, yielded great economies in the use of raw materials
and fuel, raising the productivity of capital and, as always, that of labor.

The diligent pursuit of the new technologies in Europe and Japan—
plus, in Japan, the economies derived from large-scale plants and equipment—finally gave these countries a competitive edge for many steel
products that extended even to the American market. By the end of the
1970s, the steelmakers of Japan and Western Europe were supplying
between 15 and 20 percent of the requirements of American steel-using
firms. By 1978, one out of five jobs in the U.S. steel industry had been sus-
pended or terminated.

But the underlying science and the attendant technology for the
revolution in steel production was known around the world. Why didn't
the managers of U.S. steel firms order their development and application
in their own plants? What policies and practices inhibited them?

Both West Germany and Japan have paid higher prices for raw
materials (coal, iron ore, electricity) than the steel industry of the United
States, but they use those materials more efficiently. Therefore, the materials component of total production costs—notably in Japan—is less than
in the United States. Energy-saving equipment is given high priority in
Japan. By contrast, in the factories of the American steel industry, equipment is older and therefore less efficient in extracting the energy potential
of fuels and the metal content of ores.

By 1979, 33 percent of U.S. steel production facilities were more than
twenty years old and 12 percent were more than thirty years old.[6] That
age of U.S. steel industry equipment must be set against the eleven years
required to recover (depreciate) the cost of new plant and equipment in
the U.S. industry. In West Germany, the cost-recovery period is ten
years; in Japan it is eleven years.[7] Steelmaking facilities of the major U.S.
steel firms were also milked for cash flow that was accumulated and used
for investment elsewhere, for dividends, and for large senior executive
salaries.

The Office of Technology Assessment concluded the following, in a
wide-ranging and sober report to Congress:

> More often than not, steel industry executives express a desire to be
> second with proven technology not first with new technology...
> domestic firms also tend to sell whatever innovative technology they do
> create as quickly as possible, in order to maximize immediate profits,
> instead of keeping the technology proprietary and thereby gaining a
> competitive advantage.... One explanation for these and other such
> shortcomings is a lack of dedicated, long-range strategic planning by
> domestic steel companies, particularly by integrated producers.[8]

In the absence of a substantial commitment to research and development by steel management, it is unreasonable to expect much ability among these firms either to innovate technology or to make timely use of innovations developed elsewhere.

Up to this point, the focus has been on components of production cost. But price must, of course, include administrative costs and profits. The costs of managing, though an important factor in the total picture of modern industry, are seldom mentioned in analyses of the steel industry. By 1977, for every one hundred production workers in the U.S. steel industry, twenty-six people were employed in administrative, technical, and clerical occupations. Studies of the steel industry in the United States and other countries have established that there is a *negative* correlation between administrative employment and steel industry output.[9] Administrative costs in this industry have been rising. The ratio of administrative to production employees in the steel industry was fourteen in 1947 and had risen to twenty-six by 1977.

Within the management of steel industry firms, the tendency has been to improve the position of accounting and financial executives. The steel industry "employs only about 60 percent as many scientists and engineers as the average manufacturing industry."[10] Of these technical personnel only about 5 percent are in the top management organizations of the industry. In the operation of steel firms "financial considerations are given priority, operating considerations are secondary, and technology is at best ranked third. . . . Technological change per se is generally not a primary concern of steel executives."[11]

The managements of the major U.S. steel firms have focused on short-term profit, and in these terms they have succeeded admirably: "Despite major technological and economic difficulties, domestic steel industry profit levels have been higher than those of foreign steel industries, although they are only about half the U.S. manufacturing average."[12]

Thomas C. Graham, president of Jones and Laughlin Steel Corporation, says that the U.S. steel industry is the most "economically efficient" in the world, by which he means the most profitable.[13] But this kind of efficiency has been achieved at the price of serious technological obsolescence that has finally led to the inability of the industry to serve about one-fifth of the U.S. market.

How could the steel industry of the United States produce basic steel at a lower average cost per ton, earn higher profits than chief competitors, and, at the same time, experience major plant closings during the late 1970s, with many managements bewailing their inability to compete—even in the United States domestic market? What appears as a contradiction is resolved when one understands that the industry-wide performance data that have been reviewed here are *averages* for many firms and factories. The efficiency of steel mills has, in fact, been highly varied. A unique tabulation for 1967 of productivity for separate blast furnaces and steel mills shows that, when ranked by productivity, the top 25 percent of factories had 2.3 times the productivity of the lowest quarter.

Obviously, the wave of steel mill closings was concentrated in the lowest quarter of factories, ranked by productivity. This reflects the pattern of management neglect of renewal, by reinvestment, of production facilities and the preference of top managers for moving profits out of the steel industry.

In many countries, including West Germany and Japan, whose steel industries are mostly privately owned, the managements operate within the framework of a national policy administered by the government for the purpose of making sure that the local steel industry is a fully competent supplier of products for the rest of the economy. In these countries the steel enterprises are not merely organizations for production and profits. They are subject to a governmental determination to sustain employment levels and the technical economic vitality of key components or the industrial system.

One might well ask, Where has the U.S. government been during this period when the U.S. steel industry fell steadily behind until, in the years 1977 to 1979, there were wholesale closings of entire steel plants? Government managers, it seems, have been busy with enlarging and managing their own economy: the military economy. That is where resources and administrative attention have been lavished without stint.

In the very important realm of research and development, one steel industry R&D executive has concluded that: "There is a trend toward more defensive type of research...more time being spent on shorter-ranged projects and projects designed to meet government mandates and regulations, and less time being spent on the kinds of long-term, high-risk, innovative projects which will lead to the new ways of making steel in the future."[14]

What is crucial is not only the U.S. steel industry's conviction that R&D be focused on short-range, quick-payoff operations but also the relatively impoverished level of this activity. In 1972, the average R&D expenditures amounted to $1.30 per ton of raw steel produced. At the same time the European Community spent $1.46 per ton, and Japan $2.26 per ton.[15] More than that: During the 1960s and 1970s there was a continuous decline in the U.S. industry's R&D activity.

Research and development personnel in the industry have little voice in strategic planning, even when it pertains to major new technology. The R&D function, such as it is, is often linked closer to sales and marketing than to production or corporate planning. By contrast, in European and Japanese steel industries, there tends to be a close association between production and R&D staffs. Furthermore, the European steel industries observe a tradition of mobility for engineering and scientific staffs, who move about among firms, universities, and government facilities. Working in R&D has high prestige and attracts top-grade scientists and engineers.

Moreover, in those countries, managements in steel and in government see research and development as a valuable instrument for developing innovative solutions to competitive problems. Thus,

> much of R&D effort in European universities and research institutes is government funded; in the United States, there has been a decline in academic steelmaking programs, largely because of a lack of government support. There are no national institutes for steel R&D, such as those in West Germany, in which companies join with university personnel in long-range R&D projects, including a great deal of basic research.[16]

In the United States,

> the training and development of technical staff are geared to managerial and executive development rather than to on-going education in technical specialties. These are the areas viewed by management as the industry's backbone, an orientation reflected in mobility patterns that generally de-emphasize R&D.[17]

The steel industry has accounted for about one-fifth of all domestic industrial pollution, and independent observers note that it has unusually high rates of occupational illness and injury. This is an important part of the hostile management-labor relationship that has long prevailed in the industry.

In 1911, Frederick Winslow Taylor published his proposals for setting industrial work standards, based upon his experience as a manager in the Midvale Steel Works. He emphasized the importance of removing all planning of work from the workers. As one justification for this general policy, he offered the following: "...the pig-iron handler is not an extraordinary man difficult to find; he is merely a man more or less of the type of the ox, heavy both mentally and physically.... The work which this man does tires him no more than any healthy normal laborer is tired by a proper day's work...."[18]

Despite the formalization of relationships between the managements of the steel industry and the United Steelworkers of America, the traditions of the early steel masters still weigh heavily. At the nation's number two steel company, Bethlehem, reporters for the *Wall Street Journal* learned from a local union official that

The steel industry's biggest problem is management's attitude toward the workers. Last year, when Local 6787 asked to be allowed to use the Sand Creek Club, a Bethlehem golf and swimming club for management, 'we were turned down flat,' he says. 'They told us, we don't want you people using the Sand Creek Club.' As Mr. Wilborn, the local's president said, 'You could just sense the discrimination in the way they turned us down. They offended a lot of people with that one.'[19]

The U.S. Steel Corporation, after closing its Ohio works in 1979, was confronted by a new kind of problem in relation to the trade union. In cooperation with various community groups, the union had developed plans for buying the Ohio facilities, the financing to be a combination of private funds, community funds, and federal loans or grants. The management of U.S. Steel refused to consider the proposal, saying that, on principle, it did not wish to sell to any party that would use federal funds to compete against U.S. Steel. A local union official reported: "The company wouldn't even let any of our members walk through the plants with our engineers and bankers."[20]

Suppose the proposed reorganization, re-equipping and reopening had been achieved, under the control of a union–community-based ownership. The way would have been open to operating with lower profit margins and lower administrative costs than are acceptable to the managers of U.S. Steel. Those factors, plus the cooperation induced by shared controls over operations, could have made possible a steel plant producing a saleable, quality product while maintaining employment and assuring long-term economic viability. The strategies for those objectives would be rather different from the short-term profit maximizing, enlargement of managerial controls, and maximum return on investments from whatever enterprise seems handy for the purpose.

Virtually assured of a healthy domestic market, the managers of U.S. steel firms agreed after World War II to steel wages well above those of any other manufacturing industry. In return for a 1959 no-strike agreement, steel management offered wages linked to the cost of living. By 1979, inflation had escalated steel wages to 56 percent above the average for manufacturing workers overall. Steel management, however, was ill-equipped to offset that cost increase with productivity growth.

Steel industry management has been aggressive in seeking out major financial concessions from the federal government. Unembarrassed by any appearance of contradiction with free enterprise ideology, they had, by August 1981, extracted a series of major concessions:

- Tax law was revised to permit the write-off of steel plant in five years instead of the previous eleven.
- Tax credits on steel investments were raised.

- Rules governing the leasing of equipment were changed, making that strategy more advantageous to the steel companies.
- Pollution-control standards were relaxed for three years, saving the industry $170 million a year.
- "Trigger price" mechanisms, administered by the federal government, had the effect of increasing steel prices and raising profits.

The first three of these changes in federal regulations could add about $500 million per year to the treasuries of steel industry firms. However, steel industry managers indicated that these gifts from the federal government were still not sufficient incentive to encourage major investments in really new, integrated steel plants.

In their search for short-term profits, regardless of source, steel industry managers have relied increasingly on diversification. The 1980 annual report of the United States Steel Corporation showed that of its total "identifiable assets" only 51 percent remained in the steel industry. There is more of that to come. U.S. Steel and Armco have announced a continuation of the strategy; in 1980 the National Steel Corporation paid $241 million for a savings and loan company.[21]

From 1977 to 1980 the nonsteel assets of U.S. Steel grew by 80 percent, while steel assets increased 13 percent. In 1979 and 1980 the corporation showed the way for profit making with less steel production. It lowered steel production from 29.7 to 23.3 million tons while reducing its blast furnaces from forty-six to twenty-seven, and its employees from 170,000 to 155,000.[22]

According to steel management, the sharp increase in imports as a percent of U.S. steel consumption hurt them mainly because of unfair pricing by foreign competitors. However, industry analysts judge that the salability of steel products from Western Europe and from Japan in the United States is more related to efficient technology (as in Japan) and the high quality of the Japanese and Western European steel products.

A continuation of the policies and practices exhibited by the U.S. steel industry's managers during the last quarter-century will assuredly force deterioration to a point where, by the end of the 1980s, imports of steel could account for about one-third of U.S. industry's requirements, while employment would decline "by about 20 percent, or some 90,000 workers from the 1978 level."[23] Meanwhile, the major U.S. steel firms, having protected themselves financially with investments of all sorts outside their own industry, would still be able to maintain levels of profitability that were sufficiently attractive to investors and to financially oriented top managers.

Brushing aside all these considerations of steel and autos, many people believe that the future of U.S. prosperity depends on the newer high technology industries. That, they say, is where the United States can and should excel. How, then, is it doing in the realm, for example, of integrated circuit production?

In the spring of 1979 Richard W. Anderson, general manager of Hewlett-Packard's Computer Systems Division, caused a considerable stir when he disclosed that, in his firm's experience, integrated circuits delivered by U.S. manufacturers had five to six times the failure rate of comparable products available from Japanese firms. In October 1980 he reported an improvement among the U.S. firms amounting to a 50 percent reduction in the failure rate for the U.S. products.

What caused this quality difference between U.S. and Japanese producers of electronic components? In response to higher wage rates in the United States, "American integrated circuit vendors typically moved their labor-intensive operations offshore, to areas of low technology and low labor rates where it's very hard to exercise the control that's required to maintain a high level of quality. What the Japanese did was automate these operations, and surround them with highly trained supervision."[24] The Japanese approach to cost reduction was once the classic American pattern. It was the one that gave American industry its world supremacy in productivity.

The solution adopted by the American firms secured immediate short-term cost reduction without the long-term commitment associated with investment in new facilities. The Japanese firms, by contrast, secured cost reduction in their own factories by making a long-range commitment to new production equipment and to the training of a more sophisticated work force.

The U.S. producers of microchips and the computers that use them must expect a gathering storm of Japanese competition. The chief citadels of U.S. leadership in the world computer industry are now under challenge. Will the American managers of "silicon valley" and the great computer firms marshal the research, design, and production competence that is needed to hold a front rank position? Or will they too slip into the familiar patterns of industrial decay that have spelled catastrophe for major parts of the consumer electronics and other industries in the United States?

One test of production deterioration is the inability of U.S.-based factories to hold on to the home market. This has come about from the inability of managements to design, produce, and market competitively in terms of technology (quality of product) and economy (cost and price). The following table shows the extent of this declining competence, giving for each product the proportion of U.S. purchases that was supplied from production outside the United States during 1979–80. In each case, the

TABLE 2–1. Percentage of U.S. Consumption Produced Abroad (1979–80).

Product	%	Product	%
Apparel	20	Leather gloves	37
Automobiles	27	Machine tools	25[a]
Bicycles	22	Microwave ranges and ovens	22
Calculating machines, desk-top and printing	39	Motion-picture cameras (1977)	74
		Sewing machines (1978)	51
Calculating machines, hand-held	47	Steel mill products	15
Communications systems and equipment	16	Tape recorders and dictation machines, office type	100
Flatware	50	TV sets, black and white	87
Footwear (non-rubber)	45	X-ray and other irradiation equipment	24
Integrated microcircuits	34		

a. As of 1982, this figure was 42 percent.

imports displaced former U.S. production. For each class of product, the percentage of imports implies a substantial—for the most part permanent—loss of employment opportunity in the domestic industry.

This list of products and industries, while a small sampling, includes a number of industries whose basic importance is obvious (steel, machine tools, electronics). It also shows that the decline of production competence has not been limited to any particular class of product. The disabling of U.S. industry has proceeded in both producers' and in consumer goods, in hardware and in software, in "traditional" and in newer high technology industries. By 1980, it is clear, the U.S. industrial economy had suffered a debacle.

Many individual industries, to be sure, have been holding their own, and then some, in both the U.S. and world markets. These include a number of important machinery industries—electrical industrial apparatus, construction and mining machinery, miscellaneous mechanical equipment—as well as large chemical industries (industrial, pharmaceutical, plastics). Other U.S. industries that have maintained strong positions, technical and economic, abroad as well as at home are ones that have received massive government subsidies for research and development and for capital investment—mainly as part of the military-space economy. These industries include the manufacturing of aircraft, electrical equipment, engines, communications equipment, ordnance, and professional and scientific instruments.[25]

During 1978, there was a marked change in the composition of U.S. imports. Petroleum, long this country's leading import item, dropped to third place behind machinery, transportation equipment, and manufactured goods. The machinery ranged from machine tools and electronic equipment to motor vehicles, railroad equipment, and ships. The manufactured goods included iron and steel, nonferrous metals, alloys, plastics, medical and other instruments. The suppliers for both categories were located mainly in Japan and Europe.

These depleted industries reflect a development that is unprecedented in the American economy. The history of industrial capitalism records a succession of "business cycles," of booms and busts, but no instances of massed production incompetence. Until the present era no American manufacturing industry ever died from an inability to produce competent products at acceptable prices. A pattern emerges, in which each industry's decay may be likened to a particular production of a classic drama. In each production the actors wear different costumes, the stage settings vary according to industry and locale; as in the theater, the quality of the performance varies from one presentation to the next. But all these differences exist within essentially the same framework of plot and action.

The top management becomes increasingly finance- and short-term-profit-oriented; research and development activity is limited; investment in new equipment is deferred, and the age of manufacturing facilities increases; product variety is enlarged and opportunities for meaningful standardization are avoided; production equipment is pushed beyond limits of reliable performance; quality is controlled in a way to set acceptable percentages of defective products; work and workers are accorded low status and, therefore, the organization of work is of secondary importance; decision-making by workers is resisted as diminishing the decision power and effectiveness of management; profits are maintained by seeking investment opportunities outside the original product sphere of the firm; production facilities are abandoned after systematic withholding of maintenance and equipment replacement; management seeks improvement in overall efficiency by intensifying administrative controls and supervision; wage rates are described as the prime cause of noncompetitiveness; opportunities for productivity of capital and labor through stabilization of operations are characteristically ignored, being mainly unknown to industry management; management attempts to pass along cost increases to customers. When all else fails and profits as well as management's position are in peril, management turns to government for subsidy and rescue. All the while, as these processes unfold, management seeks its self-justification in pronouncements about postindustrial society, sunset industries, and the like.

I have referred repeatedly to data from West Germany and Japan in order to establish that the conditions in U.S. industry are not without alternatives. To grasp these alternatives it is important to focus on the common features of West Germany and Japan and contrast them with the United States. In the United States, management typically claims a sole "right to manage," even as unions have been recognized as the representatives of workers—thereby making effective decision processes bilateral in character. In West Germany and Japan, management concedes the worker some part in decisionmaking. The way of doing so differs widely, according to the different cultures of the two societies. In West Germany, a network of laws includes those providing for *Mitbestimmung,* for the functioning of works councils and the relation of these institutions to trade unions. In Japan, a network of hard-fought management-labor agreements, institutions, and usages defines rights and obligations of workers and managers, against a background of strongly production-oriented management.[26]

In the American industrial pattern, a real effort is made to effect a sharp separation between the decisionmaking and production occupations. Engineers are strongly oriented toward management careers and typically have no part in direct production operations. The German/Japanese pattern creates less separation between decisionmaking and producing. Engineers often participate directly in production. German and Japanese management systems are more congruent with modern technology than the U.S. Taylorite managerial model.

In all the above contrasts, the controlling difference is the attitude of these societies to workers and work. The other elements defined in this overview are consistent with and linked to the differences in that fundamental area.

Among Americans with a strong nationalist tradition, the spectacle of industrial decline has evoked a barrage of mainly irrelevant "explanations." High wages is the explanation usually advanced first. For two centuries, workshops, then manufacturing industries, in the United States prospered while paying the highest wages in the world. This was notably so during the twentieth century, when there was no question about the ease of transporting industrial goods, even across oceans. Product design and productivity in manufacturing in the United States were fully adequate to offset the lower wage costs enjoyed by manufacturers in all the other industrialized countries.

The reason for this decline does not lie in demands for high wages but grows out of normal managerial operations. When the cumulative effects of the developments in management, technology, and productivity are taken into account, a surprising prospect for the United States must be considered: The deterioration in production competence can become irreversible. Management has been expected to organize work and in exchange has been permitted to control production and to take a large share of the profits and power. But managerialism, oriented with primacy to profits/power, has developed a trained incapacity to organize work. The traditional basis for legitimacy of managerial power is being destroyed by the controlled deterioration of the U.S. production system and the parallel efforts of management to sustain its money making in the presence of a growing workless population. Once the social contract breakdown is displayed for all to see, there will come a national demand for alternative ways to organize work and rebuild the American economy.

NOTES

1. Unpublished data made available by U.S. Department of Labor, Bureau of Labor Statistics.

2. National Machine Tool Builders Association, *Economic Handbook of the Machine Tool Industry*, (1980–81), p. 250.

3. Michael Boretsky, *U.S. Technology: Trends and Policy Issues* U.S. Department of Commerce, October 1973, Table 21.

4. Sebastian B. Littauer, "Stability of Production Rates as a Determinant of Industrial Productivity Levels," *Proceedings of the Business and Economics Statistics Section*, American Statistical Association, 10–13 September 1954.

5. William J. Harahan, Director of Technical Planning for Manufacturing Staff, Ford Motor Company, quoted in *Business Week*, 14 September 1981, 97.

6. U.S. Congress, Office of Technology Assessment, *Technology and Steel Industry Competitiveness* (Washington, D.C., 1980), p. 130.

7. Ibid., p. 59.

8. Ibid., p. 95.

9. Nelson Fraiman, "Growth of Administrative Employment and Output in the U.S. Steel Industry," *Journal of Economic Issues* (June 1977).

10. Office of Technology Assessment, *Technology*, p. 364.

11. Ibid., p. 5.

12. *The New York Times*, 20 March 1981.

13. Office of Technology Assessment, *Technology*, p. 273.

14. Ibid., p. 278.

15. Ibid., p. 77.

16. Ibid., p. 369.

17. Frederick W. Taylor, *The Principles of Scientific Management* (Harper & Bros., 1911), p. 137.

18. *The Wall Street Journal*, 17 April 1981.

19. Ibid., 23 September 1980.

20. *The New York Times*, 17 August 1981.

21. Ibid., 19 February 1981.

22. Office of Technology Assessment, *Technology*, p. 36.

23. From a summary of remarks by Richard W. Anderson, General Manager, Hewlett-Packard Computer Systems Division, at H.P. press reception, Cupertino, California, 21 October 1980. By special communication from the Hewlett-Packard Company.

24. Office of Technology Assessment, *Technology*, pp. 276–81.

25. *The New York Times*, 5 July 1978.

26. Steve Lohr, "Japanese Earned Labor Harmony," *The New York Times*, 13 February 1982.

3

Labor and the Military— A History

Lance Compa

From the end of World War II to the recent Kissinger Commission report on Central America, the American labor movement has affirmed its official support for high levels of military spending and an interventionist foreign policy. To many American labor leaders and rank and file workers, jobs, patriotism, and a healthy union movement seem intimately interconnected. The heady experience of full employment and large-scale organizing during the Second World War, when union membership jumped from 8.5 million in 1940 to 13.5 million in 1945, induced the unions to support the arms race and the worldwide deployment of U.S. bases, weapons, and troops since then. By the mid-1950s union membership rose to 16.5 million. Over one-third of the total labor force, and half of the manufacturing labor force, were union represented. In 1954 the Congress of Industrial Organizations (the more liberal of the then-separate labor federations) complained about Eisenhower administration "penny pinching" in Pentagon spending and resolved that "the Government immediately drop its policy of attempting to measure defense expenditures against revenue receipts." While the rate of union growth slowed in the 1960s, continued economic expansion, new organizing gains, and significant contract advances appeared to parallel the growing U.S. involvement in the Vietnam War.

According to the supposed equation of wartime-scale production and trade union growth, the Reagan administration's huge buildup of missiles, aircraft, warships, and other weapons should be sparking a revival of union organizing and contract gains. Instead, the opposite is the case. Decades of collective bargaining breakthroughs have been eroded by employer-imposed contract concessions, and a fivefold increase in decertification votes in the past decade has eliminated hundreds of union bargaining units each year. Indeed, one of the government's first labor-related acts was to liquidate an entire union of air traffic controllers.

The rate of new union organizations is at a fifty-year low point.

33

Growth sectors of the economy, such as service and high technology, are resolutely nonunion. From representing one-third of the work force in the 1950s, organized labor has slipped below one-fifth. Perhaps most disturbingly, the worst setbacks have occurred in traditional labor bastions— mining, manufacturing, transportation, and construction. In a lost strike against concessions, Phelps-Dodge copper miners in Arizona, members of the United Steelworkers, have seen their union nearly broken. Auto workers, steel workers, rubber and electrical workers, and others in basic manufacturing have suffered from contract concessions, plant closings, and runaway shops. Airline employees have had huge concessions imposed on them, and Greyhound workers suffered a bitter strike defeat at the end of 1983. "Double-breasted" construction companies—whereby an organized contractor sets up a nonunion alter ego to avoid collective bargaining agreements—have moved massively into heavy construction projects that were formerly a union preserve.

Instead of offsetting this trend or even retarding it, the big increase in military spending promotes it. The "reverse transfer" of funds from social programs to the Pentagon has slashed union membership in what was the fastest growing part of the labor movement: public employee and service sector unions. Thanks to unrestrained military spending, a $200 billion federal deficit has created escalating interest rates that, in turn, depress construction activity. The same deficit, and the resultant overvalued dollar, have priced U.S.-made products out of international markets, making foreign imports irresistible bargains for American consumers.

Moreover, a disproportionate share of Pentagon largesse is showered on the antiunion South and Southwest. Especially in the growing high technology sectors, some of the biggest military contractors are completely nonunion. Even those unionized workers who work on military projects are subject to the quirks of a contracting process that can eliminate thousands of jobs at the clip of a terminated contract. Finally, a 1983 policy directive from Pentagon officials ordered contractors to force substantial concessions on their organized workers, commanding them to "accept work stoppages if that's what it takes."

Although this new attack on labor has taken many union leaders by surprise, such management and government assaults have inevitably followed tentative union advances during periods of a military buildup. Indeed, labor's attempt to fend off employer charges of foreign influence, radical domination, and subversive disregard of the "national interest," through official patriotism, support for high military budgets, and military intervention abroad has never brought more than temporary gains.

Official labor patriotism goes back to the early days of the American Federation of Labor (AF of L). Constituted in 1886 from a federation formed five years earlier, the AF of L sought to gather the elite of the labor movement, especially its skilled crafts (though mineworkers, brewers, and other industrial groupings were also a part of it), and find a safe haven where unions could conduct their business without exhausting themselves in losing battles. The AF of L stood for craft autonomy, a narrow scope of economic activity, and reliance on "friends of labor" in the political arena rather than independent labor political action.

Careful always to distinguish themselves from the more class-conscious, socialist-oriented unionism of labor radicals in groups like the Industrial Workers of the World (IWW) and the Western Federation of Miners (WF of M), AF of L leaders thought to gain acceptance from employers and government authorities. Samuel Gompers, the cigar makers' union leader who presided over the AF of L for nearly forty years after its founding, declared that corporate and political leaders should cooperate with the AF of L "or they will have the alternative of being forced to take the consequences of the so-called IWW with all that that implies." And indeed, while the Knights of Labor, the IWW, the WF of M and other radical labor formations broke under the weight of government repression and their own organizational ineptitude in the late nineteenth and early twentieth centuries, the AF of L, despite occasional setbacks, patiently consolidated its strength and sharpened its business union ideology.

In spite of the dominant AF of L conservatism, Eugene V. Debs (later a Socialist Party candidate for president) and many other socialists led individual federation affiliates in its early decades, livening labor activity in those years. Debs led the 1894 Pullman strike, which spread from the luxury passenger car maker to a nationwide railroad strike, one of the landmark labor struggles of the last century. When Debs and other strike leaders appealed to the AF of L for support after a federal court injunction broke the strike and landed them in jail, Samual Gompers demurred with a pithy statement of the federation's philosophy: "In the eyes of the public mind the working classes are now arrayed in open hostility to the Federal authority. This is a position we do not wish to be placed in."

Until the eve of World War I, the AF of L reflected the country's prevailing isolationist mood. But as the United States prepared to enter the European conflict, Gompers abandoned his previous pacifist views. He accepted an appointment in 1916 to the Council on National Defense, an advisory commission on war preparedness. This marked the beginning of a special relationship between American labor leadership and the U.S. military. Shortly before the U.S. declaration of war in April 1917, Gompers convened a special conference of AF of L unions to resolve all-out support for Wilson administration policy. Upon the dispatch of American troops, he called the war "the most wonderful crusade ever entered upon by men in the whole history of the world." In fact, this crusade held out great promise to Gompers and the AF of L.

The need for uninterrupted production promoted creation of a War Labor Board, a special commission set up to prevent or help resolve labor disputes. The War Labor Board protected the AF of L and helped destroy what was left of their opposition in the IWW. In return, the AF of L endorsed emergency espionage and sedition laws that were used to jail or deport IWW leaders and other antiwar activists. There were hundreds of AF of L union strikes during the war, including in war-related industries, but the government never charged AF of L unions with disloyalty. Federal authorities protected federation union leaders from arrests and the unions themselves from strikebreaking.

Even in AF of L unions with strong antiwar sentiments, opposition was muted or suppressed as the War Labor Board handed out its favors. Union shop and maintenance-of-membership clauses were forced on recalcitrant employers. Recognition of unions was encouraged, and government contracts were awarded with favored unions in mind.

The Amalgamated Clothing Workers, for example, was a struggling union at the beginning of World War I. Yet, by the end of the war, it has organized the bulk of the industry and become one of the major unions in the AF of L. To a great extent this was due to the efforts of Sidney Hillman, then an emerging young officer of the union who, twenty years later, became the most influential labor leader under Franklin Roosevelt. Hilliman led a drive to silence the antiwar forces in the Amalgamated especially among the union's many immigrant, socialist members. In return, the government adopted a policy of awarding major contracts for uniforms and related military apparel only to union-represented firms and thus helped the Amalgamated gain its position in the industry.

The labor movement was recharged when the war ended in 1918. AF of L labor's optimism was part of a general surge of euphoria that swept the nation at war's end. Having helped win the war, unionists joined other liberal forces to seek progressive reform. Liberal stalwarts, *The Nation* and the *New Republic* called for a labor-progressive alliance, continuation of government planning efforts, and democratic controls on corporate investments. Confident of its place, the AF of L adopted a policy statement in December 1918 calling for government ownership of public utilities, controls on corporate power, and a federal housing program. The United Mine Workers demanded nationalization of the mines, and the railroad brotherhoods sought government operation of the rail system.

Instead of progress, a wave of repression greeted the labor and progressive movements, pulling even the loyal AF of L in its wake. In 1919 government troops crushed the Seattle general strike, the Boston police strike, and the first national steel strike. Threats of more federal strikebreaking ended a nationwide coal strike and prevented a rail strike the same year. By the end of 1919, strike incidence was at a six-year low point. In the notorious Palmer Raids of January 1920, thousands of workers and union activists were arrested and many deported for their radical leanings, or merely for being foreign born.

Gompers and the AF of L leadership hoped that their wartime cooperation would insulate the federation from the new antilabor offensive. They were, however, disappointed. The AF of L reform program was dismissed, and unions were relegated to their prewar supplicant status. Without its favored wartime treatment, and ruling out militant organizing tactics in the growing mass production industries, the AF of L lost 25 percent of its members. It fell from over four million in 1919 to fewer than three million in 1923, where it stagnated for the rest of the decade in the midst of an economic boom. The union security clauses that had been the plum of the wartime collaboration were rolled back by a massive open-shop drive by employers, tellingly called "the American Plan."

In spite of these setbacks, there was no slackening in the support that the AF of L gave the U.S. military. Samuel Gompers lectured annually at the Army War College from 1919 until his death in 1924, and his successor, William Green, carried on the tradition. Notwithstanding the Legion's extensive involvement in strikebreaking and antiunion agitation around the country, the AF of L formed a de facto alliance with the newly formed American Legion in the 1920's.

In 1926 the AF of L endorsed the Citizens Military Training Corps—in effect, a national militia sponsored by big employers—although its program included antiunion indoctrination and training of strikebreakers. Seeking a quid pro quo for its patriotism, the AF of L petitioned for a new wage board, patterned after the War Labor Board, to help civilian employees of the War Department. An Army liaison officer recommended such a board on the grounds that the AF of L was "conservative and patriotic" in contrast to the menace of more radical labor activists who were "definitely military" and "definitely pacifistic." The War Department's denial of this modest request demonstrated the frailty of labor's reliance on official patriotism to shore up its organizational and collective bargaining weaknesses.

To remedy AF of L's growing weakness, its leaders turned to an old ally, the National Civic Federation (NCF), for succor in its 1920s crisis. A tripartite business-labor-public alliance, the NCF was formed at the turn of the century to combat radical elements in the labor movement and, supposedly, to rein in renegade antiunion companies. The NCF sent a nationwide mailing to American employers in 1924 begging for an end to union-busting. The labor movement of every other industrial country, it pointed out, was in the hands of communists and socialists who were "harrassing their governments" whereas the AF of L supported U.S.

military might, fought against diplomatic recognition of the new Soviet state, and opposed the formation of a labor-based political party. Complaining of continued employer hostility to unions, the NCF urged something be done "to allay this bitterness between two forces which, logically, should be working together against common foes whose philosophy spells the taking over of all their property, and the government as well." There is no evidence of any response, other than continued union-busting campaigns.

Desperate for acceptance and respect, the labor movement touted every gimmick imaginable to bolster its prospects. Worker ownership, labor management efficiency committees, the "B&O Plan" for labor-management cooperation, union welfare funds, labor banks—all were held out as the salvation of the labor movement. So pervasive was its desperation that in 1928 the AF of L Executive Council actually issued a statement declaring that "at no time in its history has the trade union had greater influence in industrial circles. The constructive policies which we advocate and follow challenge the attention of employers in this country and abroad." In an unguarded moment, however, Metal Trades president John P. Frey confessed, "We have been so 'good' that we have become almost no good."

Frustrated rank and file American workers finally blew past the craft-union AF of L leadership in the great strikes and organizing drives of the 1930s. That upsurge of industrial unionism took organizational shape in the new Congress of Industrial Organizations (CIO), based among mine, auto, steel, rubber, and electrical workers. AF of L leader Frey, earlier concerned whether the federation was too "good," regained his senses and declared to the newly formed House Un-American Activities Committee in 1938 that 248 Communists controlled the CIO. The AF of L moved quickly to its own program of industrial organizing. The older federation soon organized as many industrial workers as did the CIO, in formerly craft-line AF of L unions such as the International Association of Machinists, the International Brotherhood of Electrical Workers, the United Brotherhood of Carpenters, and others.

World War II was another period of opportunity for patriotic trade unionism. Left-wing CIO union leaders, initially opposed to U.S. involvement in the war, switched when Nazi Germany attacked the Soviet Union in mid-1941. By the December attack on Pearl Harbor, the labor movement was united in support of the war effort. For the most part unions honored a no-strike pledge, restraining their demands and cooperating with a new War Labor Board. They were again rewarded, while the conflict was underway, with the stabilizing force of union shop and maintenance-of-membership clauses in labor contracts for military production, forms of union security that they had not been able to standardize in the

1930s organizing surge. As many new workers came under contract during the war as were organized in all of the great 1930s drives.

At the close of World War II, pent-up consumer demands at home and the need for reconstruction abroad made the shift from wartime to civilian production a matter of mechanics more than one of creative policy changes. Besides, the emerging cold war and revolutionary struggles in China and the Third World European empires made for continuing demand for high levels of military production, so the change was not as abrupt as it might have been.

Angered over what they saw as wartime profiteering by corporations, combined with steep postwar inflation, the CIO unions led nationwide strikes in the steel, auto, electrical, and other mass production industries in 1946, winning large wage increases to restore purchasing power lost in the wartime austerity. Employers responded to the CIO effort with their own political offensive. Cries of a too-powerful labor movement helped give Republicans control of Congress in the 1946 elections, leading to passage of the Taft-Hartley Act in 1947. The new law reversed many of the principles of the Wagner Act, the original New Deal legislation that protected workers' rights to organize and bargain collectively.

Taft-Hartley took organizing out of the workers' hands and gave employers license to campaign openly against union organization. Because of the inherent intimidation that flows from the employment relationship, the power to wage an antiunion campaign inside the workplace gave employers an overwhelming advantage in NLRB elections.

Taft-Hartley also required the National Labor Relations Board (NLRB) to automatically seek injunctions against unions for unfair labor practices but left injunctions against employers optional, a choice the board has rarely used to help workers. It permitted "right-to-work" laws in the states, which prohibit employers and unions from negotiating union shop clauses in collective bargaining agreements, which would require the payment of dues to the bargaining representative. It outlawed solidarity work stoppages called "secondary boycotts" by union members supporting other workers' struggles. Finally, the 1947 Act required all union officers to sign non-Communist affidavits in order to enjoy what little protection was left in the law, in particular the right to appear on an NLRB election ballot.

Anxious to forestall further attacks, the labor movement embraced the cold war. The CIO expelled eleven left-wing unions in 1949 and began moving toward accord with the AF of L. Their 1955 merger created a united labor movement of cold war liberals and old-line craft unionists.

Walter Reuther of the United Auto Workers, who led the drive to oust the left unions from the CIO, summed up the traditional longing of labor leaders for respectability when he told the 1947 CIO convention that "the thing that is weak with American foreign policy is in how it is being sold to the people of Europe.... My plea is that they have to bring labor into this, give us our place around the councils in Washington just as they did during the War..." Reuther's plea was answered; the right kind of labor leaders were accepted: those who adopted a hard-edged cold war ideology and accepted direct CIA involvement in the labor movement.

Passionate anti-Communism and compliance with CIA policy directives thus became litmus tests for labor patriots in the late 1940s and early 1950s. The labor movement's foreign and military policies were managed by ex-Communist Jay Lovestone, George Meany's director of international affairs, and by ex-World Federalist Cord Meyer, head of the CIA's labor section.

During the war, the Soviet Union had been an ally and the European resistance was led by Communists and Socialists, many of them labor activists. Labor staffers in the OSS, World War II's predecessor to the CIA, had been drawn largely from liberal and left forces in the CIO. After the war, however, they were purged. Lovestone's chief aide Irving Brown (who is now in charge of the AFL-CIO Department of International Affairs) and AF of L loyalists took over European labor work. Using CIA funds, they established right-wing labor groups to break the power of Communist-led unions in Europe. After its 1955 merger, the AFL-CIO went on to create foreign labor "institutes" in Africa, Asia, and Latin America, using U.S. government money to develop a cadre of right-wing labor leaders in those continents.

A degree of self-satisfaction was understandable as labor leaders surveyed their prospects in the mid-1950s. The merger of the two federations ended years of fratricidal raiding and promised new, unified organizing drives. Key industrial sectors were almost fully unionized, and labor had a great deal of bargaining clout. Just as Keynesian economics seemed to stabilize the business cycle and end the threat of depression, labor statesmanship had stabilized the unions' place in society and ended the threat of widespread union-busting.

In the postwar period of expansion, there seemed, indeed, to be enough wealth to spread around to everyone in the mainstream of the U.S. economy. But when the expansion ended and U.S. companies began facing a strong challenge from Japanese and European manufacturers (and the more advanced Third World nations, as well) American companies began looking inward in the 1970s to a new source of profitability: weaker unions and lowered union demands.

One event above all others illustrated the weaknesses of labor's postwar strategy: the demise of the Labor Law Reform Bill in 1978. The labor reform bill had been pursued by unions since the Taft-Hartley days.

It provided several legal boosts to organize new workers; for example, expediting representation elections, giving union organizers "equal time" opportunities to address workers, and denying federal contracts to repeat labor law violators. Corporate attacks on the bill mocked the premise of its labor proponents that unions had become an equal and accepted partner in the American power structure.

The labor movement gathered all its resources and put them on the line for the labor law reform bill. Union leadership declared it the acid test for politicians seeking labor support, and many union leaders expected the bulk of the management community to support the bill. "Nothing is more important to the labor movement," declared AFL-CIO President George Meany at this point in its history, "nothing." The corporations agreed. They made the bill their own top priority—and worked to defeat it. A massive employer lobbying campaign overwhelmed union accounts of rank and file workers who had suffered under management abuse of the loophole-ridden Taft-Hartley law.

Stung by this betrayal, the AFL-CIO leadership pleaded with big business to hold up its end of the postwar deal. In an "open letter to the wise and intelligent leaders of the American business community," George Meany begged:

> Why do you let the hate mongers and law violators falsely claim to speak in the name of America's business leaders?... Do you support the law breakers and the law evaders in the business community? Do you want to destroy American trade unionism? Do you secretly seek a death sentence for the collective bargaining system you so often hail in public forums?

Unable to accept the business community's answer, then-Secretary–Treasurer Lane Kirkland bravely claimed that blue chip business leaders really supported labor law reform. Unfortunately, as Kirkland explained after union leaders could not break a Senate filibuster that killed the bill, "organized pressures on company executives by customers, suppliers, and bankers have compelled them to hold their tongues in spite of their better instincts."

These better instincts notwithstanding, business leaders have followed their campaign against labor law reform with a campaign to weaken labor further through plant closings, runaway shops, and decertification drives. Corporate officials have enlisted the help of sophisticated union-busting consultants to snuff out organizing drives at the newly built plants of the Fortune 500. Using misapplied bankruptcy laws, dummy "double-breasted" corporations, and other paper maneuvers, they have successfully evaded collective bargaining with established unions. With massive unemployment, cutbacks in unemployment insurance, welfare, pensions, and the deterioration of entire sections of the economy and the country, the labor movement is suffering the worst crisis it has faced since the 1920s.

The American labor movement is thus confronting some hard choices. In the 1920s, the issue was craft versus industrial unionism: organizing the millions of workers in the mass production industries into single unions or clinging to a craft system limited to skilled trades workers. At that time, only an insurgent movement, led by John L. Lewis, was able to organize breakthroughs and build the CIO.

No less a revolution in current labor strategy (though it need not require an institutional break) is needed to solve the new crisis in American trade unionism.

Dealing with military spending and foreign policy is critical to labor's future. Military spending is robbing the civilian economy and destroying union jobs. American support for right-wing military regimes creates havens for runaway shops from American plants. Ideological barriers to trade with socialist countries cut off one-third of many potential world markets to U.S. workers. The refusal by AFL-CIO leaders to confer with Communist trade unionists—the mainstream labor leaders in many capitalist countries—impedes the building of trade union unity against the multinational corporations.

There can be no revival of the American labor movement without solutions to these and other foreign and military policy problems. The new willingness of many union leaders and union members to speak out on foreign and military policy issues suggests that there is hope for such a revival.

By the end of the 1960s, many union leaders were challenging the unwavering hawkish line of the AFL-CIO and the federation's support for the Vietnam War. A thousand labor leaders, many of them national officers of major AFL-CIO Unions, organized a "Labor for Peace" initiative in 1972. While conservatives remained firmly in control of the AFL-CIO's official foreign and military policy apparatus, the passions of the antiwar movement generated a new spirit of weighing, challenging, and questioning within the labor movement

Today, nineteen international unions, including most of the largest AFL-CIO affiliates, have come out forthrightly in favor of a bilateral, verifiable freeze on the production, deployment, and testing of nuclear weapons over the opposition of government officials and top AFL-CIO leaders. These unions forced the national federation to amend an equivocal, staff-prepared resolution on defense policy to acknowledge that "among our membership, as in our society, a majority favor a verifiable bilateral nuclear freeze." At the local level, many rank and file union leaders have been active in freeze referendums and other local initiatives aimed at halting the arms race.

A new, progressive wing is taking shape in the labor movement, ending a lock-step compliance on foreign and military policy issues. For some top labor officials, the change is threatening. American Federation of Teachers President Albert Shanker, a top federation insider who proudly proclaims himself a labor hawk, has lamented to a conference of retired generals and admirals that "there is a tremendous softening toward the left" in the labor movement. He warned against "the possibility in some unions of fairly significant infiltration of groups that say, 'We're helping you on labor laws, we're helping you on these various social programs, we'd like you to work with us on the reduction of defense expenditures.'"

The healthiest development in the labor movement is precisely this new alliance of labor and peace groups, though it has nothing to do with the ominous implications of the infiltration suggested by Shanker. Labor's new peace movement instead grows out of the hard blows unions are suffering in the workplace due to military spending and to the realization by many in labor's rank and file, as well as leaders, that the present course of our foreign and military policies could end in disaster.

Just as a break with craft unionism was needed to spark the CIO organizing burst in the 1930s, a break with the labor movement's historical compliance on military and foreign policy issues is key to an overall revival of the labor movement. Unless they face up to the consequences of high military spending and its damage to their own members (let alone the threat of nuclear annihilation and what *it* means for their members), AFL-CIO and other union leaders' attempts to formulate viable economic policy positions and to build progressive political coalitions are doomed. There can be no broad social advances by labor and its allies—each of which is indispensable to the others—if the trade unions do not take up leadership in the most potent mass organizing current of our time: the movement to halt the arms race and prevent nuclear war. The principles of economic conversion from military to human needs production can unify these movements and help make trade unionism once again a growing, organizing, aggressive force for reform in American society.

PART II

Why Conversion

4

The West and the Rest: Conversion and Third World Development

Clyde Sanger

The experience of two development decades—the 1960s and the 1970s—has shown that, of all the factors that might produce restraint in military expenditure by the major spenders, the least persuasive so far has been the need for greater developmental aid. The big spenders have not responded, and will not respond, to louder calls for what they may regard as charity. The task is to convince the governments of industrialized countries that a greater commitment to world development, as well as to disarmament, is in their own best interests.

Proving this case is not too difficult, but translating it into a basis for policy is more so. Governments have to acknowledge first that accelerated economic growth in the industrialized countries has become increasingly dependent each year upon more balanced development throughout the world. Secondly, they need to accept that the new factors aggravating the security problems of states cannot be resolved by military strength: the prospect of shortages of raw materials, particularly in the energy sector; pollution and other strains upon the environment; and impatience over the widening disparities between the wealthy and the poor.

There is still a broad resistance among the western industrialized countries to a phrase coined in 1974, when developing countries began to call for "a new international economic order" (NIEO). The Brandt Report[1] tried to soften this antagonism by speaking of the "mutuality of interests" between industrialized and developing countries, thus suggesting that all parties will be winners from the changes that have to come. Another phrase that has recently come into use—it is favored by the UN Group of Experts—is "the cooperative management of interdependence." Both are rather ponderous phrases, but their importance cannot be denied.

Excerpted from Clyde Sanger, *Safe and Sound: Disarmament and Development in the Eighties*, (Deneau Publishers, Ottawa).

REALLOCATING RESOURCES

Every government must have a lengthy list of programs to which it would invest larger resources if it felt able to embark upon a steady reduction of military spending. There are long-established social programs—housing construction, public health, social security—that many planners believe require increased funding; in the United States, even before the Reagan administration's cutbacks, it was being argued that, to meet priorities, allocations to these three programs should be raised by between 32 and 58 percent in the early 1980s.

Of newer programs, environmental protection should have strong claims on any resources released by disarmament. The Organization for Economic Cooperation and Development (OECD) has warned that air pollution in Western Europe will rise by 70 to 80 percent during the early 1980s if protection measures remain at the expenditure level of the 1970s. The U.S. National Planning Association has estimated that, for an effective program of environmental protection against industrial and nuclear pollution in the United States, a budget of some $45 billion will be needed. And the world in general has yet to discover a reliable way to dispose of nuclear waste.

In recent years, seven to eight times as much has been spent on military research and development around the world as on research on energy conservation and on alternative sources of energy. With the approach of higher cost energy, of whatever sort, all industrialized countries face broad requirements for reindustrialization: their manufacturing technology, their plant and the location of their factories, as well as the networks of transportation and distribution, all belong to the era of cheap energy. Estimates released by the UN Economic and Social Council suggest (probably conservatively) that the Soviet Union and Eastern Europe need to increase their investment in the energy field, including transport and distribution, from 4 percent of net material product in 1979 to at least 4.5 percent in 1990.

As for the United States, the 1981 National Economic Survey calculated that between $40 and $80 billion of capital investment would be required each year to bring industry to reasonable levels of productivity and cost efficiency in the era of higher energy prices. Obviously, most of this investment—amounting to between one-quarter and one-half of all nonresidential fixed investment in the United States—would come from the private sector. But this great process of reindustrialization needs to draw to some extent on public funds.

A study for the United Nations Institute for Training and Research (UNITAR), *Eastern Europe and the New International Economic Order,* by Ervin Laszlo and Joel Kurtzman points out how small a share of world trade the Soviet Union and the six countries of Eastern Europe hold, considering their state of industrialization. In 1976, the authors state, the portion of the world's industrial production that they possessed was nearly 26 percent; their share of the world's gross product was 17 percent, and of world exports, a mere 8.8 percent. Studies submitted to the UN Group of Experts confirm that one of the greatest obstacles in Eastern Europe and the Soviet Union to the full mobilization of all internal factors for development—manpower, capital, raw materials—has been the enormous diversion of resources for military purposes. The release of manpower from the military sector can relieve the labor shortages foreseen in these countries' industries during the 1980s, and the reallocation of material resources will help an industrial overhaul that should enable them to compete more effectively in international trade and should also provide a better range of consumer goods for their citizens. There is, in sum, a great number of domestic priorities to which resources can be put in the industrialized nations of the world if balanced reductions are made in military spending.

For developing countries, it is difficult to generalize. Their levels of military expenditure vary greatly, and some governments do not see much prospect of reducing expenditures, even if there was general disarmament, arguing that their possession of scarce natural resources makes them vulnerable to subversion or outright attack. It is true that military activities in some developing countries can have considerable ancillary benefits, such as the training of manpower in certain skills; and there are other structural constraints to development that would not be simply cleared by the reallocation of resources from the military sector.

But having said all that, most developing countries would certainly benefit, even in the short term, if they were able to reduce their military spending and allot more resources to satisfying basic human needs. Those countries that are spending relatively large amounts on importing arms, and which are consequently short of foreign exchange to buy capital goods and technology for vital sectors of their economies, can hope for considerably greater economic growth if the problem of balancing their civilian trade in imports and exports is relaxed.

Between 1967 and 1976, a period of major military clashes in the Middle East and South Asia as well as of the first energy crisis, less than one-third of the seventy-one countries that were importing weapons had a positive trade balance.[2] The reduction of balance of payments constraints is at the core of the Leontief/Duchin projection of economic consequences of reduced military spending, and its results provide several dramatic examples of improved economic growth following the easing of these constraints and a reduction in arms expenditure, most notably among the eighteen countries of arid Africa but also in low-income Asia.

DISARMAMENT AND THE NIEO

The larger part of investment in the economic and social advancement of developing countries will continue to have to come, as it always has done, from their own domestic sources. But even a substantial reduction in their military spending (and some cannot cut much, because they are spending a negligible amount anyway) will not by itself clear the way for accelerated development. There is a sharp need to transfer resources from the industrialized world. These can take several other forms than balance-of-payments credits; for example, increasing investment in industrialization and measures to stimulate export trade in the developing countries. The OECD and the World Bank agree that an annual 5 percent rate of increase in the flow of official development assistance—now totalling $30 billion—is an indispensable minimum to bolster the economic growth of the developing nations.

This brings us back to the New International Economic Order, for these are elements in the Program of Action that was worked out during the sixth special Session of the UN General Assembly in April–May 1974. A number of steps have been taken since then to alter the existing system and compensate for the heavy inequality of conditions it has produced over many years, by some measures of positive discrimination in favor of developing countries. Certain tariffs and other trade barriers have been reduced. In 1979 it was agreed to establish the Common Fund, the price stabilization element in an Integrated Program of Commodities for the eighteen most important primary products of developing countries. In the Rome Convention of 1975, the European Community negotiated with forty-six African, Caribbean, and Pacific countries an improved form of association, which included trade promotion, industrial cooperation, and an innovative (if inadequately funded) scheme for stabilizing export earnings. The International Fund for Agricultural Development was set up in 1974 to improve food security in developing countries, and the North-South Summit at Cancun, Mexico, in December 1981 renforced this objective. A few other measures have been added, such as the forgiveness of some foreign debts on development loans.

But overall, progress on the goals behind the Program of Action for a new international economic order has been slow and uneven. In 1980, the average per capita income for all developing countries was just one-thirteenth of that of the industrial countries—$850 compared with $10,660—and for the low-income countries of Africa and Asia the gap in per capita income is an enormous 50 to 1 since their average income is only $220. The divergence, in fact, widened visibly in the 1970s, the second development decade.

This falling backwards is particularly noticeable in foreign trade. While some OPEC members have built up a large surplus, the low-income oil-importing countries of Asia and Africa have suffered dismally. In 1980, when payments for fuel imports had been made, these countries had only $11 billion worth of foreign exchange to pay for all other imports, compared with $16.2 billion in 1970. *The World Development Report 1981* estimates that, even in the high (i.e., optimistic) case of trends projected to 1990, in that year these countries will have only $12.3 billion of purchasing power for imports. (All these figures are comparable, being calculated in 1978 dollars.)

There are exceptions to this sorry tale. A few developing countries have strong and productive manufacturing industries, a principal goal in the 1974 Program of Action and the subsequent Lima Declaration adopted by the Second General Conference of the United Nations Industrial Development Organization (UNIDO). But there are not many: By 1977, eight countries and territories—Brazil, Hong Kong, Malaysia, Mexico, the Philippines, Singapore, South Korea, and Taiwan—accounted for almost 75 percent of the manufactures exported by the developing nations. And even with these countries, the benefits were unfairly concentrated, because investment went into industrial enclaves that employed a small fraction of the work force in comparative prosperity.

Disarmament and conversion measures can and should give a fresh start to efforts to bring in a new international economic order. No one denies the increasing interdependence of states. Cooperative management is the only wise course on many matters, from the exploitation of seabed resources ("the heritage of all mankind") to environmental protection. Where there is apparent conflict of interest—for example, competition in manufactured goods and the recent trend in industrialized countries toward protectionism rather than offering greater access to markets—the present period of adjusting industry to higher energy costs may provide unexpected grounds for cooperation. For, when seen in the broad context of change and reindustrialization, making it easier for developing countries to reach wider markets is a far less disruptive course.

The release of many scientists and technicians from military activities can also speed the transfer of modern technology, especially if satisfactory codes of conduct are worked out so that transnational corporations conform to the national development plans of their host governments. Also, greater benefits to developing countries from research and development can surely be expected as a by-product of disarmament and conversion and a part of increased official development assistance. So little research has been devoted to the specific problems of developing countries—to improving, for instance, the yield and nutritional value of staple foods rather than conducting research on export crops—that even a small increase could produce significant benefits.

Few would argue, and even fewer would expect, that more than a minor part of the "disarmament savings" should or would be transferred to developing countries as official development assistance. The advantage that developing countries may hope to gain from these savings is an indirect one: a more equal system of world trade after industrialized countries have put resources into industrial adjustment in the general conversion from military production.

What is important, above all, is the attitude of cooperation. If agreement can be researched on a comprehensive and balanced program to reduce global military expenditure, there is no reason why the spirit of cooperation cannot carry over into a comprehensive program of economic development. And, in this spirit, the mutuality of interests between the industrialized and developing countries will become more evident.

DISARMAMENT AND WORLD TRADE

This mutuality is best seen in patterns of world trade. The pattern much simplified, is a triangular one of West, East, and South.

East-West economic relations have been greatly affected by the clouds of the arms race and the sunshine of detente. During the noontime of detente, there was a sixfold increase in the turnover of East-West trade, but the dismal times of fear and suspicion have produced (according to calculations by the Polish Institute of International Affairs) some 2,000 groups of items excluded from the East-West trade list on political-strategic grounds.

Trade between East and South has been as meager as the level of development assistance. When developing countries have stressed the importance of the centrally planned economies becoming more involved in international economic discussions, and specifically expanding their aid and trade with the South, the reply has often been to point to the global arms race as a reason for their not being able to do so. The Council for Mutual Economic Assistance and the Development Process[3] expressed the hope that the seven countries would double their present share of imports from developing countries during the 1980s and also considerably increase their own exports, but the authors add that "it would hardly be possible to implement the plans for the 1980s in a world embarked upon an extremely costly and escalating arms race."

The West-South trade relationship holds great promise for times of recovery and of disarmament. In 1976, before the present recession, some 2,400,000 jobs in the seventeen OECD countries were directly attributable to exports to developing countries, while about 850,000 jobs could be considered lost or nonexistent because of imports; the favorable balance of employment to OECD countries from this trade was a net 1,550,000 jobs.

The growth of the arms trade in the later 1970s has certainly provided jobs in Western exporting countries at a time of high unemployment. Weapons bought by Saudi Arabia from the United States are said to be providing 112,000 Americans with jobs over the next five years. The study of Professor Rolf Krengel of West Berlin estimates that in the Federal Republic of Germany the effect in jobs lost of a 10 percent reduction in worldwide military spending would be no more than 0.4 percent of the labor force. This loss is small compared with the great potential for trade in nonmilitary goods and services, particularly with the South.

Each of the three points of this trade triangle acts upon the other. It is sometimes said that East and West meet as competitors in the markets of the South, and also that the export patterns of the East are similar to those of the South. The positive aspect is a growing realization in the East that its economic policies must be coordinated with both the market and developing country economies, and this can perhaps best be done in the framework of the New International Economic Order.

A more stable South, capable of sustaining its independence through a better economic performance, can reduce the possible areas of political conflict between East and West. If the expansion of trade flows, then, help to put future detente on a sounder basis, additional investment in the development of the South is an indirect contribution to detente. The negative triangle of armaments–insecurity–underdevelopment can be replaced by this much more promising pattern, but it requires political will and a determination to embark upon "the cooperative management of interdependence."

PLANNING FOR CONVERSION

One major purpose of planning and preparing for conversion is to minimize resistance to disarmament measures. It is important that those affected realize three things:

- That the disarmament process will be thorough and cumulative, not sporadic and liable to be revoked by some sudden reaction to a crisis
- That it is almost certain to be gradual, for conversion will not involve having to replace $500 billion of military demand at a single step or to absorb tens of millions of workers into the civilian work force

- That conversion is feasible and economically beneficial because it offers the prospect of more jobs and a steadier demand for products.

Before considering measures that can minimize the transitional problems of conversion, we should look at five important characteristics of the arms industry:

1. It is highly concentrated, in about twenty countries. Arms production in developing countries amounts to only 4 percent of the total world arms production, while the industry in the United States, the Soviet Union, Great Britain, and France accounts for some 80 percent. It is also often concentrated in certain regions of these countries; for example; around the White Sea, where most of the construction of the Soviet Union's nuclear-powered submarines takes place, or in Southern California. The global output of this industry was about $130 billion in 1980. Some five million people are directly employed in producing weapons and specialized military equipment.

2. The arms industry is also heavily centralized in certain industrial sectors, principally those industries that can supply major weapons systems—aircraft, missiles, warships, and tanks. There are wide variations between the major producing nations, but data from NATO countries show that military demand accounts for between 40 and 80 percent of production in the aerospace sector and between 20 and 30 percent of electronics business.

3. Proportionately, much more is spent on research and development in defense industries as in others, and they employ a much higher percentage of engineers, technicians, and skilled workers.

4. There is a growing dependence on exports in the defense industries of some countries, particularly the four main arms suppliers; these, though fluctuating in volume year by year, now make up more than 20 percent of the world's production of military goods and services. The export share of military goods produced in selected industries of countries providing data for the later 1970s is in the range of 40 to 70 percent. If this is the general pattern for arms-producing countries, it complicates the problems of conversion.

5. The defense industry in all countries is largely under either direct or indirect state control. This control is complete in the Soviet Union, while in France and Great Britain about half the workers directly engaged in military production in 1980 were employed in nationalized or state enterprises. Even in the United States the federal government owns much of the plant space and manufacturing equipment of the aircraft industry. Besides, the government as the buyer of a weapons system assumes all the financial risks, since a contract is normally based on specifications and

the price is established later, after the cost of meeting the specifications has been worked out.

These five characteristics provide a background for some of the problems that have to be faced when conversion programs begin.

Attitudes of Specialized Workers

In particular, scientists and engineers in the military sector in all important producing countries are taught to emphasize quality and performance standards rather than high production rates or cost-effectiveness, as in the commercial world. Managers in military industries have also become specialists, because of the technical complexity of the things they are manufacturing; often they have some special skill, ranging from systems management to familiarity with particular governmental procedures. Retraining and a change of attitudes will be needed, but some of the particular skills can be applied with benefit to civil projects.

Specialized Capital Equipment

Over the past thirty years, the great effort of military research and development and the very particular standards of performance have produced a technological capacity in the military sector quite separate from civilian industry. The conversion problem will be lessened if, during the lengthy period of transition, military and civilian production takes place side by side at the plant level. This will mean curbing the military appetite for high performance and technological excellence at almost any cost; and doing that will greatly help to slow down the arms race, because it will begin to remove the qualitative imperative. Capital equipment can be turned over directly if it is government owned; if it is owned privately, various incentives can be offered to firms to sell or scrap it and then reinvest for civilian production.

Greater Financial Risks

Most defense work is paid for on a continuing basis, providing a favorable cash flow for the contractor. Military research and development is also carried out at low risk, because of government support. And the rate of profit is fairly certain, once a military contract is secured, because it is based on cost-plus pricing. In most markets for civilian products there is uncertainty on all these matters.

Companies that have specialized in military work may well be apprehensive about conversion because they will have two legitimate fears about their own competitiveness. They carry large overheads, with a work force top-heavy with managerial, scientific, and engineering staff; and they lack experience in marketing civilian products.

MEASURES TO MINIMIZE THE PROBLEMS OF TRANSITION

It is clear enough by now that the conversion process needs to be carefully planned at all levels, from the central government to the munitions factory, and then to a community that has become dependent on military spending. Only by thinking through the difficulties likely to arise from a reduction of military activity will a comprehensive strategy be prepared and responsibilities be allocated so that the conversion is as effective and painless as possible.

Responsibility for conversion rests ultimately with the central government. But, while it should take the lead in preparations for a conversion program, it must make sure that industry, trade unions, and officials in the most military-dependent areas all discuss the problems of adjustment and devise measures to cope with them. Where regions of a country are heavily dependent on military spending, a particularly thorough scrutiny is needed to trace how this spending works its way through the regional economy and how many jobs it affects, indirectly as well as directly.

The nature and extent of government involvement will vary from country to country, depending mainly on the type of economic system. But all governments can exploit the flexibility gained from broad disarmament measures to address major economic and social problems, both at home and internationally.

Some analysts have suggested that the large-scale units in the arms industry will have to be broken up during the process of conversion, because their structures—including a top-heavy work force and a marketing organization oriented to government procurement—are frequently unsuitable for the civilian sector. Others, however, predict that the military capability in systems management will be put to special use. These skills can be employed profitably in major projects, such as developing new sources of energy, exploiting the ocean's resources, environmental protection, and new systems for transportation and sanitation in big cities.

Many believe that the most significant dividend that disarmament will bring is the opportunity to apply science and technology more directly and systematically to economic and social development. The following section goes more deeply into this question, but here we should mention two worthwhile preparatory moves. First, the formulation of a national science policy that reflects economic and social priorities would be extremely useful in giving a focus to the conversion effort. Second, the declassification of military scientific and technical information should begin early, so that it can be made available for civilian application as soon as possible.

There is no shortage of alternative uses to which the resources released by disarmament can be put. The world ended the 1970s with a long list of urgent economic and social problems: oil substitution, the replacement of other nonrenewable raw materials, environmental pollution, and the enormous requirements for development of the poorer countries. The problem is one of choice, of setting priorities.

Many accounts, based on solid experience, indicate that it takes up to two years to refashion for civilian work resources that have been used for military purposes; that is, retraining scientists and technicians and redesigning factories. Any plant can be converted, any person retrained. It needs time, money, and will. What can encourage the process and strengthen the will is a specific list of alternative products that fit the technical criteria—occupational skills and industrial facilities—of the companies that will be converting.

Developing Countries

Several developing countries have achieved success with demobilization (e.g., India at the end of World War II) and conversion (e.g., Singapore and Malta after the closing of British military bases). But the amount of conversion that developing countries in general can undertake is much less than industrialized countries can do, mainly because they still account for only 16 percent of the world's military expenditure and because the production of major weapons is significant in only a few countries, while their research and development for military purposes is negligible.

Nevertheless, the reduction in their military spending, which must be part of world disarmament, would release sizeable amounts of money (developing countries spent $73 billion on the military sector in 1980) and able-bodied manpower for more socially useful programs. Foreign exchange saved from arms imports would ease the financial constraints that now hamper development plans; bottlenecks to industrialization and expanded agricultural production would begin to disappear.

International Cooperation

There is growing support for the view that a more balanced pattern of world growth and development would be very much in the mutual interests of industrialized and developing countries, for both economic and political reasons. Moreover, the collaborative management of interdependence should involve East-West, East-South, South-South, as well as West-South relations. It seems clear, also, that many of the transitional difficulties associated with conversion would be lessened if they were cast in the framework of international cooperation. Indeed, it is hard to think how much of this alternative work could be tackled within national boundaries; a good deal of it will have to be done in the global community shared by all mankind.

Research and development is the most promising field for the direct conversion of resources from military purposes to economic and social development projects in developing countries. The importance of science and technology for development cannot be overstated. At present, less than 3 percent of global expenditure on research and development is spent in developing countries, where only 12 percent of the world's scientists and engineers are engaged in this research. At the same time, a great deal of research into technology transfer is needed to avoid the costly and harmful mistakes made when large-scale, capital-intensive industries are transported to countries with economies based on peasant agriculture, only serving to reinforce power in the hands of an elite.

Unfortunately, people who have worked in military research and development would generally be accustomed to those attributes—wide-ranging, capital-intensive projects—so that particular care will be needed to prevent a bias towards inappropriate, even damaging, forms of technology transfer.

Those words of caution said, a short list follows of fields in which technology familiar to scientists in the military sector could help them grapple with major problems in the developing countries.

Renewable Sources of Energy

The greatest need is for small-scale devices, easy to operate and maintain in rural areas. But technical and managerial skills are also needed in some countries to develop an energy strategy, and high technology (including satellite imagery) can be useful in geophysical surveys and other work on minerals.

Food Production

Food import bills are increasing alarmingly in many developing countries, draining away their foreign exchange and hampering economic growth. Research and development can contribute enormously: developing high-yield varieties of staple crops to suit local conditions; improving methods of pest control, food storage, and food preparation; experimenting with water development and irrigation technology; and building farm equipment with local materials.

Communication Networks

Developing countries are at a great disadvantage in the use of radio frequencies for communications and education. Industrialized countries have the transmitters, the technical skills, and the lion's share of allocated frequencies. They have also made the greatest use of the geo-stationary satellite orbit along which satellites are anchored above the equator. In 1979 the World Administrative Radio Conference made a start in reviewing procedures governing the use of radio frequencies and satellites. Its work could be followed up by further research and development on behalf of the developing countries.

Health Care

The military have paid a great deal of attention to infectious diseases, food hygiene, and the management of water and waste under field conditions. One reason, until recently at least, was to prepare for the possible use of biological weapons in warfare. Much of the knowledge they acquired and the preventative capabilities they developed can be applied to the task of improving health conditions in developing countries.

Refugees and Natural Disasters

The international community has cooperated for years over these distressing and recurring human problems. The logistical efficiency of the military sector can find a great deal of scope for alternative work here.

Even with a huge effort to mobilize their own resources, combined with an imaginative program of technology transfer and collaborative research and development, such as that outlined above, the developing countries are going to be in need of vastly increased capital flows.

In its World Development Report 1980, the World Bank made projections for 1990, setting up comparatively modest targets for economic growth in middle-income and low-income countries (significantly lower than in the International Development Strategy) and making a number of optimistic assumptions about policy in industrialized countries. It estimated that the shortfall in resources between domestic savings and the investment needed to achieve the targets of growth would amount to $177.9 billion in 1990. If this gap were filled by foreign capital flows in the present proportions, one-third of that sum would be provided as grants or under concessionary terms, and two-thirds on commercial terms. But because of debts accumulated by 1990, 85 percent of this inflow would have to pay the interest and principal.

Clearly the present pattern of capital transfers is becoming intolerable. Disarmament and conversion measures provide the opportunity to change it. They will ease constraints in developing countries where, until now, most investible resources have been siphoned off to the military; and also in industrialized countries, where the volume of developmental capital has been restricted by heavy military spending. With disarmament and conversion, the industrialized countries should be freed to provide a much larger share of the foreign capital requirements of developing countries in the form of grants or "soft" loans.

The moment when all countries face economic hard times can be the time to goad them either to shrink into protectionism or else to reach out to seek more balanced growth together. At this point it is questionable whether the already industrialized countries can regain a steady footing without the help and support of the developing countries—as much in the great new markets they can offer for manufactures once their own earning power has increased, as in the raw materials they possess. It will require imagination to use the present period of recession as an opportunity. But times of crisis have been used before now for new departures in policy, to the good of the great majority. With resourcefulness and some trust, this period also may be turned into the nearest the world has recently come to good times.

NOTES

1.   The Independent Commission on International Development Issues, composed of politicians, diplomats, economists, bankers, officials, a trade unionist, and a newspaper publisher from twenty countries, worked under the chairmanship of Willy Brandt, former Chancellor of the Federal Republic of Germany, from 1978 to 1980 on a report presented to the UN Secretary-General and published under the title of *North-South: A Programme for Survival* (London: Pan Books, 1980).

2.   *Arms Race and Global Problems of International Economic Relations* (Polish International Affairs, 1980).

3.   A report prepared for UNITAR by the Institute for World Economy of the Hungarian Academy of Sciences, 1981.

5

Coping with Technology

International Association of Machinists and Aerospace Workers

INTRODUCTION

Whether you call it automation, computerization, or technological change, new technology is being used by employers to change the jobs of both white-collar and blue-collar workers across America and around the world. Contrary to the myth that contends that technology is neutral—driven by its own internal momentum and thus uncontrollable—this new technological revolution serves the interests of a certain group of people at the expense of others.

For example, many workers are finding that their power to protest the effects of new technology is being reduced as management becomes more able to maintain production without their skills. Indeed, union strength—and the existence of unions at all—is seriously threatened.

As demonstrated by this excerpt from the International Association of Machinists' new book, *Let's Rebuild America,* considering the kinds of technological processes used in alternative production is crucial to any successful conversion effort. If conversion is not merely to produce a new line of products but also to help workers cope with the kinds of alienation they experience on the job, then any new production processes must not replicate the kind of alienating conditions so often found in industrial settings. This means building human-centered machines that utilize workers' intelligence rather than minimize worker input. It means working to create technologies that will again link the hand and the brain in the productive process and thus enhance the creativity of the producer.

It also means, as those involved in the Lucas Corporate Plan recognized, including workers not just in the process of deciding what new products they will make but also in designing the technology that will be used in a particular manufacturing facility. For as long as engineers and designeers are the only people who determine technological progress, workers will be the victims of technology rather than its beneficiaries. As

David Noble has so eloquently stated, "It matters a great deal whether or not designers and users are the same people, whether or not they work together as equals and view each other as such, whether or not some have power over others, and whether or not all have a voice and a hand in the design process."*

It also matters a great deal whether or not new technology is a solution to problems of structural unemployment or exacerbates structural unemployment. As this chapter points out, new technology, as it is currently used, does not put people back to work: It robs them of precious jobs as well as precious skills. Thus, if conversion is to be a solution to the kind of unemployment that would result from any successful disarmament campaign, preparing for new technology is essential. Clearly, a conversion program that uses the kind of technology that puts people out of work in increasing numbers will never win the support of workers who are concerned about job security and skill maintenance.

—The Editors

In the late 1970s, before Americans began talking about deindustrialization and reindustrialization, corporate America was often heard talking about "restructuring the economy." The message was that corporate America intended to get out of the "smokestack" industries and go into something nice, clean, and easy like the "knowledge business" or the "information revolution." Academics and pundits were hailing the post-industrial society. The promised land, they said, was to be found in silicon chips, computer-driven machines, word processors, and the new technology.

As a matter of hindsight, we now recognize what restructuring the economy actually meant. To be sure, it partially meant a transition to a service economy, and it also meant the rise of a new high technology growth industry dealing with the knowledge business and the information revolution. But that is only half the story. The other half, not mentioned until after the 1980 presidential election, is the technological invasion of smokestack industries and the manufacturing sector.

The robot is a highly visible symbol of this technology invasion in the workplace, but the new technology goes far beyond robots. James O'Toole of University of Southern California Graduate School of Business described the invasion for *Fortune* magazine: "The application of computer technology to office and factory will affect almost every job and almost every aspect of work."

The key to the validity of that statement, of course, rests with the

---

* Mike Cooley, with an introduction by David Noble, *Architect or Bee?: The Human Technology Relationship* (Boston: South End Press, 1980), p. xv.

degree to which U.S. employers reequip their offices and factories with machines and tools that are a function of printed electronic circuits and information storage systems on tiny, almost microscopic, silicon chips. Chip technology or microcircuitry has immense potential in the workplace to displace and make obsolete scores of skills and literally millions of semiskilled and unskilled jobs.

The auto, rubber, and steel industries have already been invaded by computerized equipment and robots, which may themselves be computers or "smart" robots. *Fortune* describes job displacement and job loss due to this invasion: "Such a revolution would be hard to deal with under normal circumstances, but these enormous changes in the workforce are coming on top of an already high level of unemployment. Even after recovery [sic] takes hold, millions of manufacturing jobs—many of them in the auto, steel and rubber industries—will vanish. . . ." *Fortune* goes on to argue that ". . . millions of new jobs will be created, mostly in information systems, but they'll be so different that today's laid-off workers will be hard pressed to fill them."

Here, finally, we have an explanation of the meaning of restructuring the economy, and technology has a key role in it. It means replacing people with machines and extended unemployment for millions of workers, coupled with an economic depression that is causing business bankruptcies and failures among small and medium businesses. This reduces competition and allows the giants in the supereconomy to practice corporate cannibalism on each other through acquisitions, mergers, and unfriendly stock purchase raids.

The difference between today's new technology and the automation of the early 1960s is that the former affects service sector jobs as well as manufacturing jobs.

The oft-repeated advice to workers in manufacturing not to worry about losing their job, they'll find jobs in the nice, clean service sector, is no longer valid. People are being displaced by computerized equipment in both sectors, and skill requirements for newly created jobs are drastically changed.

The tragedy is that no government agency or any other organization has yet surveyed the scene in depth to find out which jobs will be banished and to what extent. However, in May 1982 the U.S. Government General Accounting Office (GAO) issued a report that surveyed some superficial work done by the Department of Labor. The results of that GAO survey were inconclusive as to the ultimate impact of new technology on employment. However, it did uncover a partial listing of thirty-three skilled occupations that the Department of Labor said would be adversely affected—that is, unemployment would increase—by new technology. In the manufacturing and industrial categories, molders, machine tool operators, machine set-up workers, and all printing trades skills were listed as hard hit, with declines in employment ranging from 5 to 24 percent by 1990. That list is woefully inadequate and incomplete when one considers the total number of occupations found in manufacturing.

The impact globally is speculative, too, but a recent report by the International Metalworkers Federation at Geneva, Switzerland, came to a startling conclusion. Within thirty years only 2 to 10 percent of the world's current industrialized labor force will be needed to produce all the goods necessary for total demand. No wonder Japanese workers are having second thoughts about their ready acceptance of the new technology, contrary to academic and corporate portraits of the docile, smiling Japanese worker, eager to make friends with robots and computers.

In the United States, this much can be said for certain: Since 1980, the development and installation of computer-aided manufacturing and robotic assembly has been accelerating at an increasing rate. Pioneering and leading the way for the introduction of this manufacturing technology is none other than the Pentagon.

A project begun in 1978 at Wright-Paterson Air Force Base, Dayton, Ohio, is called ICAM, for Integrated Computer Aided Manufacturing. ICAM's charter is to develop computer-aided manufacturing methods, processes, tools, machines, and automated systems for the aircraft industry. Its goal is to raise the United State's ranking for computer-aided manufacturing (CAM) from nineteenth in the world to number one. Naturally, since ICAM is paid for by U.S. taxpayers, the Pentagon bills it as not-for-profit and states that all development items are to be made available to the U.S. aircraft industry "at no charge."

How much is ICAM costing U.S. taxpayers? In 1982, it was funded at about $18 million a year. In 1983, its funding level was scheduled to increase to $55 million and stay at that level until 1985, when a totally automated sheet metal center factory is scheduled to be completed.

What will a completely automated sheet metal factory center do? According to the Air Force, it will accept raw sheet aluminum in the front door and deliver a chemically cleaned and coated, completely fabricated and assembled air-frame structure out the back door—untouched by human hands.

Note that this automated Sheet Metal Center Factory will probably displace sixty-two IAM members. When the Air Force first announced this program to the trade press, it called it the "workerless factory" or the "factory of the future." That led John Logue, formerly at Kent State University, to muse, "Now, if they can just design people-less wars."

A close relative of the Pentagon's ICAM system is the CAM-i system being developed in Arlington, Texas. It will do the same things ICAM will do, but it is for methods, processes, and tools that have general purpose application in industry at large. It is nonprofit, too, and will be given away to the automotive, civil aircraft, farm implement, and machine tool industries. By coupling computerized equipment and machine tools with robotics, CAM-i is slated to eliminate manufacturing and assembly personnel in those industries.

Because workers must survive in the short run, the IAM is calling for a Technology Bill of Rights to amend and redefine official U.S. labor policy in light of the restructuring of industry and the work force that is being foisted upon us — so far with little or no discussion of the welfare of the workers impacted, or how it may or may not contribute to rebuilding America in the national interest.

The Technology Bill of rights requires employers to use the new technology to promote full employment. It requires that savings in unit labor costs and productivity gains be shared with workers at the local enterprise level and not enrich solely the management and shareholders. It requires that impacted workers be trained and retrained for productive work. It bars the export of new technology before it is applied to the U.S. industrial base. And it requires that new technology be subject to collective bargaining *before* an employer introduces it in the workplace.

The following are the ten articles in the Workers' Technology Bill of Rights:

> Congress hereby amends the National Labor Relations Act, Railway Labor Act, and other appropriate Acts to declare national labor policy through a New Technology Bill of Rights:
>
> I.   New Technology shall be used in a way that creates jobs and promotes community-wide and national full employment.
>
> II. Unit Labor Cost savings and labor productivity gains resulting from the use of New Technology shall be shared with workers at the local enterprise level and shall not be permitted to accrue excessively or exclusively for the gain of capital, management and shareholders.
>
> Reduced work hours and increased leisure time made possible by New Technology shall result in no loss of real income or decline in living standards for workers affected at the local enterprise level.
>
> III. Local communities, the states and the nation have a right to require employers to pay a replacement tax on all machinery, equipment, robots and production systems that displace workers, cause unemployment and, thereby decrease local, state and federal revenues.
>
> IV. New Technology shall improve the conditions of work and shall enhance and expand the opportunities for knowledge, skills and compensation of workers. Displaced workers shall be entitled to training, retraining and subsequent job placement or re-employment.

V.   New Technology shall be used to develop and strengthen the U.S. industrial base, consistent with the Full Employment goal and national security requirements, before it is licensed or otherwise exported abroad.

VI.   New Technology shall be evaluated in terms of worker safety and health and shall not be destructive of the workplace environment, nor shall it be used at the expense of the community's natural environment.

VII.   Workers, through their trade unions and bargaining units, shall have an absolute right to participate in all phases of management deliberations and decisions that lead or could lead to the introduction of new technology or the changing of the workplace system design, work processes and procedures for doing work, including the shutdown or transfer of work, capital, plant and equipment.

VIII.   Workers shall have the right to monitor control room centers and control stations and the new technology shall not be used to monitor, measure or otherwise control the work practices and work standards of individual workers, at the point of work.

IX.   Storage of an individual worker's personal data and information file by the employer shall be tightly controlled and the collection and/or release and dissemination of information with respect to race, religious or political activities and beliefs, records of physical and mental health disorders and treatments, records of arrests and felony charges or convictions, information concerning sexual preferences and conduct, information concerning internal and private family matters, and information regarding an individual's financial condition or credit worthiness shall not be permitted, except in rare circumstances related to health, and then only after consultation with a family or union-appointed physician, psychiatrist or member of the clergy. The right of an individual worker to inspect his or her personal data file shall at all times be absolute and open.

X.   When New Technology is employed in the production of military goods and services, workers, through their trade union and bargaining agent, shall have a right to bargain with management over the establishment of Alternative Production Committees, which shall design ways to adopt that technology to socially-useful production and products in the civilian sector of the economy.

6

Making Peace Possible: The Legislative Approach to Economic Conversion

Lloyd J. Dumas

INTRODUCTION: THE LEGISLATIVE IMPULSE

Whenever a public issue of major significance arises, we feel an impulse to address it through the legislative process. Problems as wide ranging as racial discrimination, alcoholism and drug abuse, environmental pollution, workplace health and safety, and consumer protection have all been subjected to attempts at legislative solution, or at least amelioration. As well-intentioned as these attempts have been, an honest evaluation of their degree of success would reveal mixed results. On the one hand, the Prohibition amendment not only failed to solve the problem it addressed but was also probably one of the greatest single boosts to organized crime in the nation's history. On the other hand, though civil rights legislation has clearly not come close to eliminating racial discrimination, it has been a key component in the substantial gains in that direction that have been achieved over the past quarter century.

Well-conceived, well-designed legislation must recognize the limits as well as the power of the legislative process to influence human behavior. It must be grounded in a clear understanding of the nature of the problem it addresses and must be sensitive not just to the conceptual difficulties involved but also to the very down-to-earth problems of successful implementation. There is little doubt that legislation so conceived and so grounded can make a valuable contribution to positive social change. But in our rush to right even the most grievous of wrongs, to pursue even the most laudable objectives, we must not forget to take the time to make sure our proposals are clearly thought out and carefully drawn. After all, laws do not solve human problems; people do.

The arms race is one of the premier public issues of the day. Its dogged pursuit over the latter half of the twentieth century has seriously undermined the productive competence of the U.S. economy and begun what looks to be a long-term cumulative deterioration in the nation's standard of living.[1] More importantly, it has led to a massive reduction in national and world security, threatening the termination of human society and perhaps the total extinction of the human species by intention or even by accident.[2] Thus, the attempt to reclaim some of both our lost security and our economic well-being requires shifting a significant fraction of the nation's productive resources out of military and into civilian-oriented activity. To do this efficiently and smoothly, with minimal disruption and pain during the transition, is the mandate of economic conversion.

Legislation has a critical economic and political role to play in this process. To understand why that is and what that is, we must begin with a brief analysis of the essence of the conversion problem itself.

THE CHANGING NATURE OF THE PROBLEM

At the close of World War II, the U.S. economy underwent a very large-scale and remarkably successful transition from military to civilian-oriented production. As Kenneth Boulding has pointed out, "...in one year, 1945–46, we transferred 30 percent of the GNP from the war industry into civilian uses, without unemployment ever rising above 3 percent, an astonishing testimony to the flexibility of the American economy and also to some wise planning by the Committee for Economic Development at the local level."[3] This experience is certainly a very important demonstration of the general feasibility of even massive redirections of the nation's economy toward civilian production, yet it must be interpreted with some care as a guide to present-day policy. For, in the immediate post-World War II period, the U.S. economy underwent "reconversion," and this is quite different from the problem of "conversion" we face today.

As U.S. involvement in World War II grew—initially as a weapons supplier and later as a combatant—firms normally oriented toward civilian production began to convert to producing for the military. All of the labor force at such firms, from production and maintenance workers to engineers to managers, were trained to serve civilian commercial markets. The production facilities and equipment were also designed and set up for civilian production. Though modifications were made, during the war facilities and equipment for the most part remained geared toward effective civilian production. When the war ended, these firms went back to doing what they were used to doing—producing civilian goods. They "reconverted."

The picture is very different today. Today's arms industry includes generations of managers, engineers, scientists, production and maintenance workers who have never done anything but military-oriented work. Still others have spent at least the major fraction of their working life so engaged. Many present-day military industrial firms have never operated in civilian commercial markets. And even those firms that are major producers of both civilian and military products—firms such as Rockwell International, Boeing, and Texas Instruments—have operationally separated, insulated divisions that function as, in effect, wholly owned subsidiaries reporting to the same overall top management. For the modern, military goods producing firm, military production is no short-lived aberration—it is the norm.

Furthermore, during the World War II period both the means of production and the technologies applied in producing military goods were fairly similar to those of civilian production. Over the nearly four decades since, these facilities, equipments, and technologies rapidly diverged. The physical plant and machinery of, and the technologies applied in a modern military industrial firm are far different from what is commonplace in civilian commercial firms. The technologies embodied in the designs of the products themselves have diverged much farther. Thus, the problem of shifting from military to civilian production has become one of "conversion," not "reconversion"—that is, one of shifting to something new, not of returning to something familiar.

CONVERSION AND ECONOMIC POLICY

A simple-minded policy of sharply cutting back on military expenditures would thus create considerable economic distress in an economy as militarily oriented as that of the United States. Not only would those workers laid off from their jobs in military industry suffer, but their loss of income would lead to a cutback in their consumer spending that would also generate further layoffs in industries supplying consumer goods. Similarly, lowered purchases by the military-industrial firms for which they work would generate negative multiplier effects that would add to growing unemployment.

Government decisionmakers have a variety of so-called macroeconomic policies available to them to deal with situations of rising unemployment. Policies like cutting taxes, increasing government spending (in nonmilitary areas), and increasing the money supply should stimulate the economy and work against the rising unemployment. Why are they not sufficient to cope with the economic problems generated by the military cutbacks? Why is it necessary to worry about economic conversion as a separate issue that must be given special attention?

There are really two answers to this question. The first lies in the geographic pattern of military industry and bases; the second, in the matter of what could be called "trained incapacity."

The effects of general macroeconomic policies such as those outlined above tend to be averaged over the nation. That is not to say that all areas of the country or for that matter all sectors of the economy are affected equally. That is typically not true. But it is true that these policies are not directed at specific industries or geographic areas. Their effects spread out across the economy and across the nation.

Military industry and bases, however, are not spread evenly throughout the country. Gathered in tightly concentrated pockets, they are located in every major geographic region of the nation. Such pockets include, among others, the Dallas–Fort Worth metroplex (military electronics and aerospace) and San Antonio (military bases) in Texas; the "silicon valley" (military electronics) in northern California and the Los Angeles (aerospace) area in southern California; the Groton–New London area (military shipbuilding) in Connecticut; Seattle (aerospace) in Washington; St. Louis (aerospace) in Missouri; Pascagoula (military shipbuilding) in Mississippi; and the Boston–Cambridge so-called "route 128" area (research labs, "think tanks," and military electronics) in Massachusetts.

Economic policies that average their stimulating effects across the nation cannot reach into these specific areas deeply enough to prevent regional recession in the event of major military spending cuts. Advanced, contingency planning for conversion can prepare military-oriented facilities and their work forces to move strongly and effectively into productive and profitable civilian-oriented activity, with all of the attendant economic and other societal benefits of such a shift. At the same time, such planning can avert the economic anguish that the work force and the surrounding communities have felt in previous "bust" periods in the military spending roller coaster.

That such conversions can produce substantial local as well as national economic benefits is, for instance, illustrated by a Pentagon study showing the creation of 123,777 new civilian jobs to replace the 87,703 civilian jobs lost as some ninety-four military bases were converted to a variety of alternative uses in the United States over the period 1961–81.[4] The flavor of the local impact of these conversions is illustrated by the following, taken from a *New York Times* article reprinted in that same Pentagon document:

> Mobile, Alabama—When Brookley Air Force Base was closed in 1969 with the loss of 13,600 civilian jobs, there were bitter protests and acute

apprehension...a decade later...many leaders in this city would not have Brookley back even if the Government came begging.

The base has turned into a prospering industrial-aviation-educational complex; the city government has become an industrial landlord with a major new source of revenue, and the departure of so large a military presence has made the city more diverse and independent.[5]

Macroeconomic policies are also insufficient to deal with the economic problems generated by large-scale cutbacks in military spending because a significant fraction of the work force at military-oriented facilities is hampered by a "trained incapacity" to function in civilian-oriented activity. Especially true of management personnel, engineers, and scientists, it is not, for the most part, a serious problem for production workers, maintenance personnel, and lower level administrative and clerical employees.

Trained incapacity results from both off- and on-the-job training suited only to the peculiar world of military-oriented activity. For managers, engineers, and scientists, there are many differences between the kind of training and orientation that is appropriate in a military serving as opposed to commercial civilian context. Put succinctly, the military "world" is characterized by selling to a single (government) customer, extreme pressure for maximum product performance capability, and relatively little attention to cost; the civilian "world," by multicustomer markets, attention to good but not extreme performance capability, and very great emphasis on minimizing costs.[6] Retraining and reorientation of engineers and scientists is thus prerequisite to successful conversion. Macroeconomic policy has little to offer in coping with this crucial issue.

Macroeconomic policy does, however, have a role to play in successful large-scale conversion. Such policy can make the transition either easier or more difficult. In general, stimulatory policy is probably a good approach. Keeping interest rates low, for example, will tend to facilitate the financing of the perhaps substantial capital investments necessary in modifying facilities and equipment. And economic stimulation will avoid holding down demand in markets to which military firms are converting. Purposeful stimulation may not be appropriate if the economy is at the time in the "boom" phase of the business cycle. But even in such a situation it is important not to restrain the economy too strongly or the early phases of conversion may be made more difficult.

Oddly enough, for much the same reasons generalized shifts in centralized economic plans will also not cope with the conversion problem in the Soviet Union. It is difficult to evaluate the geographic concentration argument because of the inaccessibility of Soviet society, particularly with respect to military matters, but it is clear that the problem of trained incapacity for civilian production is just as serious in the Soviet Union as in the United States. The problem with respect to engineers and scientists is remarkably similar; that of managers has some different dimensions as well as some direct similarities. However, the chief policy implications are very much the same—that decentralized and particularized conversion planning is prerequisite to successful conversion, and that general centralized economic policy is relevant mainly in terms of providing a facilitating context for conversion.[7]

THE ROLE OF LEGISLATION IN CONVERSION

While it is not possible to legislate effective conversion in the United States directly, it is possible to strongly encourage and institutionalize planning for economic conversion on an advanced contingency basis. And it is certainly possible to set up mechanisms for implementation of these plans and to legislate the sort of cutbacks in military appropriations that will trigger them.

Since the federal government is the center of the military system, it seems obvious that legislation on the federal level holds the key both to setting up the mechanisms of conversion planning and to creating the pressure to convert by reducing the military budget. However, state and local governments do have a role to play, for both can facilitate certain aspects of the conversion process. Perhaps more importantly, state and local governments can certainly encourage the institutionalization of conversion planning and implementation by serving as a legitimate, responsible source of political pressure on the federal government. Because the local impacts problem is so serious, one could argue it would be irresponsible of state and local government to do otherwise.

Both conceptually and in a pragmatic political sense, several key issues arise in the design of federal legislation aimed at the planning and implementation procedures required for smooth and effective economic conversion:

1. Should the planning be done on a centralized or decentralized basis?
2. How can there be some assurance that the planning will be taken seriously and done properly?
3. To what extent should the conversion process itself (as opposed to planning) be subsidized? How and by whom?

These three issues were the major points of contention among those involved in the original design and subsequent discussion of the most sweeping attempt at conversion legislation in recent years, the Defense Economic Adjustment Act. This bill, first introduced into the Congress in late 1977, has been reintroduced every year since. A number of more modest legislative proposals have resulted from the discussions initially generated by its introduction. To date, none has become law.

DESIGNING CONVERSION LEGISLATION

Centralization vs. Decentralization

Effective planning for conversion of a given facility and work force requires detailed information about that facility and work force. Plans must be tailor-made. The best plan for converting an Air Force base in Texas may have serious drawbacks if applied to converting an Air Force base in Kansas. Likewise, a superbly drawn conversion plan for a military electronics firm in California may not work well when applied to a military electronics firm in Massachusetts. It is not merely a question of geography. Though there are substantial generic similarities between air bases or electronics firms, there are also many individual differences. Every facility, every base is somewhat different in its mix of structures and equipment, their capabilities, their condition, and their layout. There is also considerable variation in the size and skill mix of every associated labor force, and the economic as well as geographic characteristics of every surrounding community. Even the local political and legal situations may differ in a variety of relevant ways (e.g., zoning laws, pollution regulations). These differences in detail are crucial to the development of a workable, well-constructed conversion plan.

All of this argues strongly in the direction of highly decentralized conversion planning. For this level of detailed knowledge is most readily assembled by the local managers of the facility in question, its work force, and the leaders of the surrounding community, who will already know or have access to much of the information required. They will have some background knowledge and operating experience helpful in processing it. It therefore seems logical that the planning should be done at the local plant or base site, by some conglomeration of local managers, work force, and community advisers.

The most common and strongly stated objection to this kind of highly decentralized local planning effort is one of competence. Many argue that only the federal government has both the resources and expertise available to ensure serious, effective planning. Only some centralized planning body has the economic overview necessary to coordinate properly all of these plans in order to avoid, for example, a situation in which all military aerospace firms planned to convert to producing mass transit vehicles, oversaturating the market and guaranteeing failure of at least some of these converted enterprises.

It is commonly assumed that "experts" employed by the federal government are more competent in any given area of expertise than those available locally or regionally, or even nationally from nongovernmental sources. The mission, power, prestige, and resources of the federal government supposedly allow it to draw to its employ leaders in all the various fields of expertise relevant to analyzing the nation's problems. Without casting any aspersions on the quality of federal experts, it is clear that this is simply not true. Nearly all the leaders of practically any field of expertise that focuses on social issues in fact lie outside the direct or indirect employ of the federal government. Thus, if local conversion planners have limited funds available to them to hire expert consultants when their in-house expertise needs a boost, they will certainly have a wide range of quality consultants from which to choose.

As to the issue of coordination, it is highly unlikely that a very large fraction of the nation's military facilities and bases would be converting at one time. Thus, all that is really necessary is that conversion plans cover a range of possible alternatives to which the firm or base plans to convert, and that they be periodically updated. If that were done, a firm would have a number of already planned alternate product lines and could choose one or two whose markets still looked open and profitable at the point of actual conversion. Updating will give further assurances, allowing the firm to strike from its list of alternative products those to which enough other firms have already converted. Done in advance of its own conversion, the firm would have time to explore new product lines that would replace those originally planned. There is no need for centralized planning.

An intermediate proposal is to have the actual planning done on a highly decentralized basis but to have centralized oversight of these plans. In other words, some federal agency would be given the responsibility to evaluate the conversion plans drawn up locally. Thus, objective federal experts would pass judgment on the acceptability of the plans, giving the assurance of a double check on plan workability.

Aside from objections that might be raised on grounds of the inherently proprietary nature of these plans and fears of their possible leakage to potential competitors, this proposal founders for more straightforward reasons. Any serious federal effort to evaluate these conversion plans would be extraordinarily expensive and would create a huge new bureaucracy while conveying minimal benefits. Even a rough partial and conservative estimate makes this clear.

There are approximately 20,000 prime military contractors, 100,000 subcontractors, and on the order of a few hundred military bases. Suppose the evaluators were to review the conversion plans of all prime contractors and only half the subcontractors once every two years (ignoring military bases). There would thus be roughly 35,000 plans to be reviewed every year [$0.5 \times (20,000 + 0.5 \times 100,000)$].

The minimal staff of professionals needed for the serious evaluation of any given detailed conversion plan would be about four people (e.g., an economist, an engineer, an accountant, and an organizational management specialist). Each team would have to spend at least two weeks at the facility in question, with perhaps a week more required for report writing. There would thus be about a 3-week cycle time. Assuming a 48-week work year, one team could at most evaluate about sixteen conversion plans per year. Therefore, some 2,190 teams are required (35,000/16), for a total professional staff of about 8,750. Assuming a support staff of 4,000 and an administrative staff of perhaps 1,000, total staffing requirements would be roughly 13,750 people.

Remembering that nearly two-thirds of the staff are professionals, $25,000 per year (including fringe benefits) is a reasonable yet conservative estimate of average salary. Annual salary expense would hence be $343,750,000 ($25,000 \times 13,750$). Travel costs would add roughly another $148,000,000. Thus, total personnel and travel costs alone would be roughly $490,900,000 per year! And if the evaluation team judges the plan defective, all that it is in a position to do is to tell the decentralized planners to try again.

If it is true that a simple system of centralized *oversight and evaluation* is so cumbersome and expensive, it is clear the cost of centralized *development* of detailed conversion plans would be more cumbersome and far more expensive. Conversion planning should thus be carried out on a highly decentralized basis. It can be done more effectively this way, and at much lower cost.

Assuring Serious, High Quality Conversion Planning

Today, neither military-serving firms nor military bases plan in advance for conversion. Given the possibility that military demand for their product may decline—even without an overall cutback in military spending—why do the firms at least not take planning for this contingency seriously?

There are a number of reasons. First, it is the firm's management that decides whether or not to consider alternative product planning. In the current situation they have little incentive to do so.

The managers of military industrial firms are aware that the Defense Department now provides them with large sums of money under very loose control. The combination of full reimbursement regardless of cost and guaranteed profit over the long term despite products whose performance often falls substantially short of original specifications is, to put it mildly, hard to find elsewhere.

Moreover, they distinctly benefit from lack of conversion planning. Now it is possible for firms to argue that their particular project should be funded or thousands of jobs will be lost. This politically powerful argument often plays at least as large a role in securing budget funding as arguments concerning the contribution of this particular project to national security. To have conversion plans readily available would undercut the political clout of the jobs argument. Thus, it is not surprising that managements of military firms are less than enthusiastic about conversion planning.

Furthermore, when military contracts are prematurely cancelled, the firms involved typically receive generous "termination payments." Employees at these facilities, at the same time, receive little more than pink slips and standard severance pay. The surrounding community, if it is highly defense-dependent and has experienced a substantial net loss of military business, faces a serious and perhaps elongated recession. Economic hostages to military budgets, they have positive interest in fostering advance conversion planning. Yet there is presently no mechanism by which they can activate, let alone participate in, the conversion planning process.

First then, we must alter the incentives of management so as to encourage them to engage in conversion planning. Second, we must provide a planning mechanism that will incorporate the already existing interests of employees and the community at large to increase pressure for the planning to be done seriously and well.

One possible legislative solution begins with a kind of paradox. It is possible to use management's desire to remain in the business of military production to press them into planning for conversion. This can be done by simply making the establishment of a conversion planning committee a prerequisite for eligibility for military contracts. Any firm that wished to remain in the military business would thus have to begin contingency planning for eventual conversion. To prevent such committees from being pro forma operations set up only to satisfy the legal eligibility requirement, the legal mandate could require the establishment of an independently funded conversion committee with equal participation by management, representatives of the work force, and community leaders. The independent funding provided by some preestablished formula would prevent management from crippling the committee financially. The equal tripartite structure of the committee would eliminate sole management control over disbursement of the funds allocated to the committee as well as providing a potentially useful balancing of influence of the various parties at interest that could do much to assure a serious and efficient conversion planning process.

It is not so much that each of the three parties to the committee would be expected to be continually plotting and scheming to subvert the committee that makes the tripartite structure useful. It is simply that each has a separate interest in the outcome of the planning process, and each particular interest leads to some extent in a different direction. It is thus useful to reassure each against domination by the other's interest, while simultaneously preventing it from drawing the conversion planning process off track in its own preferred way.

• While important, differences among the parties to the committee should not be overemphasized. They actually have much more in common than may be apparent. If serious conversion planning will be underway, then management has strong reason to cooperate to make sure that the alternative products chosen are those that have strong markets and solid profit potential; that the financing plan is well conceived; that the conversion plan is workable. Employees have strong incentives to assure that an economically viable plan results or conversion will not protect their jobs. Similarly, an effective conversion plan will help to protect the surrounding community from the loss of income and tax base that normally results from the shutdown of a significant employer.

Subsidy

There are two categories of subsidies that might well lubricate the process of conversion: subsidies to the employees and direct subsidies to the firms.

Even with well-drawn plans for conversion available, the actual conversion of a facility and its work force takes some time. Though there is considerable variability in time required, it is reasonable to estimate that most conversions will take one to two years. There seems to be little disagreement that subsidies to the employees displaced during the changeover are crucial to mitigating the economic trauma both they and the surrounding community would otherwise face. Specific types and level of subsidies may be debated, but it would seem that the essential elements of a solid system of transition support would include income maintenance (at some substantial level); continuation of medical insurance, pension, and other major employee benefits; and retraining allowances. For those employees who could not be accommodated at the same facility by the conversion plan, relocation allowances and reemployment services would be of great value. With this type of support, the work force and community would be well cushioned against the shock of transition.

Various safeguards to prevent abuse of this employee subsidy system should be considered. Perhaps the most important among them would be a provision setting a specific time limit on the receipt of this support, say two years or until reemployment at the converted facility (or at another civilian-oriented job), whichever is shorter.

There has been considerably more controversy surrounding the issue of direct subsidies to the firm. Supporters of direct subsidy to firms argue that such subsidies smooth the conversion process, facilitating the kinds of capital investment required to purchase equipment and modify structures. They also "sweeten the pot" for management, lessening their resistance to conversion. Finally, since these firms currently service the military and hence the federal government, the federal government should take responsibility for the effects of the shift in federal policy that terminated their military mission. Opponents of such subsidies argue that the firm would already be subsidized indirectly since its employees receive subsidies—including, especially, retraining allowances. Further subsidies would give the firm an unfair advantage in competing with those firms already operating in the relevant civilian markets. This is economically inequitable and politically damaging since it might cause potentially disadvantaged civilian firms to oppose conversion legislation.

Furthermore, such a direct firm subsidy program would strengthen the pressures for taxpayer subsidy on the part of firms undergoing various sorts of economic pressures in a variety of other industries. This increase in "welfare for the corporations" adds another potentially backbreaking burden on the nation's taxpayers. Finally, whether or not the pressure for subsidy spreads, these kinds of subsidies are directly antagonistic to the basic principles under which market economies operate. Subsidy relieves pressure for efficient production by lessening the penalty for inefficiency and in extremis even making inefficiency lucrative. Already a problem in industrial firms that service the military, it should not be encouraged in their new civilian-oriented incarnations.

The arguments against at least large-scale direct subsidization of firms during conversion seem far stronger than those in favor. One of the major arguments for conversion is that it replaces the cost escalating, subsidized, inefficiency of military industry with the cost minimizing orientation so crucial to strong, economically viable, efficient civilian production. Direct firm subsidies tend to undermine this goal. Subsidizing conversion of the work force gives the firm ready-to-go, civilian-oriented employees. This degree of indirect subsidy puts them on a more equal footing with the already civilian firms with which they will be competing after conversion without giving them unfair advantage.

A MODEL CONVERSION BILL

It is useful at this point to trace out what the main provisions of a comprehensive conversion bill might be. The model offered is essentially that embedded in the original version of the Defense Economic Adjustment Act introduced into the Senate in the late 1970s by George McGovern (D–SD) and Charles Mathias (R–MD) and into the House of Representatives by Ted Weiss (D–NY). While this is surely not the only workable design possible for effective federal conversion legislation, it is sensitive to the crucial requirements for successful conversion.

There are three main components to the design. The first established a Defense Economic Adjustment Council in the Executive Office of the President. The council is chaired by the secretary of commerce and consists of six cabinet officers, six representatives of the business management community, and six representatives of organized labor. The council has no planning function and no oversight function with respect to conversion plans. Its main functions are twofold. First, it encourages preparation of plans for civilian-oriented public projects by the various civilian agencies of the federal government and by state and local governments. This list of projects that it then prioritizes and makes available to those doing the actual conversion planning constitute potential markets that a converted facility might seek to service. These potential markets will only become actual if funds released from military purposes are channeled to other government agencies. But this is nevertheless valuable information to the planning committees.

Second, the council's function is to produce a conversion guidelines handbook, as an aid to successful conversion planning. Available as a set of guidelines, not regulations, this handbook would then be offered to the planning committees, which may follow or ignore its suggestions as they see fit.

The second main component of the bill establishes so-called alternative use committees at every military base and military industrial facility (including research laboratories, "think tanks", and the like). These are the planning committees. They must consist of at least nine members: one-third representatives of the local management, one-third representatives of the nonmanagement labor force, and one-third representatives of the community appointed by the chief executive of the local government (and not otherwise associated with the facility). Provided with autonomous funds at the initial rate of $50 per employee, the main function of the alternative use committee is to analyze the facility and its work force and develop a comprehensive plan to convert these to efficient civilian-oriented activity. Facilities and equipment modifications and purchase, work-force retraining requirements, product marketability studies, and a financing strategy must all be included in the plan.

The third main component of the bill establishes a Workers' Economic Adjustment Reserve Trust Fund in the Treasury Department. Each defense contractor is required to pay 1.25 percent of the gross value of its contracts into the fund each year. The fund is then available to finance all of the worker adjustment benefits provided by the bill. These benefits include income maintenance at a level equal to 90 percent of the first $25,000 and 50 percent of the next $5,000 of regular annual salary,[8] vested pension credit, maintenance of medical and life insurance benefits, retraining allowances, and employment services and relocation allowances for all workers not reemployable at the same facility under the plan. These benefits begin upon activation of the conversion plan and last until it has been completed, to a maximum of two years. No individual is eligible for more than one conversion-related program of benefits.

There is much left out of this brief sketch, but it should suffice to illustrate the central elements of a legislative design that would regularize and institutionalize advanced planning for conversion as well as facilitate plan implementation when cutbacks in military programs occur.

THE POLITICS OF CONVERSION LEGISLATION

After the initial introduction of the Defense Economic Adjustment Act in 1977, a series of informal discussions with interested parties were held. They included meetings involving representatives of a dozen or so major labor unions, staff members of the Congressional offices involved, the designers of the legislation, and other knowledgeable individuals. Among the labor unions represented were the International Association of Machinists and Aerospace Workers (IAM) and the United Auto Workers (UAW)—two of the largest unions organizing workers in military industry—as well as the Oil, Chemical, and Atomic Workers Union (OCAW), the United Electrical Workers (UE), and the American Federation of Government Employees (AFGE). As a result of these discussions and others, a variety of modifications in the original design were made. Over the next several years these were introduced into the Congress, with varying sponsorship, as substitutes for the originally proposed legislation. None of these versions of comprehensive conversion legislation has to date even been voted out of committee.

The difficulties encountered in trying to move comprehensive conversion bills through the Congress led a number of supporters of the concept of planned conversion to try a different legislative approach. Without question, the most successful attempt to date at partial conversion-related legislation was that mounted in 1978–79 by Connecticut Congressmen McKinney and Dodd (the former a Republican, the latter a Democrat).

Both of these Congressmen attached their proposals as amendments to the renewal of the Economic Development Act, the 1965 legislation that had established the Economic Development Agency (EDA), the primary federal agency assisting communities in recovering from sudden economic dislocations. The Dodd/McKinney amendments essentially required at least ninety days and normally one year's advance notice to the communities involved of plans to close a base or cancel a military contract. In addition to the availability of advance community diversification planning grants, a worker assistance program was to be set up in the Department of Labor to aid workers laid off because of a base closure or contract termination. At the same time an Office of Economic Diversification was to be set up as part of the EDA administrative apparatus. This office would provide technical expertise to aid local communities in planning strategies to diversify their economies. The basic local diversification planning groups would include representatives from business, labor, and the community at large.

The EDA renewal legislation was passed by the House of Representatives in 1979, with the Dodd/McKinney amendments attached. Unfortunately, the Senate-passed version of the EDA legislation did not include comparable provisions. Thus, the bill went to a House-Senate conference committee. There the House conferees stood firm on the Dodd/McKinney amendments, refusing to accept watered-down versions proposed by the Senate conferees. The Senators were split on this issue. Ultimately, rather than accept these amendments they preferred to let the EDA renewal legislation fail.

In late 1979, the Defense Production Act (DPA) of 1950 was due to expire: This act provided the basic framework for federal mobilization during national emergencies. Reasoning that an act that provided for mobilization also had an obligation to address the issue of demobilization, an attempt was made to try to forward efforts at conversion planning through the vehicle of the DPA renewal legislation. For a time, this approach looked promising, but it proved unsuccessful.

In May 1961 the Department of Defense had initiated an Economic Adjustment Program to assist communities in recovering from the economic impact of base closings. Since 1970, this function has been carried out through the President's Economic Adjustment Committee by its permanent staff, known as the Office of Economic Adjustment (OEA) headquartered in the Pentagon. On the whole, the OEA has served a useful function as liaison between representatives of the impacted communities and various federal agencies whose programs might be of use in aiding these local efforts. They have also served as expediter in community contacts with the Pentagon. However, though of some use, they have done little more than to encourage local initiative in after-the-fact recovery from base closings.

On 23 March 1978 President Carter issued Executive Order 12049 strengthening OEA somewhat and more importantly providing for "economic impact analysis and analysis of community requirements for federal economic adjustment resources" *in advance of* base closings. This executive order was apparently spurred by growing interest in conversion legislation in the Congress and may also have been a reaction to a prior meeting on the issue of advanced conversion planning at the White House between the President's domestic affairs advisor and the designers of the Defense Economic Adjustment Act, as well as others. It is not clear whether the executive order was an attempt to head off serious conversion legislation or was intended for other purposes, but it is clear that it has had little practical effect in encouraging contingency planning for conversion. Furthermore, it seems clear that as long as the Office of Economic Adjustment lies within the Department of Defense, independent of the competence, funding, or even desire of its staff, it is unlikely to be able to move in a serious and sustained way to encourage widespread decentralized, advanced planning for conversion.

Finally, there have been attempts at the level of state and local government to encourage conversion planning. Notable among these were proposals introduced into the state legislatures of Connecticut, California, and Washington during the late 1970s. California is by far the state receiving most prime military contracts, while both Connecticut and Washington state are also heavily defense dependent.

The California bill called for the creation of an interdepartmental group to encourage and facilitate alternative use planning in California's defense-dependent communities. The Connecticut bill, the Economic Conversion and Employment Security Act, called for the creation of a labor (25%)–community (25%)–management (50%) committee to plan for alternative uses at military-related plants and facilities. The Washington state bill was an appeal to Congress and the President urging passage of conversion planning legislation similar to the federal Defense Economic Adjustment Act proposal, as well as further expansion of the Office of Economic Adjustment.

There are, of course, serious limits on what this level of government can do in the area of conversion. They do not fund the military bases, nor are they the source of military contracts—these are the province of the federal government. Yet neither are these proposals without use, for state and local legislative proposals can serve as a prelude to public hearings that can potentially perform an educational function, making the public at large (as well as more focused economic interests) aware of the seriousness of defense dependency in the local economy and the usefulness of conversion planning as insurance against the vulnerability that dependency implies. This grass roots educational function is not to be minimized, for a broader public understanding of the issues is fundamental to the success of national conversion legislation. Even nonbinding appeals of these levels of government for federal action help to raise awareness of this issue and apply additional pressure on the federal government to stop shirking its responsibilities in this area.

FREEING THE HOSTAGES

As things presently stand, independent of political party, ideology, background, or personal judgment millions of people in the United States find their economic security held hostage to the military budget. Through the geographic pattern of high concentrations of military dependency spread throughout all major regions of the nation, the employers and organizations of these individuals and the representatives of their communities are able to exert disproportionate influence on Congress and the president. The political power of the perceived economic threat of lowered military spending should not be underestimated. This point was rather dramatically illustrated not long ago when Senator John Tower, Chair of the Senate Armed Services Committee, sent a letter to many members of the Congress who had been talking about the need for cutbacks or at least restrictions in military expenditures—a position with which Tower, of course, strongly disagreed. In his letter, he requested these members of Congress to respond with a specific list of military programs *in their own districts* that they believed should be eliminated. He reported receiving no replies.

The political importance of the economic argument can be further independently verified by noting that virtually every newspaper account of curtailment of military activity, whether a base closure or contract cancellation, contains a statement about job loss, if not in the headline, then in the first sentence.

Advance planning for economic conversion is a strategy for making peace possible by concretely reassuring those who directly fear loss of their own jobs as a result of cutbacks in military spending, as well as the much larger segment of the population who fear that such cutbacks will generate broader economic recession or depression. It can and will free the work force and thus the Congress from their current hostage position.

How much of the support for ever larger military budgets would evaporate if conversion legislation generated the kind of planning that would render the job loss argument meaningless? It is hard to say. But it is clear that the debate on weapons systems, military posture, and the like would be moved from the arena of myopic economics to that of legitimate security requirements where it belongs. The military is no economic welfare agency, nor should it be. National security issues should not be entangled in local economic dependencies. There are always more effective, more productive ways of creating or maintaining jobs and income than by building unnecessary military hardware or keeping an unneeded base open.

Furthermore, conversion planning can itself be very empowering, particularly if done by the multiparty, highly decentralized approach that has been embodied in comprehensive legislative proposals like the Defense Economic Adjustment Act. Conversion planning does not allow a simplistic "shut it down" or "keep it going" approach. It requires the far more complex and creative process of searching for viable alternatives and offers in its very nature at least the potential for a highly participatory decision-making process.

The legislative approach to economic conversion has thus far been less than spectacularly successful, but there have been some partial successes, some hopeful signs. The plain fact is that the nation's economy will never more than temporarily emerge from its continuing long-term decay until it is relieved of the crippling burden of heavy military spending. National security will continue to deteriorate as long as we persist in the fantasy that our safety lies in continuing to amass sophisticated weaponry to add to our already incomprehensibly destructive stockpile. Yet until the fear of unemployment and other severe economic disruption can be permanently laid to rest, it will be exceedingly difficult to develop the political support necessary to transfer resources from the military to the civilian sector. Conversion legislation thus has a potentially pivotal role to play, not only in rebuilding the nation's economy, but also in putting us on a more viable path to survival.

NOTES

1.   L.J. Dumas, *The Political Economy of Arms Reduction: Reversing Economic Decay* (Boulder, CO: Westview Press, 1982), ch. 1.
2.   See L.J. Dumas, "National Insecurity in the Nuclear Age," *Bulletin of the Atomic Scientists* (May 1976) and "Human Fallibility and Weapons," *Bulletin of the Atomic Scientists* (November 1980) for arguments on the decline of security; see also Carl Sagan, "The Nuclear Winter," *Parade* (30 October 1983) for arguments on effects of nuclear war.
3.   Kenneth Boulding, "Foreword" in Dumas, *The Political Economy*, p. xiii.
4.   President's Economic Adjustment Committee, Office of Economic Adjustment, Office of the Assistant Secretary of Defense (Manpower Reserve Affairs and Logistics), *1961–1981, Twenty Years of Civilian Reuse: Summary of Completed Military Base*

Economic Adjustment Projects (Washington: The Pentagon, November 1981). Note that these data must be interpreted with some care since a small fraction of the "civilian" reuses were by military industrial firms and such other "civilian" agencies as the National Guard.

5.   John Herbers, "Cities Find Conversion of Old Military Bases a Boon to Economies," *New York Times,* 26 April 1979.

6.   For a much more detailed discussion of this question, see Dumas, *The Political Economy,* ch. 2.

7.   For a much more detailed discussion, see Seymour Melman, "Conversion of Military Economy: the USSR," in Dumas, *The Political Economy.*

8.   These numbers are slightly updated from the 1977 version of the bill.

PART III

Case Studies in Conversion

7

The Lucas Plan: The Roots of the Movement

Dave Elliott and Hilary Wainwright

"There is talk of crisis wherever you turn. I think we have to stand back from that crisis for a few moments and see where we are in relation to it. For it is the present economy that has a crisis. We don't. We're just as skilled as we were: miners can still dig coal, bricklayers build houses, and we can still design and produce things."

So argued Mike Cooley, a design engineer from a North London factory of Lucas Aerospace. It was January 1975, and Cooley was addressing a weekend meeting of more than sixty shop stewards from the design offices and workshops of all seventeen Lucas Aerospace factories who had come together to work out a strategy to reverse the drastic decline in jobs at their company.

The company they worked for—Lucas Aerospace—is one company within the large conglomerate, Lucas Industries. The largest designer and manufacturer of aircraft systems and equipment in Europe, the company manufactures fuel systems, flying control instrumentation, and electrical equipment. It has been involved with work on Concorde, the Russian TU144 supersonic airliner, the A300B airbus, the Lockheed Tristar, the RB211, the Anglo-French Jaguar, the European Multi-Role Combat Aircraft, and, more recently, the Sting Ray missile system. About 43 percent of its business is related to military aircraft, 7 percent to other defense work, while approximately 45 percent of its work comes from Rolls Royce and 27 percent direct from the Ministry of Defense.

In 1970, the largely unionized Lucas work force—over one-third skilled engineers, design technicians, draughtsmen, and research staffers—totalled approximately 18,000. Job security had never been a threatening issue. But after hearing of rumors that management was having secret talks with the Labour government's Industrial Reorganization Corporation concerning rationalization of the Lucas Aerospace Division, Lucas

Excerpted from Hilary Wainwright and Dave Elliott, *The Lucas Plan: A New Trade Unionism in the Making?* (London, Allison and Busby, 1982).

shop stewards organized a cross-plant, multiunion combine committee to fight the implicated decline in jobs. The committee convened for the first time in December 1969, representing the interests of 13,000 shopfloor workers in all seventeen Lucas Aerospace factories.

Over the next five years, the combine carried out active dissent against the company's ongoing rationalization plans. Despite some short-term victories, however, management was always able to implement its desired policies, and the shop stewards soon learned that they would have to find more lasting solutions to control or at least influence decisions about investment or employment. In 1975, with a Labour government again in office, they were faced with another crisis. The Labour government manifesto had promised to nationalize the aerospace industry and cut back on military contracts.

In order to find out whether this forthcoming nationalization would secure or erode employment, shop stewards had crowded into Minister of Industry Tony Benn's office the previous November. Benn explained that he did not have the power to include Lucas Aerospace in nationalization proposals. He went on to suggest that the combine committee be involved in drawing up a corporate strategy for Lucas Aerospace. "We should be thinking of ways of producing our way through a slump," he counseled. "We must be prepared to diversify and we cannot ignore intermediate technology." Benn said he would try to arrange meetings between the company and the combine committee and the government to discuss any alternative proposal drawn up by the committee.

Thus, when the combine met in January 1975, they had two possibilities. Either they could push exclusively for further nationalization including Lucas Aerospace, or they could develop a new approach that would defend jobs and improve work conditions more effectively in the short run and, at the same time, prepare the ground for a genuinely democratic form of social ownership in the long run. Which, Cooley and others asked their coworkers, did they favor?

Few delegates were able to report much enthusiasm for proceeding only with nationalization, but delegate after delegate stressed the need for a new approach. As the meeting began to develop its ideas about this "new concept," they talked of an alternative plan—one, they decided, that would not include management, however. No matter how dubious some were about their own ability to design such a corporate plan, to draw up a plan with management, they felt, could easily undermine trade union independence and create a situation in which the unions were simply doing managerial job for the managers. "If we were dependent on management in drawing up a plan we'd end up doing it on their terms. We would be cutting our own throats," one shop steward argued.

Since industrial democracy had been an important theme in the

Labour party's election campaign, it seemed possible to use the creation of a union-based plan as an opportunity to give substance to a suggestion that seemed to have only form and little content. Although a great many workers were skeptical of their ability to draw up a plan on their own, the stewards decided to take the risk. "Let us draw up a plan without management," Mike Reynolds, an AUEW shop steward from Liverpool, put forcefully. "Let us start here from this combine committee; after all, over the years it has grown and grown. It has ability not only in industrial disputes but also to tackle wider problems. Let's get down to working on how we'd draw up a plan, on our terms, to meet the needs of the community."

And so the Lucas corporate plan was born. After hours of discussion the committee voted on a resolution stating that "We reaffirm our policy that Lucas Aerospace be nationalized with full worker's control. We further instruct the executive committee to prepare a corporate plan for the protection of our workers until the full nationalization of Lucas Aerospace is achieved."

To begin their mandated work, the combine executive committee formed a corporate plan subcommittee, whose first act was the distribution of a questionnaire to all shop stewards and office committees. The straightforward questionnaire requested information about the size of the factory, the number and types of machines, and details of the work force, and ended up with questions about alternative products and ways of running the factory.

Designed not only to elicit practical answers, the questionnaire led shop stewards to think in ways that were entirely new. "The planning process," one steward explained, "is as important as the plan itself because it involves questioning existing assumptions and generating alternative options." Such questions as: How could the plant be run by the work force itself? Could existing line managers still be used?—even questions as simple as a request for information about machinery and skills— proved remarkably valuable. "They wanted to know what machine tools we had," said Mike Cooley. "It was quite amazing that no site knew what they had. The reason for this is that this information was for planning. Now planning production is a fundamental part of running a business. But management does the planning. Workers do the production. To do the alternative corporate plan we were having to think as if we were planning. It really made shop stewards sit up."

At the majority of sites the shop stewards created a corporate plan committee that investigated the answers to questions of information and received ideas for alternative products. Notices were put up asking members for ideas. The overall idea of the plan was explained at mass meetings, section meetings, and in leaflets. It was not always easy for the corporate plan committee to meet during company time since its work did not count as official union business. And involvement would have been restricted if they had held the meetings in the evenings. Consequently, meeting time had to be snatched during lunch hours. At Burnley the committee used to hold its sessions, which were open to any interested member of any union, in the canteen on Friday during lunchtime and the afternoon. It was an informal affair and sometimes none too sober, but over the six months during which the plan was drawn up these Friday afternoon discussions led to a common commitment on the part of shop floor and staff to the ideas of the plan.

The company-wide audit of skills and equipment revealed the wide range of technologies—spanning almost the whole of the engineering field—in which a modern high technology company like Lucas Aerospace is involved. It manufactures, for example, mechanical and electrical control equipment for aircraft flight controls, aircraft electrical generating systems and associated electrical switch gears, jet engine ignition and fuel control systems, jet engine thrust-reversing systems (for braking), de-icing equipment, cockpit instrument lighting, and display equipment. The breadth of technical expertise required to produce these products is extensive: aerodynamics; stress and structural analysis; engineering design; mechanical, electrical, and electronic engineering associated with hydraulic systems; servo-mechanisms and actuators for aircraft control systems; and fluid control and combustion science for fuel management. The emphasis in aerospace is on technical flexibility and also on relatively short runs or batches rather than on mass production. Prototype projects are common.

In some cases it was fairly clear how some of the aerospace technologies could be utilized for other purposes. For example, the recirculating ballscrew (manufactured at Lucas-Rotax) is a device used for the precision control of aircraft flight controls (e.g., flaps), but it can be and is also used in industrial machine-tool control systems. Servo-mechanisms generally can be used for remote control devices where remote precision control over the position and movement of some component or tool is required; for example, in undersea oil rig maintenance, mining, or firefighting using robotic devices. Since the emphasis in aerospace is always on minimizing weight and size, some aerospace "remote control" expertise might also be expected to be relevant to the problems faced in the design of improved artificial limb controls.

Some other potential applications of aerospace technology are more obvious. For example, the combine's plan included proposals for developing windmill technology using aerospace, aerodynamics, and aerofoil design expertise as well as basic electrical and mechanical skills. Windmill production is an area in which aerospace firms in the United Kingdom and more notably in the United States have subsequently begun to be increasingly interested. The more general mechanical, electrical, and electronic skills of the Lucas work force could have myriad other applications, many of which were suggested by the shop stewards. For example, the combine proposed to use their fluid-control expertise for the development of pumps and a control system for use with domestic solar-heat collecting units. Combine members also felt that much of their expertise in hydraulic systems could be used to provide power takeoff for the rotor blade speed control in some types of windmills. Small "ducted fans" wind turbine systems are used in some aircraft to provide auxiliary power— essentially a small windmill tapping energy from the slipstream. These provided another potential area for development—that is, ducted fan windmills.

Lucas's experience with various types of small conventional power packs (used in aircraft) and fuel cells (used in spacecraft) could be put to a wide range of uses. So too could its knowledge of heat-pump technology. The combine also felt that some of the expertise associated with aircraft blind-landing systems might prove relevant to the provision of sight substitution aids for the blind.

Management itself had at one time made use of the varied potential of aerospace technology to diversify into nonaerospace products. In conditions of boom and labor scarcity in the 1950s, management needed to ensure that it maintained a good team of technical workers in spite of periodic military cancellations. One way of doing this was to allow the design teams to develop civilian products until defense orders picked up. Within Lucas, prototypes for a heat pump, a guidance system for a road-rail vehicle, a total valve system for the gas or oil industry, and brake retarders for coaches and trains had all been developed, but there were never the resources to support sustained production. One of the questions in the combine's questionnaire was intended to gather information on these past products at each site, asking workers to assess the relevance of these products, both socially and technically, for the combine's corporate plan.

Some of these past products, in modified form, were chosen as part of the corporate plan. In many cases they had originated as ideas by individual designers responding to a social need they believed they could meet. For example, one of the earlier diversification projects was an improved railway level-crossing barrier, the idea of a designer at Willesden. He had noticed the primitive and unsafe barriers used in many areas and decided that some of the aerospace technologies with which he worked could improve their safety. It was exactly this kind of experience and stimulus, spurred on by a collective determination to resist redundancy, that lay behind the ideas of the combine's corporate plan. The difference, however, was that in the past the designers with ideas that could help to solve social problems were entirely dependent on management's goodwill for seeing the project through. They had no power with which to fight for resources for a socially important project once the "private" objectives of the company had squeezed it out.

The same would be true of any proposal that a shopfloor worker put into the company's suggestion box. More often than not such a proposal would be stimulated by social concern, a concern about safety, or a concern to reduce wastage. However, whether or not and how it was taken up would depend on the company's view of how its own best interests were to be met. Without the power of a workers' organization these private criteria could never be challenged. Workers seemed to realize this difference. At the Bradford site, for example, the suggestion box in the corner of the workers' entrance to the factory is gathering dust, yet workers there proposed around fifty different ideas to the corporate plan committee.

In addition to these, the combine was also able to draw on and give constructive vent to a more general frustration among designers and skilled workers with the limits on innovation in the arms industry. There are periods when the arms industry is the source of major technological advances and consequently a dynamic force within the economy. But the conservatism of government defense departments and the armed forces on the demand side and the intense competition between a small number of prime contractors on the supply side have produced an approach to technological change that retards radical innovation. This combination of competing suppliers for a monopolistic and traditionalist customer has, for the last decade or so, led to trend innovation rather than the more fundamental product or process innovation.

Lucas Aerospace, as a prime supplier of components to the prime contractors, is even more rigidly locked within this traditional thinking because it has to meet the technical requirements set by prime contractors. The result for imaginative engineers is frustration. First, most of their innovative project ideas are turned down by management, and secondly, as projects become more elaborate, the contribution of individual engineers becomes more restricted, more fragmented, and less satisfying. This kind of frustration did not provide the initial impetus behind the plan. However, once the combine set an unofficial design process in motion, this frustration surfaced. Even where engineers—especially more senior engineers—felt unable to contribute directly to the plan, they looked upon it benignly and often provided indirect help—even if only by not being obstructive.

The process of drawing up the corporate plan involved the social interests and commitments of apprentices and shopfloor workers as well as design engineers. At several sites, most of the initial ideas came from the shopfloor; technical workers would often follow up these ideas by looking through technical journals for background information. The work on the plan, moreover, created a framework in which people could connect their own and others' needs as producers with their needs as consumers. It suggested ways of overcoming the contemporary plight of many who have to perform alienating tasks only to produce throwaway products that, in effect, exploit people as consumers.

In two cases, for example, local connections between workers and a local hospital or home for disabled people proved an important stimulus. At Wolverhampton there had been a long association between a nearby handicapped children's center and a charity club based in the factory. In 1966, one of the apprentices in the factory designed a vehicle that could be used by children in the center suffering from spina bifida. The apprentice was able to mold the back of the bast to suit the shape of the child's back. The "Hobcart" could have made a huge difference to the lives of these children had it been manufactured on a large scale. Lucas would not consider it, even though the Australian Spina Bifida Association had placed a large order. Although the designer had moved to the United States his colleagues suggested the cart be part of the plan.

At Bradford, too, there had been a robust tradition of charitable activities in support of a school for handicapped children. The plan tapped some of the same social concern that led people to support the charities. "In my mind," explained an AUEW steward, "when I first heard of the corporate plan, the two went together. Now I've shifted my involvement more toward the corporate plan and the combine committee. Charities are well and good, but they often feel like a drop in the ocean. With trade union power behind some of their ideas I think you've got a greater chance of getting something done."

The planning committee also made fruitful use of outside technical expertise. After sending out a letter to 180 organizations and individuals well known for their interest and expertise in alternative technologies, and the use of technology in a socially useful way, three responded—David Elliott of the Technology Faculty of the Open University, Richard Fletcher of the North-East London Polytechnic, and Professor Thring, who was working on remote-control devices at Queen Mary College.

At that time the idea of close relationships between academics and workers was unusual, though now this direct involvement of researchers with shopfloor and local trade union groups has become more common. Each of the three people who responded provided details of alternative technologies they considered to be relevant. David Elliott outlined possible options for alternative energy. Richard Fletcher's proposals for a road-rail vehicle and Professor Thring's for telechiric devices were also discussed and incorporated into the plan. Thring's ideas on hybrid electric engines were also used, and subsequently the Lucas stewards informally provided technical help on the development of a test unit at Queen Mary College. The proposals from these sympathetic individuals were not, however, incorporated without modification. The combine's response to some of the alternative energy options, which Elliott drew from alternative technology movement literature, was critical. The combine felt that some of these would be relevant only to small, self-sufficient, experimental groups; they did not want to produce what one of them described as "gimmicks for individual architect-built houses" or "playthings for the middle class."

An orthodox corporate planner would not recognize the combine committee's alternative corporate plan as authentic. It is a corporate plan in the sense that just as a managerial plan sets out the objectives and strategy of the company over, say, a five-year period and on this basis makes its month-to-month operational decisions, so the combine's plan sets out the foreseeable needs, objectives, and strategy for the work force that then provide the basis for particular bargaining and campaigning positions. The combine's plan, however, has a different starting point and different objectives from those of a traditional corporate plan. Unlike management's corporate plan it does not start from an overriding commitment to increasing the dividends and the value of the shares of Lucas Industries. On the contrary, in the long run most combine delegates would prefer to see Lucas Aerospace under some form of social ownership and democratic control. In the short and medium term the combine's objectives are to fight for secure, useful, and dignified jobs for all those who work at Lucas Aerospace; to create such jobs for those whose skills and energies are at present wasted; to establish training facilities for such jobs for youth and women who at present have limited access to skilled jobs; and to make products that help to solve rather than to exacerbate human problems.

For the purpose of summarizing the plan, it can be divided into four parts, although in actual fact these parts are interwoven throughout the plan. They are:

1. A documentation of the productive resources of Lucas Aerospace;
2. An analysis of the problems and needs facing workers at Lucas Aerospace as a result of changes in the aerospace industry and the world economy;
3. An assessment of the social needs that the available resources could meet;

4. Detailed proposals about the products, the production process, and the employment development program that could contribute to meeting these different needs.

The plan starts with a summary of the skills of the work force, the numbers and type of machine tools, and the research and development facilities at Lucas Aerospace. Full details were provided in the detailed appendixes that backed up the main argument and proposals. The latter were presented at the combine committee in a fifty-page document.

Fear of losing their jobs was one problem facing Lucas Aerospace workers; the other problem that the Plan identified was the declining skill content and interest of the jobs that remained. The introduction to the plan argues that the past seventy years had seen systematic efforts to fragment jobs into small, narrow functions and to perform them at an increased tempo: "This process, which oddly is known as "Scientific Management," attempts to reduce the worker to a blind unthinking appendage to the machine or process in which he or she is working. . . ." The combine identified with the resistance of workers whose work had long ago tied them to the pace and requirements of the machine. The plan gives examples of the ways in which these workers are refusing to be treated as subhuman.

As the combine's plan points out, these problems are not confined to the shopfloor. The past ten years have seen the extension of various forms of "Taylorism" into the fields of white-collar and mental work. Already in the early 1970s it had become clear, the combine argued, that management's attempts to replace human intelligence with machine intelligence by emphasizing the universal importance of computer-controlled machine tools as against human skill have had disastrous results. One purpose of the corporate plan was to campaign for radical job redesign that would protect combine members from this deskilling process and enable them to extend their skills.

The plan then goes on to document social needs in the wider community, which Lucas has the technology to meet. It argues that "the aerospace industry is a particularly glaring example of the gap which exists between that which technology could provide and that which it actually does provide to meet the wide range of human problems with which combine members were familiar from their own experience." The plan then lists some of the ways the gap could be closed. These are divided into six major areas: medical equipment, alternative energy sources, transport systems, braking systems, oceanics, and telechiric—remote control—equipment. The proposals within these areas are drawn from the 150 or so ideas that combine delegates gathered together in response to the questionnaire.

Clearly, the plan's emphasis lay in "socially useful production." The combine committee delegates spelled out one definition of a socially useful product:

- The product must not waste energy and raw materials, neither in its manufacture nor in its use.
- The product must be capable of being produced in a labor intensive manner so as not to give rise to structural unemployment.
- The product must lend itself to organizational forms within production that are nonalienating, and without authoritarian giving of orders. Instead, the work should be organized so as to link practical and theoretical tasks and allow for human creativity and enthusiasm.

The Lucas stewards illustrated that the present way in which product choices are made and market power is distributed leads to social needs going unmet, even when there are the resources to meet them. Options are closed off that are both technologically feasible and socially desirable.

Consider, for example, the combine's proposal for a hybrid vehicle. The technology for it has been known for decades. The need for it has existed for even longer. People would very likely have been buying it, had they had the option. The problem is they would not have been buying it in sufficient numbers for it to be profitable for the mass-production giant car firms to make the extra investment required. And the car industry is such that the giant mass-production firms determine the options that we face on the market.

Until the energy crisis possibly makes the hybrid vehicle profitable for the major corporations, this option of a nonpolluting town car is not available on the "free" market. The implication of this and many similar examples highlighted by the Lucas stewards is that products are not only things; their existence and their design are the consequence of social purposes and social values, however hidden and implicit these values often are.

The Lucas stewards are not the first to have challenged the social values behind product decisions. The disarmament movement challenges the production of the bomb; feminists have identified and challenged the degrading assumptions made about women in the decision to make, for instance, vaginal deodorants and in the marketing of many other cosmetics; and the antinuclear movement focuses on the moral and political issues of energy policymaking. The newness of the Lucas workers' initiative is that they are challenging these values as producers as well as as citizens, users, and consumers. It is for this reason that their notion of socially useful production refers not only to products but also to the production process itself, which leads to the final aspect of their corporate plan.

At least one-quarter of the plan's proposals insist on an employee development program. In particular the combine called for the creation of working organizations "in which the skill and ability of our manual and staff workers is continually used in closely integrated production teams, where all the experience and common sense of the shop-floor workers would be directly linked to the scientific knowledge of the technical staff" (combine press release, January 1976). They also made proposals for retraining schemes for both blue- and white-collar workers, including women and young people, to help break down divisions and develop skills. In relation to retraining, the plan argues that it is essential to develop "the capabilities of our people to meet the technological and sociological challenges which will come during the next few years." It proposes that "in the event of work shortage occurring before the alternative products have been introduced, the potential redundancy could be transformed into a positive breathing space during which re-education could act as a form of enlightened work-sharing."

On employee development, the combine points out that there is no indication that the company is working on an adequate program of apprenticeships and the intake of young people. It adds:

> the company is making no attempt to employ women in technical jobs and, apart from the recruitment of these from outside, there are very many women doing routine jobs well below their existing capabilities. Quite apart from the desirability of countering these discriminating practices, the employment of women in the male-dominated areas would have an important 'humanizing' effect on science and technology.

It concludes: "it is our view that the entire work force, including semiskilled and skilled workers, are capable of retraining for jobs which would greatly extend the range of work they could undertake."

On 9 January 1976, in the conference room of the Lucas Aerospace Shaftmoor Lane factory, seven members of Lucas Aerospace top management received a delegation unlike any it had received before. Representatives of staff workers and shopfloor workers from every site—thirty-seven shop stewards in all—had come to present to management their plan for the long-term job security of their employees. In the two-hour meeting that followed, the shop stewards presented a summary of the plan. They held back the technical details for each group of products until—as they hoped—negotiations had got underway. This technical work, especially the work on those products that were likely to be profitable as well as socially useful, was one of the combine's negotiating weapons. Unless the combine kept it under their control, management would pick and choose from the plan on its own terms, gaining a free consultancy service out of the combine's work.

Who manages Lucas was a nonnegotiable issue. So too, as far as management was concerned, was the corporate plan. Management would not even meet the combine to present their reply. The promised second meeting, initially arranged for 27 April, was cancelled. Moreover the reply was sent not to the combine committee executive but to individual convenors, presumably to avoid de facto recognition of the combine's committee. The reply argued that the only way to secure jobs was to continue with the existing product range. It stated that the combine's product proposals were not compatible with the company's product lines, since the company emphasized short runs of high added value products, whereas the combine's ideas—as the company depicted them—implied a move to mass production of less sophisticated low added value products.

Although the company tried to stall action and prevent national negotiations, it did continue to meet with the combine. Lucas needed a channel of communications with the unions across all its diverse units, and it preferred to deal with its own shop stewards rather than outside officials. As time went on, however, the company began to place more obstacles in the way of meetings between management and the entire combine. The company also tried to divide the combine by trying to establish different negotiating regions for the South and North and by refusing to allow staff to participate in certain meetings, even though the outcome concerned staff members. Management also tried to play off national officials against the combine committee.

The Labour government, of course, could have put pressure on Lucas management to consider seriously the plan and produce some of its products. The industrial policies talked about during the first year of the Labour government had caused some anxiety in the boardrooms of companies like Lucas, especially when the talking was done by those on the left of the Labour party like Tony Benn and included proposals of compulsory planning agreements with trade union involvement. The precise meaning of such a policy may not have been clear, but it would certainly have obliged Lucas to consider the combine committee's plan more seriously, if only to be sure of future government subsidies. By the beginning of 1975, however, Prime Minister Harold Wilson had allayed their fears. He had set up a cabinet committee under his own chairmanship to take charge of the direction of industrial policy, thus restoring business confidence in the government itself. Planning agreements became voluntary and the trade union role in their creation became an optional extra. In July

1975, Wilson removed the remaining obstacle: Tony Benn. So by 1976, when the shop stewards' plan, itself encouraged by the Labour party's policies, was ready, management was under no pressure whatsoever to give it serious consideration. As a result the committee lost one of its most powerful negotiating levers.

In spite of management's resistance to national negotiations over the plan, the committee was able to secure several important local victories. Flexible in its position of favoring national over local negotiations, the committee had decided to negotiate locally when major redundancies took place in the autumn of 1975 at two sites, Birmingham and Hemel Hempstead. In both sites, campaigns successfully prevented redundancies and generated a long-term commitment to the alternative plan as part of a practical strategy for resisting redundancies.

At Birmingham, for example, the publicity around the fact that there were practical alternatives to layoffs kept workers from accepting voluntary redundancies, and the combine helped workers successfully press the company to create more jobs and move into a new factory. At Hemel Hempstead, the company wanted to eliminate the industrial ball screw division. By explaining how this product could be used in other alternative products and in other industries, workers not only refused to take the voluntary redundancies the company promoted but also convinced the government to oppose Lucas's proposed shutdown.

Persuaded by the combine's arguments, Lord Beswick, a minister of the Department of Industry, made it clear to management that the government would not look favourably on Lucas, in other respects, if they continued with their plan to close the ball screw division. Negotiations then began between management and the unions, and the latter's bargaining position was backed up by industrial sanctions and the threat of a refusal to work on the aerospace ball screws that the company wanted to keep. By the end of September 1976, the industrial ball screw division was saved.

Finally, at the Burnley site, the combine was able to force management to undertake negotiations about alternative production.. Between October 1976 and January 1978, a new-products committee met on the average of every six weeks. When management tried to lay off 300 workers, the existence of detailed work on alternative products provided stewards with a strong argument against layoffs. Armed with concrete alternatives, they built up sufficient support from the members to force management to withdraw the threat of redundancies.

Moreover, with this kind of support the trade union representatives were able to press for development of one specific product—the heat pump. Originally, stewards wanted to produce two small prototype pumps (one air-to-air machine and one air-to-water unit) that would serve as an efficient form of heating in overall energy terms. After months of struggle over details, the Department of Energy's Energy Technology Support Unit provided a grant to pay for the subsequent development and testing work, and Lucas themselves put up an initial £5,000 sterling for materials and provided a development engineer and a machinist and fitter to build the unit.

In spite of problems that resulted from such a low level of financing, the prototype was ready by the end of 1979. With a proven basic technical concept, the stewards wanted to use a larger, cheaper mass-produced car engine for a unit suited to providing heat for a group of houses, rather than just one. Burnley stewards and the combine committee had hoped that even if Lucas did not produce such units, they could at least obtain work on design and component controls. Lucas management, however, remained unmoved. Nevertheless, Burnley stewards saw the overall exercise of having successfully forced the company at least to develop a prototype as an important precedent. Subsequently, each time the company talked about shortage of work, the stewards were able to say, "Why not develop the heat pump?"

After ten years of struggle, management has never manufactured the heat pump or any other alternative product. The company refused to negotiate on the plan, commenting, "We are very unresponsive to a deliberate attempt by a group of workers to achieve a de facto situation to achieve bargaining rights across one of our companies." After Tony Benn had been removed from the Department of Industry, the Labour government accepted the company's point of view. With the election of Margaret Thatcher 3 May 1979, any hope of government support ended. The company no longer had to make any concessions to the political influence of the combine's corporate plan. Indeed, the abrasively antiunion atmosphere of the Thatcher government meant that the company could not only undermine the combine's strength but trade union strength as well.

Unfortunately, the company's staunch resistance to the Lucas corporate plan was not countered by the trade union movement as a whole. The Transport and General Workers Union (TGWU)—Britain's largest union—was the most supportive, and TGWU stewards at the Lucas Aerospace Shaftmoor Lane factory in Birmingham passed a resolution calling on their union to give full support to the alternative plan. At the TGWU's 1977 biannual conference, the general executive council recommended the union support the initiative and encourage similar initiatives elsewhere. The union has furthermore given backing and publicity to the alternative plan in its publication of the record and has used it in educational material.

AUEW members and members of other unions did not find their leadership quite so responsive. Because of long-standing political conflicts in the union and because the combine committee bypassed traditional trade union hierarchy and protocol, the union's General Secretary Ken Gill and other union officials were hostile both to combine leader Mike Cooley, and to the initiative itself. After long delays, the 1978 AUEW national conference finally passed a resolution in support of the plan. However, this was too late to effect critical negotiations between the company and the unions involved. And when the company fired Mike Cooley in 1981, the union was halfhearted, at best, in its attempts to defend him.

Although the plan ultimately failed to produce any alternative production it has succeeded on a number of levels. First, it allowed workers to fight successfully the company's efforts to lay off workers during the years of intensive campaigning and publicity. Second, it gave workers a sense of self-confidence, a clear example that they could, in fact, influence the design and production process and take part in the corporate decisionmaking process. Finally, it created an important working model of conversion activity. This model has not only helped other trade union activists initiate successful conversion campaigns in Britain and other countries, it also provides a point of departure for a discussion about the potential and problems of conversion activity.

The Lucas Shop Stewards Combine Committee was in an ideal position for developing and fighting for a workers' plan. The company employed a particularly high proportion of design engineers, scientific and technical workers, and highly qualified shopfloor workers who could participate in the construction of a proposal for alternative production. The technological requirements of an advanced aerospace company like Lucas also permitted the kind of flexibility that is valuable in the creation of alternative production. Aerospace components are produced in small batches to meet special orders, and to meet the specific requirements of each order the machine tools and production processes have to be adaptable. Most of the machine tools at Lucas are "universal" machine tools, which can be used to carry out many different engineering jobs.

Apart from these factors concerning the production side of the combine's plan, there are also specific features that concern the financing and purchasing side. Lucas Aerospace's main customers are governments or government-owned companies. In the case of the companies owned by the British government—Rolls Royce and British Aerospace—Lucas Aerospace has a near monopoly on the supply of several components.

Consequently, the combine committee was in a more favorable position to put forward an alternative plan than trade unionists faced with more genuine competitive pressures. In effect the combine already faced planned economic relations; the combine plan was merely challenging the content and the control of these relations. Since the government was already both subsidizing and purchasing from Lucas, the idea of a Labour

government committed to defense cuts switching more of their purchasing powers to, for instance, medical and transport products did not at
first seem to pose insuperable problems. Moreover, when a company has
such close relations and support from government, management's justifi-
cations for redundancies by reference to market forces lost much of their
force. The need to consider profit and loss as part of a social balance that
includes the cost of unemployment is a persuasive argument when much
of the company's profitability comes from the taxpayer in the first place,
and political considerations, albeit ones that the combine considered anti-
social, already determine the company's markets.

In spite of all these favorable aspects, there is, however, a strong
case for some additional level of organization beyond but connected with
existing trade union organizations. This is especially true at a time when
trade unions have been forced back to their most defensive positions. For
example, delegates to the Lucas combine committee found that the day-
to-day requirements of collective bargaining under the last year of the
Labour government and the first years of Tory rule were of a very defensive kind. The confidence simply did not exist to put forward positive and
radical policies of the kind they had developed in the corporate plan.
However, the combine believe that work should continue to develop the
approach of the alternative corporate plan and to extend the network of
organizations involved in similar initiatives, in preparation for more favorable conditions. Otherwise they and others would be unable to turn the
opportunity of a radical Labour government, or at least an economic
expansion, to their advantage, and the cycle of disillusionment and de-
moralization, leading to another Tory victory, would once more be set in
motion. This work will involve a conscious allocation of time and trade
union personnel to prepare discussions on issues of longer term strategy
and to formulate the basis for positive bargaining positions on questions
such as technology, government funding, and corporate investment
plans well in advance of the issues coming up in collective bargaining.
This will involve the creation of some new structure, even if only exten-
sions of existing trade union organizations.

There are several arguments for this additional level of trade union
activity. First, the content of discussion and ideas in those organizations
whose main function is collective bargaining is necessarily determined by
the immediate tactical concerns of the negotiations at hand: On its own
this is too narrow a framework to encourage ideas to develop about the
future of the industry, the social needs that the industry could meet, and
alternative products and technologies to press on management and government. Such a discussion needs stimulus and coordination outside of
the procedures and agendas of collective bargaining. In the case of Lucas
such a stimulus was provided by the combine committee when it sent

out a questionnaire and thereby introduced a new dimension on to the agendas of the factory trade union committees. The discussions at factory level stimulated by the questionnaire were in general more open-ended, more conducive to innovation and experimentation than the routine discussions connected with day-to-day negotiations.

A second reason for some additional level of organization concerns the fact that organizations whose main purpose is collective bargaining—including collective bargaining over proposals flowing from more broadly based workers' plans—need to parallel the power structures of the employers. By contrast the objective of developing alternative plans based on meeting the social needs of producers and users requires a form of association that cuts across different employers and across the different but interdependent sectors of the economy. If workers' plans were produced only on an enterprise basis there would be a danger of including proposals that if implemented would simply put other workers out of work. There would also be a danger of implying that the producers alone had the right to determine what was socially needed. There would also be other, more strategic problems concerning relations with the company, if workers' plans were simply focused on one enterprise: It would be harder to transcend the firms' economic boundaries, premises, and priorities. For this reason, negotiations on "planning agreements" with individual firms could degenerate into exercises in collaboration with management—as many trade unionists fear.

Clearly association with workers and, where necessary, users beyond the individual company and industry is needed. Indeed, this kind of association is beginning to be formed in local authorities in Britain—like Greater London Council, Sheffield, and West Midlands, where sympathetic technologists and engineers in local polytechnics and universities are working with trade unionists to draw up alternative proposals that will help to save or even create jobs—and in local trade councils where the idea of planning for social need is becoming popular, as well as in political parties and social movements.

The disarmament movement and the campaign against nuclear power have, for example, also stimulated and strengthened the discussion among trade unionists for alternative plans. The British Campaign for Nuclear Disarmament and European Nuclear Disarmament are beginning to work with trade unionists in the arms industry on plans for conversion. Activists in the antinuclear power movement have worked with members of many different unions affected by government energy policy to develop a trade union based campaign for nonnuclear energy policies. The new approach to energy policy that is gradually emerging moves the emphasis away from a concern with just conventional energy supply technologies (for example, centralized electricity producing power plants) to interest in local energy provisions (for example, solar energy and combined heat and power) and beyond that to a concern with the question of energy demand management and energy conservation. Transport planning, waste recycling, urban planning—all very much the concern of local authorities—are increasingly seen as relating directly to energy policy, which explains why public service unions are becoming much more interested in energy issues. This local government level concern also offers more opportunity for involvement and initiatives by community groups. Given the existing alternative plans produced by power engineering workers, it seems that the basis for democratic planning linking users and producers exists in the energy sector.

And, of course, government involvement is critical to the success of the creation of any plan for alternative production. Government can play a role in several important ways. First, government could play a catalytic role in bringing about direct association between the people, or the organizations representing them, who are concerned with the fact that existing market and planning machanisms fail to meet human needs. Such associations could try to resolve conflicting needs, to arrive as far as possible at a common policy or several different but consistent policies and build the strength to implement these policies. Given British industry's integration with the international economy, such direct associations would need to be organized on an international level: between, for instance, workers in tractor companies or agricultural machinery producers in Britain and the agricultural departments of governments in the Third World, so that machinery could be produced with a design and price to meet the needs of those countries by workers who would otherwise be laid off in Britain.

The role of government would not be limited to the provision of resources and encouragement; it would also delegate powers and legitimacy to the workers' committees formed in the process. Workers, for instance, would be empowered to monitor the implementation of policies decided nationally, regionally, or locally. Today, for example, trade union representatives have the power to monitor the implementation of the Health and Safety at Work Legislation. On a far wider scale the same could apply to industrial policy.

A further role would be to coordinate the funding for the implementation of workers' plans. Using financial and other sanctions on the companies concerned, government could support workers bargaining over proposals. And finally, in supporting the new institutions of popular planning the government would set the overall framework of economic policy, including levels of taxation, exchange rates, and the basis of international trading relations.

The Lucas Corporate Plan was the beginning of a powerful new movement. It was a vehicle that helped initiate a discussion about the need for alliances between a variety of different movements that can put pressure on government to act—to create just, democratic societies. In recent years, the need for alliances that produce such concrete conversion proposals has grown ever more urgent, for two fears now haunt people not only in Britain but also all over the world: the fear of unemployment and the fear of war. Both are the outcome of forces that often seem to be outside the control of so-called ordinary people—technological and market pressures producing the constant threat of redundancy and the momentum of the military machine carrying with it the threat of extermination. The ideas pioneered by the Lucas stewards and the workers' self-confidence they inspired have put down roots that cannot easily be destroyed. They have proved that ordinary people are capable of working to cope with their world in truly extraordinary ways.

8

Economic Conversion Activity in Western Europe

Suzanne Gordon

Like long lines of skiers making their way up a steep incline, rows of council houses cling to the hills of Sheffield, an aging industrial city in South Yorkshire, England. Built in the late 1960s, much of Britain's public housing has been steadily deteriorating in recent years. In Sheffield, shattered windows are repaired with thin sheets of plywood rather than glass; exterior partition walls that divide individual units crumble slowly in the rain and wind; and, in the interior of countless units, families battle the worst symptom of wear—a thick, blue-black mold that coats walls and ceilings and invades closets and cupboards where it rots linens, clothing, and finally, the very core of the houses themselves. Although England's damp climate naturally encourages this insidious growth, apartments constructed without adequate ventilation aggravates the problem in public housing. Vapor from a boiling kettle, steam from a bath or shower, even the exhalation of residents' breathing all combine with the general dampness in the air to form the musty, odorous fungus that is a pervasive problem for tenants and local housing authorities all over Great Britain. In Manchester, not far from Sheffield, the city council decided it was cheaper to demolish an entire housing development—the Fort Beswick estate—than to repair the effects of mold. In Sheffield, the county council has spent millions of pounds sterling repairing mold damage to a quarter of its 93,000 public housing units.

Until recently, the Sheffield Council and other metropolitan councils had two options: either follow the Manchester strategy or continue to allocate funds for maintenance work in a never-ending attempt to stem the fungus. In 1980, all this changed, however. In that year the Sheffield Council began a series of innovative public investment programs that utilized idle factories and have produced jobs for the unemployed— and, in the process, have provided a practical solution to the problem of mold. With its steel-based infrastructure, Sheffield has been hit hard by Britain's recent recession. Faced with 80,000 unemployed workers and no immediate prospect of relief from the Thatcher government's economic policies, the city's Labour-controlled council decided to act on its own to deal with growing unemployment and economic decline. Allocating a budget of £2.5 million, the council has mandated its employment department to promote conversion of unused production facilities to meet unmet social needs in the area. The department is empowered to encourage the development and production of products that the council itself can purchase—at a significant savings of tax payers' money—and it will select product lines that do not create unemployment elsewhere by competing with items manufactured in other regions in the United Kingdom.

To ascertain which product lines would fit the suggested criteria, the council consulted local engineering school faculties and enlisted the help of the shop stewards combine committee of the Lucas Aerospace group. Engineer Phil Asquith—a leader in the Lucas movement to convert Britain's largest aerospace manufacturer to socially useful, nonmilitary production—advised, for example, that the council did not have the resources to manufacture and produce one of the most famous Lucas designed products, a heat pump to be installed in council housing. The pump, which was one of 150 product ideas that Lucas stewards proposed to their company's management, would have provided a cheap and efficient means of heating housing units that badly needed efficient heat sources. After considering Sheffield's condensation problem, Asquith suggested the council help workers produce specially designed dehumidifiers instead.

A dehumidifier that would work around the clock to draw moisture from the air and collect it in a sealed container would more than fulfill the council's criteria for socially useful, marketable and cost-effective production. By utilizing a relatively small research and development budget—a mere £26,500—the council could pay an engineering professor at the local polytechnic to work full-time on supervising the research and development phase of the project. He, in turn, could recruit students attracted to the challenge of a real life—rather than manufactured—design job, and together they could produce a prototype to test and install. The project would eventually require from 200 to 400 workers, and the council as purchaser would save far more than it currently spends in repair bills to maintain damaged housing stock. Since the only dehumidifier available on the market—an American product—was too costly, cumbersome, noisy, and subject to vandalism to purchase, the council was assured such production would meet unmet social needs without simultaneously exporting unemployment.

The council took Phil Asquith's advice. Indeed, it soon hired Asquith and another former Lucas shop steward, Brian Salisbury, to work in the

Employment Department itself. After a year, designers had come up with a quiet, virtually unbreakable, sleek dehumidifier that can, as an added benefit, heat a small room or landing. In January, 1984, they mounted it on the walls of selected council housing units where it will be tested during the harshest winter months when condensation is most severe. When it passes its trial run, it will then be produced by a cooperative of machinists established after their old machine tool factory was recently closed down. The price of each unit is £250; the price of tooling up a factory to manufacture the unit is an additional £12,000 above the initial R and D expenditure. Initially, the dehumidifiers will only be marketed locally, and when they have a proven track record, the co-op will reach out to other local authorities in Britain.

Ordinarily, there would be nothing unusual about a municipal effort to initiate a cost-cutting program to maintain public property. The Sheffield experiment is, however, no ordinary program. Rather, it is part of a continentwide campaign to promote the concept of economic conversion both as a means of reversing the economic decline that threatens many workers and their communities and as a means of providing alternatives to growing reliance on military production.

All over Europe, official statistics show increasing unemployment. According to the Organization for Economic Cooperation and Development (OECD), Great Britain's unemployment went from 5.3 percent in 1976 to 12.5 percent in 1982. In Italy, the jobless rate was 7.2 percent in 1978 and 9.2 percent six years later. In the Netherlands, unemployment was 5.9 percent between 1975 and 1980 and is now up to 12 percent. France registered 2.6 percent unemployed in 1973 and 8.3 percent in 1982, while Germany, which boasted an enviable low of 1.1 percent in 1976, has now gone up to 6.8 percent. Moreover, due to what economists recognize as serious structural flaws in the global economy, even the most optimistic projections for recovery acknowledge that millions of workers will be left unemployed.

One of the most popular methods of reducing unemployment and increasing the profitability of at least some corporations has been to devote more government funds to defense production and development of an arms export industry. In most industrialized nations, therefore, numerous firms that have produced for both civilian and military markets are undergoing what peace and conversion activists call "reverse conversion" by shifting to greater military production. Less lucrative and riskier research, development, and manufacturing related to civilian product lines is being drastically reduced or eliminated altogether.

Adopting the broadest possible definition of conversion, European labor unions, political parties, peace activists, and economic planners have begun to work more closely in response to this triple threat of unemployment, rearmament, and reverse conversion. In the past, conversion has been viewed only as a means of dealing with the vicissitudes of the arms economy—as an insurance policy that would protect defense workers from the eventual outbreak of peace and help neutralize their opposition to military budget cuts. European activists are, however, now promoting conversion as a solution to the economic dislocation caused by plant closings and layoffs due to the introduction of new technology, the shift of plants to countries with low labor costs, the failure to invest in maintenance of plant and equipment as well as to the environmental damage caused by polluting industries. Conversion is also being used as a way to advance the idea that rank and file workers should have a far greater role in determining corporate investment decisions that affect their jobs, families, and communities.

In almost every European country with a highly developed arms economy and serious economic problems a number of trade unionists and politicians have encouraged public debate about conversion or some form of actual conversion activity. The one exception is France. There, the alignment of both left parties with the Mitterrand government's rearmament and pronuclear policies has been a major obstacle to the creation of a strong peace movement and serious consideration of conversion as a means to economic recovery. In France, conversion discussions are thus limited to proforma working groups—like that set up by the country's second largest trade-union federation, the CFDT (Confederation Française Democratique de Travailleurs)—which so far, have only endorsed a variety of diversification schemes that would increase civilian production in the arms industry. Some diversification plans have, in fact, produced new civilian product lines. In general, however, these diversification efforts were not worker-initiated. France thus remains a country where reverse conversion goes almost unchallenged.

In the Netherlands, Norway, Denmark, and Belgium, conversion has become far more popular since the mass-based peace movements in those countries won over a large majority of their citizens to the recent campaigns against the "Euromissiles." Through the aggressive participation of the Swedish Metalworkers Union and the Social Democratic Party, Sweden has also begun a serious conversion process. In 1979, a national committee, composed of representatives of labor, and industry, met to outline a program that would expand the civilian sector of defense firms. Two reports issued by the group included the suggestion (among others) that community groups should work with the government to encourage alternative production and that the government should purchase new civilian technologies just as it has been a major purchaser of military goods.

Because Swedish arms companies function in a very closed environment, shielded by national security regulations from public scrutiny, the Metalworkers Union believes that the state must take a leading role in promoting conversion. Financial and technical assistance are essential, and the process of researching and developing alternative products must begin long before a military contract is to be canceled—which means, of course, that the government and military contractors must provide information about current and future project plans. The Swedes estimate that as many as eight to ten years may be necessary to create and introduce substitute products that would be successful in civilian markets. To begin the necessary contingency planning, the Metalworkers have begun to set up alternative use committees in major arms factories.

One of the most successful conversion efforts in Sweden has taken place at the Oresundsvarvet shipyard in the town of Landskrona. The large shipyard, a fully state-owned facility run by the Swedyards group, had suffered from the shipbuilding crisis of the mid-seventies. In June 1981, the Swedish government decided to close down the yard, which had employed between 2500 and 3000 workers. Deeply concerned about the fate of the yard and their community, 10,000 of 36,000 Landskrona residents demonstrated to save the shipyard. Due to their protest and the work of Swedish unions and industrial policy planners, the government and the company contributed a number of grants and initiated a major conversion effort.

Because of this effort, of the 2,322 employees who were laid off, 1,650 have new jobs in the area. Fully half of these jobs are in the more than 40 enterprises established during the shut-down period. By utilizing the buildings at the shipyard, and the workers skills, and supplementing these with retooled facilities and retraining programs, Landskrona Produktion has set up an impressive series of newly converted enterprises. These include companies that produce the EWOS Giant Cage, a floating installation for raising fish on an industrial scale; the Sanol Decontamination System, a system for cleaning up both large and small scale oil spills; a truck-sweeper system for street cleaning; and an expanded container house that can provide living units or field hospitals that can be easily installed on a variety of sites.

The cooperative venture between workers, community residents, and local and national governmental authorities has produced training programs from between two weeks to four years for some 1200 shipyard employees and has been so successful that the Swedish National Labour Market Board is now interested in studying wider applications of the Landskrona model to other areas suffering industrial decline.

By far the most advanced conversion work in Europe today is going on in the United Kingdom. Britain's conversion movement is a direct outgrowth of the ten-year struggle to convert Lucas Aerospace—Britain's largest aerospace manufacturer—from military to socially useful production. As was pointed out in an earlier chapter, conversion activity at Lucas began when the company threatened to lay off thousands of workers because of cutbacks in military contracts and company rationalization plans. Without any alternatives to propose to management to maintain employment levels, Lucas workers recognized they would have very little leverage to resist the layoffs. The workers thus drew up a list of 150 alternative products and developed working prototypes of five of these products. Although the company ultimately refused to produce any of the proposed products, the widely publicized Lucas Plan nevertheless became a model for conversion activity in the United Kingdom, Europe, and the United States.

In Britain itself the Lucas experience succeeded in persuading even those organizations, union officials, and politicians who were at the outset unsympathetic to the project. Many of Britain's largest unions, for example, were initially hostile to the Lucas Shop Stewards Combine Committee because it bypassed established trade union channels and hierarchies. Since then many of these unions have endorsed conversion. Those unions who were supportive of the Lucas Plan like the Transport and General Workers Union—Britain's largest union, which represents thousands of workers in arms factories and the Ministry of Defense—now promote conversion even more aggressively in educational and coordinating campaigns. The TGWU, for example, has published and distributed a booklet on conversion entitled "A Better Future: A TGWU Strategy for Arms Conversion" and has helped workers in arms factories set up alternative use committees. Other parts of the labor movement, including public sector unions, have also joined the campaign.

The British Labour party, which gave only the faintest encouragement to the Lucas Plan when it was last in power, has adopted a proposal for national conversion legislation that it promises to enact when it regains power. Most importantly, however, key rank and file leaders of the Lucas Shop Stewards Combine Committee have moved on to positions in some of England's largest municipal governments where they are involved in well-funded, public programs for converting both arms factories and other sectors of the local economy.

Phil Asquith's role in the Sheffield Employment Department is one example of this, and the Sheffield dehumidifier is just one of the products his group is working on. Others include a "human-centered" machine tool produced by a local company; a self-contained hygiene facility for the disabled; a wash basin designed for wheelchair users; equipment for use in cancer treatment; and a combined heat and power system to heat homes and buildings in the Sheffield city center. The Sheffield Council has also set up a product development center called SCEPTRE (Sheffield Center for Product Development and Technological Resources) where workers, engineers, and members of the community can collaborate on the design and development of product prototypes. Located in a large lobbylike room in the Sheffield Polytechnic, the workshop operates in full view of passersby who are encouraged to observe work processes and contribute product suggestions or requests—to participate in the scientific and technical process of creation rather than fear it. As Asquith explains:

> What we want to do is create, in microcosm, a viable local economy that bypasses the most pernicious effects of the kind of market economy that exports unemployment, disenfranchises poor and working class citizens, and spends more money developing weapons of destruction than satisfying dire human needs. This working economy will itself serve as a prototype that can be elaborated upon and replicated when a sympathetic national government takes office and can enact national legislation to create a national program of the kind of economic reconstruction the Lucas Model outlines.

Not surprisingly, the Labour-controlled Greater London Council—Britain's largest and best funded local authority—also has the most ambitious of the country's conversion programs. Located in a building on the south bank of the Thames, directly across from Westminster Abbey and the Houses of Parliament, the London Council—quite literally—wears its Labour manifesto on its sleeve. It defiantly displays an enormous banner that daily reminds Prime Minister Margaret Thatcher of the human costs of her economic programs. In huge block letters, the banner bears the number—regularly revised upward—of Greater London's unemployed.

Since his election as the Labour party leader of the council, Ken Livingston and the Labour majority have tried to counter the military and employment policies of the national government. The council has recently declared London a "nuclear-free zone," proclaimed 1983 to be Peace Year, plastered the city with billboards asking citizens to oppose the arms race, published a realistic and frightening account of the potential effects of a nuclear war on London, and added its strong, collective voice to the recent campaign against the deployment of Euromissiles.

But council members realize there can be no global security without national and local job security. Thus, the council's manifesto includes a pledge to restructure London's industry so that long-term, socially useful employment is created. Among the most important vehicles established to fulfill this pledge is the Greater London Enterprise Board (GLEB). With a budget of £32 million for fiscal year 1983, the board's mandate is to assist the establishment of new enterprises that manufacture socially useful products, keep old enterprises and their jobs intact, or help them convert to new product lines.

Located in new office space several miles south of County Hall, the GLEB began operating in February 1983 and has already helped set up or maintain 130 factories providing over 2,000 jobs. GLEB's crucial arm is its technology division, directed by the Lucas Plan's most well-known and charismatic advocate, Mike Cooley. A blond, wispy-haired engineer whose black pin-stripe suit suggests he might be a British banker and not a trade union activist, Cooley works in a large office complex that also employs the financial experts, technical advisers, and media specialists who provide and promote GLEB's services. In the rear of the building is Cooley's pride and joy—a set of offices and workshops that comprise one of five technology networks that GLEB has created around London. At the moment, the huge barnlike space houses only a few machine tools, including a special lathe designed to maximize rather than minimize operator input. And it awaits delivery of the famous Lucas road-rail vehicle that will soon be put on display. While showing a visitor around, Cooley pauses to ask a machinist when the lathe will be available so he can come in at night and work on a project.

The technology network is the embodiment of GLEB's philosophy. There are now five of these networks—three of which are geographically based, in North, East and Southeast London; two of which are product-based, dealing with energy and new technology. The networks can, Cooley explains, "make use of the enormous skill and talent amongst people on the shop floor. This talent, which they articulate in a tacit, product and skill-oriented sense rather than abstractly, is tremendously undervalued," he contends. The networks supplement shopfloor resources with the help of the infrastructure of higher educational facilities in London. Thus, each network is associated with a polytechnic and is aided by technical specialists. However, in order to prevent domination by such experts, no network is located on university or polytechnic premises.

The networks also involve the surrounding community and attempt to respond to the needs of the community rather than of profit alone. If a tenants' group is demanding improvements in their building's heating and ventilation systems, if a community wants to prevent the shutdown of a factory that sustains the local economy, it does not have to wait passively for the state to intervene. It can approach one of the technology networks and GLEB and participate not only in maintaining its own local enterprises and institutions but also in designing, developing, and manufacturing the products it needs to do so.

Just as the networks emphasize popular participation, so too the technological solutions they propose are the mirror opposite of the deskilling, authoritarian uses of technology so common in the military-industrial complex. "Instead of concentrating knowledge in the hands of an elite," says Cooley, "we've developed technology that redistributes that knowledge. The human-centered lathe is one example. Another is a medical-diagnostic system that puts doctor and patient together so the two can review the patient's symptoms rather than the patient being the passive recipient of the doctor's divine wisdom."

Creating such systems, Cooley insists, does not challenge merely the workers who will use them but also the engineers who will help design them. "There are a great many scientists and engineers who would prefer to work on constructive rather than destructive projects, but they simply have no opportunity to do so. What we feel we can do is offer even the more straight-laced scientists and technologists—whose interest may just be in their science and technology—forms of work that challenge their technical ability right to its frontiers."

Although some of the products GLEB is developing and many of the companies it is assisting produce for consumer markets, many of the products involved are made for purchase by either national or local authorities. Their ultimate success, then, will depend on creating a political constituency that will support the allocation of government funds to maintain this public purchasing power and investment role. As Cooley says:

> Very often, we can be intimidated by the notion that socially useful products won't have a market. When we began at Lucas, people argued that kidney dialysis machines had no market. Then we found out that every year 3,000 people died because they couldn't get dialysis. So it wasn't a question of need, it was a question of their inability to pay. At the same time, they were telling us it was profitable to continue making fighter planes. So we said, "All right, we're scientific people, you tell us how it is possible that one is profitable and the other is not. Obviously, the customer for both is the government. The government can decide to make kidney machines or jet fighters profitable."
>
> What happens now is that the government makes jet fighters and people have literally to go around their neighborhoods collecting pennies to buy kidney machines and the arms manufacturers get money to make jets. What must happen is that we force the government to make kidney machines and the arms manufacturers go around collecting pennies to produce arms.

In GLEB's case, the process of re-ordering budget priorities begins with the Greater London Council itself. The council has a purchasing budget of some £361.8 million. If the GLC purchases the alternative products manufactured in London, it can help provide the market necessary to make such production profitable, and—as in the case of Sheffield—it can save money not only in the cost of services to workers who would otherwise be unemployed but in meeting ummet social needs. Moreover, both London and Sheffield share the same desire not to export unemployment. All three local authorities working on conversion, therefore, have attempted to develop a microcosmal system of national planning. To make sure that no local authority produces and markets the same product lines, the three have decided not to produce identical products and, in some instances, have agreed to trade ideas that are more suited to development in another authority.

Decisions about eligibility for GLEB loans, grants, and equity participation are made with equal attention to principle and social need. James McAllister, a GLEB enterprise planner, explains that while most regional and local development agencies use their financial power solely in favor of management and to keep workers from being unionized, GLEB uses its capital to leverage worker and trade-union participation. If a company wants GLEB to provide a loan or grant or to assume an equity interest in the firm, GLEB will insist that it meet three conditions.

The company must assure trade union access. If the work force is currently unorganized, it must be organized so that workers can have independent representation and some way to equalize the imbalance of power inherent in the employment relationship. If the work force is already organized, management cannot use its financial difficulties to force a union out or to extract overly harsh concessions. The company must assure fair conditions of employment and institute what GLEB calls "enterprise planning." This means that workers and management must formulate an enterprise plan, assessing both the choice of products to be produced and the production processes utilized; management must meet periodically to discuss the firm's progress in implementing the plan; and labor must have a major share in decisionmaking. Once these conditions are agreed upon, they are put into an agreement that is then signed by GLEB, management, and the workers.

Through enterprise planning, GLEB has set up companies that vary in size. The smallest is a partnership in which two women work together on a mail order childrens' book service. Larger firms—employing anywhere from 200 to 300 workers—include companies that produce handmade leather goods sold on the American market, a worker-owned company that manufactures overalls, four furniture manufacturers, an engineering company that makes automobile components, and the new companies that will soon begin to manufacture GLEB developed and designed alternative products.

"The money we have to spend," says Cooley candidly, "would only be pocketmoney for a multinational. But if we use this money tactically, we can act as catalysts. We can begin to demonstrate, in an exemplary way, what a subsequent Labour government could do if it engaged in this kind of planning on a national level. But more than this, it will show that ordinary people can indeed have some say in creating their lives and their world."

Although some of the enterprises GLEB will eventually convert are military production facilities, neither GLEB nor the GLC focus their conversion efforts solely on the defense industry. Because, however, London is a center of military production, the GLC has set up a special, military-oriented conversion project—The Greater London Conversion Council. Directed by Bill Niven, a silver-haired Scot who is himself an engineer and formerly national organizer for the British white-collar union AUEW/TASS, the conversion council is composed of representatives from trade unions, peace groups, engineering societies, and even includes a representative from the Ministry of Defense. To further its work, the conversion council has established a number of subcommittees—a defense contract monitoring group that will gather information about government procurement plans to create an early-warning system about cancellation or alteration of contracts, a pilot-study project that will target three or four of London's seventy arms factories and work with their shop stewards to set up alternative use committees, and a marketing/demand committee that will also deal directly with the GLC about its purchasing requirements. In an effort to introduce engineering students to the concept of conversion, the conversion council has recently established an innovative engineering prize for students who successfully undertake projects that illustrate ways to convert military to peacetime production.

The Lucas model has served as an inspiration and guide to those interested and involved in promoting conversion in other European countries as well. With adjustments that reflect different cultural and political circumstances, it has become a point of departure for union-based conversion campaigns in both West Germany and Italy.

There are about fifteen conversion groups currently active in German arms factories and in other civilian-oriented manufacturing plants. They are supported by some of Germany's largest unions—particularly the IG Metall with 2.6 million members in auto, steel, electronics, aerospace, and other industries—peace researchers, industrial sociologists, economists, and political organizations like the Social Democratic party and the Green party.

Of all the groups involved in conversion, the trade unions are the most critical. Unions like IG Metall give direct assistance through research institutes and the union's "Innovation Department," which gives members advice and information about new technology; through grants and funds that finance conferences and meetings; and through pressure on management to insure that employers heed conversion proposals. But the development and strength of the conversion movement in Germany is also the product of the struggles and gains unions there have won in the past. Under the German system of codetermination, unions have for many years had representation on company boards. Workers have been given access to corporate plans, and they have had substantial say in making plant-level decisions through works councils. This has set an important precedent that workers can build on when they push for a greater role in determining production options.

Union education programs – notably a program called *Bildungs Urlaub* (education holiday or leave) – also provides a framework for conversion activists to train rank-and-file workers. Through the *Bildungs Urlaub,* German workers are given two fully paid (by the employer) weeks per year in which to take courses on subjects of their choosing. Workers can thus use this time to inform themselves about conversion strategies and practice. Similarly, union-backed legislation constructs financial and legal parameters that allow workers and communities the leeway to experiment with conversion options. Strict plant-closing legislation, for instance, makes it impossible for an employer to simply close down a plant that is not making sufficient profit or to pack up and move to a Third World country. Under German law, management must give workers significant advance notice of their plans and must provide a "social plan" – a package of benefits, severance pay, and retraining schemes that make it possible for state governments to pressure management to consider alternative production or the possibility of a publically financed worker buyout.

Within this political, legislative, and trade union context, conversion committees active in Germany today approach conversion as a means to a variety of different but related ends. As Christian Wellmann, a conversion researcher at the Frei Universitat of Berlin explains,

> In Germany, conversion is a dialectical process that combines two main factors – political and economic. In many instances, conversion groups have been inspired by the peace movement. Workers in arms factories who don't want to produce arms and want to do their part for peace approach conversion as the means to this end. In other instances, the motives of those who started alternative use committees are purely economic. They say they don't so much mind working on weapons but they feel that military contracts just aren't good for job security. In still other instances, workers work in factories that produce civilian products, and the factories are threatened with closure and so they turn to conversion for employment opportunities.

Depending on the factory involved, conversion may focus on production of socially useful products that will replace military or other civilian ones, or it may, instead, concentrate on preventing the reverse conversion going on in Germany today. The conversion work at Krupp's MAK factory in Kiel – a subsidiary that builds Panzer tanks, submarine parts, petrol engines, and locomotives – is an example of an attempt to preserve civilian product lines and prevent cyclical unemployment due to over dependence on military production. To deal with the coming cancellation of a large military contract, workers at Krupp began promoting the notion of conversion and proposed a number of energy-related products that the company could develop. When MAK announced that it would end locomotive production, the conversion committee was ready to step forward and suggest it maintain its production competence in the field, and initiate new activity in the development of road-rail cargo transport. Although management and the union are still debating the merits of producing particular alternative products like heat exchange technology and devices that will help handicapped people, the conversion committee did succeed in forcing management to continue building locomotives.

Another interesting conversion effort was initiated by workers at Blohm and Voss, a shipyard that also produces tank parts in Hamburg. In 1980, shipyard workers at another factory, HDW, went on strike when the government threatened to cancel an export permit for submarines to be sold in Chile (under German law, arms exporters can be prohibited from selling weapons to governments in dangerous areas—which Chile's junta represented). When the president of the shop stewards council at Blohm and Voss and other workers heard about this incident, they determined that workers at their yard should never be put in the position of both striking to support management's interests and the interests of a repressive, antilabor regime abroad. Conversion, then, would be their insurance policy.

But to convince a recalcitrant management even to consider conversion proposals, workers at Blohm and Voss, unlike MAK workers, felt they would have to make their struggle public. By reaching out to the media, local peace and community groups, and local churches, the committee played on management's concern about its public image. Since concentrating solely on military work appears to many to be a form of mismanagement, Blohm and Voss's reluctance to consider conversion proposals would be viewed in a very bad light. After a media campaign, they agreed to work with the conversion committee. In the spring of 1983, the group brought in consultants from outside the company and conducted a one-day seminar on new product proposals, technology, and marketing strategies. Soon, the committee began assessing the wide variety of skills and machinery used in a large shipyard with a huge machine tool division.

Selecting two main areas of production—shipbuilding and energy policy—the workers decided to investigate a plan to build anchored ships containing small windmills that would be installed in off-shore locations and could generate as much energy as a 700-megawatt, nuclear-fueled power plant.

Working to integrate product proposals into the continuing debate about Hamburg's energy policy, workers developed their second set of proposals. In this case, they advised replacing costly capital-intensive pipelines that convey heat (with a great deal of heat loss) with a more efficient system that would also be job creating. Workers distributed these proposals to the press, management, and the Hamburg Senate (Hamburg and Bremen are two city-states that make up Germany's eleven city-states). This again forced management to enter into negotiations with the Hamburg Senate and plans for energy products are proceeding.

Although there are a great many other committees working on similar ideas and strategies at other arms factories, most of these efforts are in a preliminary stage. Other conversion campaigns—have taken place in factories that produce civilian products. These illustrate the breadth and potential of the conversion model as a vehicle to relieve structural unemployment and deal with the threat of plant closings and capital flight.

One of these campaigns took place at the Voith Company, a large conglomerate. Workers at Voith's Bremen plant used the conversion model to initiate a worker buy-out when management threatened to close down the facility that produced equipment to process paper products. Freed from his other duties, the president of the workers' council begin investigating conversion options. The most feasible ideas, he discovered, included production of the company's profitable product lines and wind energy technology.

The workers felt, however, that if Voith continued as owner and manager, there could be no chance of success. So the workers approached the Bremen Senate (the state's governing body) and asked them to help negotiate the buy-out. The Senate agreed. The state of Bremen thus rented the land on which the factory is located and gave it to the worker-owned company rent-free. The workers, backed by the Bremen government, were able to persuade the company to lease its equipment to the workers for an almost negligible fee. Rather than taking over a factory whose product is no longer competitive or in demand, conversion campaigners at Voith did not engage in the usual exercise of "lemon socialism." Instead, the choice of continuing profitable product lines and branching out into new alternative production, they feel, will make their buy-out a success.

Although cases like this—where conversion has proved useful—are increasingly comon, there is also a great deal to learn from those experiments in Germany and other countries where experiments have failed. This past year, workers at AG Wesser's shipyard in Bremen lost a major conversion fight that illustrates many of the problems conversion campaigns encounter. One of five major shipyards left in Germany, the AG Wesser plant had long suffered from the same problems that afflict shipbuilding in all industrialized nations. With countries like Korea and Japan producing new ships so cheaply, construction of merchant vessels has almost ceased in the West. Long known for its shipbuilding industry, Germany had operated a great many major shipyards after World War II; now it has only five large shipyards.

In order to keep its shipbuilders employed, the German government tried to initiate "make-work" projects that it distributed equally between each yard. But the work—on five frigates—only lasted half a year. With no further contracts lined up, AG Wesser decided to close shop. Shutdown rumors soon reached the workers, and when they were confirmed, union members went to IG Metall's national headquarters for help. Through the union, the workers contacted a unique research institute at the University of Bremen where economists, sociologists, and industrial experts are under contract to the German labor movement. Following the Lucas model, the workers' conversion committee then recruited technical assistants and assembled a list of twenty-six different products—eleven in energy-related fields and sixteen in trains and other transportation equipment. The committee decided the most socially useful and saleable product was a filter to be fitted on the chimneys of private houses where it would curb the chemical emissions that contribute so heavily to one of Germany's most serious environmental problems—acid rain.

One-third of German forests have been destroyed by acid rain, and the problem causes 60 million deutsche marks worth of damage each year. Because of this, the Federal Republic has enacted stringent legislation that requires emission control devices in factories and on cars. The shipbuilders discovered, however, that these regulations do not regulate a major contributor to acid rain—private homes. With government subsidies in the form of tax rebates, the devices installed on chimneys would thus have a huge market and would also serve as a perfect illustration of how conversion can be used to create both employment and alleviate other social problems. Recruiting economists, marketing experts, lawyers, peace groups, church groups, and politicians, the workers set about putting their plan into action. Unfortunately, the plan ultimately failed.

Says Martin Osterland, an industrial sociologist at the University of Bremen who worked on the one and a half year struggle:

> The failure was due to many factors. First, we just began too late. In great part, this was due to the workers' own passivity and skepticism. For a long time, many workers simply refused to believe the worst would happen. They kept thinking the company would not let them down or that the government would intervene to save them. Many didn't want to consider conversion because they didn't want to change their jobs. They'd been shipbuilders, their fathers and grandfathers had been shipbuilders, and they wanted to continue to build ships.

Not only did it take time to recruit workers to fight to preserve the opportunity to use their traditional skills—if not to save their exact jobs—it also took time to gather the kind of technical and political support without which Osterland and others feel conversion is impossible. "You can't just say, 'Oh! Let's make this!' and then go ahead and make it. You have to know the product you choose can be sold. Moreover, you have to work on the political level as well and win over politicians and other groups friendly to the cause."

Italian conversion advocates are quick to admit that activity in their country lags behind that of Germany and the United Kingdom. Fabrizio Battistelli, a sociologist at the University of Rome and one of Italy's leading experts on the subject, explains that there is no actual conversion movement in Italy but rather a loose and growing coalition of trade union militants and peace activists who are trying to forge the kind of alliances necessary to launch a strong movement in the future.

The leading force behind this new coalition is the Italian Metalworkers Union, the FLM. FLM interest in conversion dates back to the mid-seventies when Alberto Tridente, an FLM executive board member, began to discuss the issue with FLM members in various armaments factories in Italy. Tridente and others were concerned about rapid growth in Italian arms exports (Italy is the fourth largest exporter of weapons in the world). Although the Italian government has been a signatory to international agreements limiting arms sales in certain areas of international conflict, the United Nations had found Italy guilty of serious violations of these accords on four separate occasions.

Tridente and his colleagues were struck by the glaring political and moral contradictions inherent in FLM members' involvement in arms production. The Italian workers' movement has had a long history of sympathy for struggles against repressive regimes. At the beginning of the century, many Italian unionists backed the Russian revolution; in the thirties and forties, they fought fascism at home and abroad in the Spanish Civil War; and, in recent years, Italian unions have protested against military dictatorships and supported national liberation struggles in the Third World. How then could workers who marched for peace and against imperialism on Sunday rush to produce arms that would aid military intervention and heighten world tensions on Monday?

In raising such an explicitly political question among the rank and file, Tridente and other FLM officials sought ways to resolve this contradiction. Initially, discussions outlining Italy's involvement in the arms race shocked people, says Battistelli. "We've always had this impression that we're a peaceful people. But the facts were incontrovertible."

When Tridente left the FLM, Gigi Pannozzo, the new Secretary of the International Department, continued his work. Given the trend in Italy toward the same kind of reverse conversion found in other industrialized countries, the union's promotion of education and debate on the issue is more critical than ever before.

After helping rank and file workers establish local conversion committees, the FLM developed a campaign to discourage reverse conversion. As in Germany, Sweden, and the United Kingdom, conversion campaigners made use of union negotiated programs. The Italian equivalent of the German Bildungs Urlaub, for example, allowed workers to use the 150 hours of paid time-off they can devote to educational courses, for conversion education. Similarly, proposals put forth by the conversion committees are included in the bargaining package unions present to management in their normal negotiations over pay and other personnel policies. This has facilitated a far more direct discussion of the issue than is possible in the United States, where federal labor laws sharply restrict the scope of union collective bargaining to traditional wage and benefit issues.

Thus far, the Italian campaign has produced results. At Oto Melare, one of Italy's largest arms manufacturers, the factory council—made up of workers in all the union confederations in Italy who discuss working conditions and company plans with management—has forced the company to divide production equally at its new Brindisi plant between military vehicles and agricultural vehicles (This 50–50 split compares quite favorably with the military-to-civilian production ratio at the company's La Spezia plant, which produces 95 percent of its products for the military and only 5 percent for civilian markets). At Bolvetti, a Fiat-owned factory that employs 5,000 workers in Milan, the company had for years produced speedometers for civilian vehicles. Recently, it began to phase out its civilian production in favor of fuses for military ordnance. With the support of the Italian peace movement, the factory council is now beginning to analyze other markets and propose new products that could be the basis for expanded civilian production. Similarly in the cities of Selenia, Rome, and Naples the previous 75/25 ratio of military to civilian production has been equalized and plants are now producing radio equipment for use in civilian airport facilities in Third World countries and other markets.

The union has been less successful, however, in negotiating such a balance at companies like Agusta—a producer of military helicopters. In advanced technology firms, the union has found it more difficult to find products that will sell in highly competitive markets. High technology producers, Battistelli says, present a real economic problem.

> If you're talking about converting military industry to alternative production, you're talking about highly skilled workers and very advanced technology. Italian arms exporters have made their money exporting to the Third World. But while Third World countries have purchased

advanced military technology, they don't purchase much advanced consumer technology. What this means, of course, is that you would then have to begin marketing products to European, American, and Japanese markets — all of which are highly competitive and hard to break into. You run right up against American protectionist legislation, for example, or other competitive factors. This is a real dilemma for the future.

Not only do conversion activists in the labor movement have to convince management of conversion's promise, they must also convince fellow workers. "In conversations with workers," Battistelli elaborates, "you find that they are often very sympathetic to the idea of working on something other than arms production. But, as one worker told me, 'I've been working in an aeronautics factory for twenty-five years. I'm used to a job that deals with very small materials with precision instruments. You can't ask me to move from this to producing pots and pans.' This is a very important point," Battistelli emphasizes. "You have to explain to workers that they can maintain their skills as well as their jobs and salaries. Some comrades on the left do not understand that conversion doesn't just mean giving workers any old job. It means respecting and maintaining their skills."

Others, Battistelli points out, do not understand the need to frame carefully their critique of the arms industry so they do not blame workers for war production but rather the owners who really profit from it. "Unfortunately, peace activists still haven't learned that you can't show up at the arms factory gate with signs accusing workers of sinful conduct because they continue to work in arms factories," says Battistelli.

To supplement this kind of shopfloor work that explains conversion in a compelling and convincing way, the FLM has also developed a national strategy to coordinate conversion activity and propose national actions. The FLM has held five regional conferences with its rank and file members, and a national conference this past spring. In an effort to establish international links, it has helped organize a variety of international conferences and sent representatives to a major meeting between English, Italian, and German workers who are all working on the Tornado jet fighter plane — a joint project between the three nations. There, shop stewards from the different countries discussed how they could deal with the eventual termination of this joint venture contract.

The FLM is also working with other Italian union confederations to put forth a cohesive analysis of the Italian arms industry. While many have attempted to provide such an analysis, they have been hampered by their inability to penetrate the national security restrictions that limit access to information. Thus, all three national Italian union confederations and a large Catholic cultural association, the ACLI, are trying to set up a research institute and want to force the government and military contractors to supply more information about their current production and future plans. Conversion campaigners are also considering legislative proposals that would limit arms exports, alter the current relationship between the government and military contractors, and force arms suppliers to devote a share of their profits to finance study groups that will develop alternative products.

As this survey of European conversion strategies and programs suggests, the European conversion movement defines its goals far more broadly than have most American conversion efforts. Although European activists work actively on conversion plans that specifically target arms factories and try to forge links with European peace movements, they make conversion appear to be much more than a solution to the political problems caused by the unemployment resulting from successful disarmament campaigns. Their emphasis on the issue of employment illustrates that conversion is a positive, innovative job-creation strategy that is a vital supplement to any proposals for an industrial policy designed to revive declining manufacturing industry.

This emphasis has profound implications for those working in the labor and peace movements and the movement for economic justice. Through conversion planning, organized labor can transform its image as a narrow, special interest job protector to that of job creator. Conversion enables unions to assume a new role as defenders of the rights of all citizens to decent, rewarding employment. By linking workers, community, environmental, and peace groups, conversion planning also allows unions to escape the rigid stereotypes (antienvironment, antidisarmament, and pro-economic growth regardless of the social cost) that are so often used to isolate labor from other progressive constituencies.

Through the creation of alternative products, European workers have also linked their employment concerns to those of environmental and community groups and to poor and minority citizens. This kind of cooperative, working relationship helps substantiate the promise that reduction in military spending will not hurt the economy but will, instead, generate employment. While many workers intellectually grasp the fact that less money spent on the military could mean more money for social services and other forms of socially useful production, they nonetheless do not favor such spending cuts because they have no assurance that they will get service sector or civilian production jobs when theirs in the military sector are eliminated. If, however, conversion planning moves directly into the factory and workers are able to participate in investment and production decisions that both serve the community and maintain employment, producers and consumers will be united rather than divided.

Working to put pressure on regional planning agencies to subsidize the conversion process, as the Germans have done, also represents an approach that can be effectively applied in other industrialized nations. In every country, regional industrial development agency staffers scurry about trying to secure either foreign or domestic investment. Ruthlessly competing with other countries' development agencies—or even with those in other regions of their own country—these agencies try to undercut each other by guaranteeing private companies tax breaks, financial aid packages, job training programs, and equity loans at excessively low interest rates. They also promise lower wages and more tractable work forces. To deliver on these commitments, many development agencies agree to corporate personnel testing programs that weed out previously unionized workers or identify workers who would be susceptible to unionization. Particularly in the United States, both workers and communities are blackmailed by economic decline into cooperating with such development strategies, even though they undermine rather than improve their chances of achieving a decent standard of living.

Union-backed English and German conversion efforts are thus useful models for an alternative development strategy that does not sacrifice worker and community needs to corporate priorities. Using the considerable financial leverage they possess, European conversion campaigners work with development agencies to insure a healthy work and community environment. Some critics might argue that these local and regional development agencies work only with small firms to create a handful of jobs. But when one compares their track record with those of most regional development agencies, to save anywhere from 400 to 5,000 jobs is no small accomplishment. In Germany, for example, the North Rhine Westphalia development agency is now busily trying to lure American high technology firms to an area in which 800,000 workers are unemployed. The agency promises all the usual financial bonuses and has spent hundreds of thousands of dollars on its campaign. In five years, it has secured only 3,000 new jobs. Since it launched its high technology campaign—which targets firms that employ between twenty and one hundred people and advises employers to buy a machine rather than hire a German worker whenever feasible—it has not managed to convince one high technology firm to relocate in Germany.

Such gains—realized at great expense to the taxpayer—seem paltry indeed when one considers the progress of the German conversion movement or that of the Sheffield Council or GLEB. Comparing such approaches with those of the conversion movement suggests, moreover, that a direct campaign to demand that a percentage of public industrial development funds be allocated to developing conversion projects may be a useful organizing strategy.

What is most impressive and valuable about European conversion activity is that it has demonstrated that useful, albeit limited, conversion programs can be constructed without national plans or legislation. Conversion activists have formed durable community/labor/and peace movement alliances and established informal national and international networks even where conservative governments have refused to consider national conversion legislation. All conversion campaigners, of course, fight for such legislation. Nevertheless, they recognize that the movement can set up programs that, as Mike Cooley and Phil Asquith so eloquently state, can give a sense of possibility and provide workable models until such time as national governments are changed or convinced of the necessity for legislative action.

Perhaps the final lesson derived from European conversion experiments is the importance of creating a coordinated international movement. Such coordination will, first of all, help stimulate activity in different countries. Just as the Lucas Plan served as an inspiration for workplace and community-based committees in the United States and other European countries, so information about conversion going on today is invaluable to those who want to begin conversion programs in their cities or factories.

Coordination is, furthermore, necessary if conversion activity in one country is not going to adversely affect workers in another. Because of the integration of much global arms production and the international economy, developments in one country naturally affect events in another. If Lucas Aerospace shop stewards had been successful in their attempt, for example, they would have saved several thousand jobs in an American firm producing components for products that were eventually curtailed when Lucas succeeded in its rationalization plans. If disarmament campaigns—even those closely tied in with elaborate conversion plans—stop military production in one country, they may have an impact on workers elsewhere. When appropriate then, conversion activists could create coordinated proposals that help workers—like those employed on the Tornado aircraft—initiate programs on the international level.

Despite the great potential for coordination and innovative action, and the significant number of recent successes in the conversion field, all activists involved acknowledge the tremendous problems that exist in overcoming management resistance and convincing workers that they must act to save their jobs themselves because neither government nor employers can be counted on to do it for them. With this in mind, however, conversion activity is both growing and strengthening. Thus, when Germany's AG Wesser began its first day of auctioning off equipment to manufacturers who had come from all over the world, the workers who had struggled so hard for conversion gathered at the factory gate to greet them. To commemorate their struggle, they placed a plaque inscribed with a motto that more and more European workers seem to have adopted: "Those who fight may lose, but those who don't fight have already lost."

9

Conversion in the Aerospace Industry: The McDonnell Douglas Project

Joel S. Yudken

INTRODUCTION

In fiscal year 1983, the McDonnell Douglas Corporation (MDC) was the nation's number two military contractor, with over $4 billion sales to the Pentagon, and forty-third in the *Fortune 500* list of largest corporations. The company is the product of a merger between the McDonnell Aircraft Company, a successful military aircraft manufacturer headquartered in St. Louis, Missouri, and the Long Beach-based Douglas Aircraft Company (DAC), which was bought out in 1967. At the time of the merger, the commercial aircraft market was expanding and had a projected annual growth rate of 15 percent. McDonnell believed that a merger with an established aircraft manufacturer like Douglas would give it privileged access to that market.

Once the world's premier civilian aircraft producer, Douglas's problems began when it lost its commanding lead in the jet airliner market, in the mid-1950s. Boeing introduced its 707 in 1957. By 1965 it had bypassed Douglas in its share of the market. In 1967, Douglas was in serious financial difficulty and needed a partner to keep it from bankruptcy. The deal with McDonnell Aircraft was attractive to Douglas because the ailing company thought it had found a savior.

Unfortunately, the expected turn-around for Douglas, after the merger, never materialized, and it became MDC's most unstable division. DAC failed to turn a profit in any year and suffered an accumulated loss of $450–500 million.

Managerial problems combined with other economic factors to erode Douglas's market viability. The original founder of McDonnell, and Chief Executive Officer of MDC, James McDonnell, assumed all final decisions regarding commercial aircraft, and MDC thus continued to operate

130

according to the rules of the defense market. Condescending to his airliner customers in sales negotiations, he refused to bargain over price and changes in specifications. His inflexibility lost MDC some customers to the L-1011 assuring Lockheed's entry into the commercial field. Two of Douglas's presidents resigned over conflicts with St. Louis.[1] Sanford N. ("Sandy") McDonnell, James's nephew and successor as chief executive officer since 1980, has made similar mistakes. By 1982, Douglas was considering phasing out its commercial line and closing its Long Beach plant.

The production work force, the bulk of which is represented by the United Auto Workers (UAW) Local 148, has been hit particularly hard by Douglas's market losses. Since the late 1960s, overall employment at the plant has fallen dramatically from its peak level of 33,000. The number of hourly workers covered by the UAW has dropped from over 12,000 in 1980 to below 5,000. This layoff was the largest single work-force cutback at a major manufacturing plant in Southern California during 1982.

The engineering, scientific, and technical work force, about half of which belongs to the Southern California Professional Engineering Association (SCPEA), has also been reduced from about 7,000 members to a little more than half that number, and estimates indicate that the plant is currently operating at only 15 to 20 percent of its capacity.

In the face of consistent corporate failure to maintain a reasonable level of production and employment at the plant, UAW Local 148 President Bob Berghoff began to look for new approaches for reemploying his workers. Although MDC would, at a later meeting, paint a rosy picture of the plant's future, Berghoff remains skeptical about their ability to fulfill these promises. To supplement their only active commercial transport aircraft program, the twin-engine 150–170 seat MD-80 (previously the DC-9 Super 80), management had plans for producing three new commercial jets: the twin-engine, narrow body, 100–125 seat MD-90; the three-engine, 270 seat long-range, wide-body MD-100 (to succeed the DC-10); and the D-3300, a proposed design in the 150 seat category.

In addition to its existing military aircraft production (the KC-10 military tanker and some other smaller contracts), the company said it hoped eventually to capture a major Pentagon contract for the C-17 supertransport aircraft. Earlier in 1983, the new Douglas President James Worsham, announced his goals for increasing military sales at Douglas from 29 percent to over 40 percent of its overall sales.

But, despite some airline interest, there have been no firm orders for the proposed new commercial aircraft, and Lockheed recently beat out MDC in the military supertransport category by winning a new order for its C5 planes. Yet the company had tried to argue that by the late 1980s or early 1990s this situation would be turned around, and within a decade employment at the plant could rise as high as 25,000 workers. Berghoff has countered with the obvious point that this does little for the thousands of currently unemployed Douglas workers.

Over a period of several months in 1982, representatives of the Los Angeles Coalition Against Plant Shutdowns (LACAPS), a coalition of labor, religious leaders, and community activists, had been meeting with Berghoff about the deteriorating situation at the plant. Introducing the idea of conversion planning, they familiarized him with the Lucas Aerospace workers' attempts to resist layoffs by developing alternative product plans. Through LACAPS Berghoff made contact with Catherine Squire, an economic adjustment specialist with the California Department of Economic and Business Development (DEBD).

Squire helped Berghoff contact the Mid-Peninsula Conversion Project (MPCP), a Santa Clara County, California-based group with nine years' experience in the alternate use planning and conversion process. In conjunction with the State, MPCP and the UAW would explore the possibilities of developing alternative product ideas for creating new jobs at the plant.

THE MCDONNELL DOUGLAS PROJECT

MPCP and Squire began to meet with the UAW in its offices in Lakewood, California, adjacent to the sprawling Douglas facilities, and the airport in Long Beach. It was clear from the beginning that during the first stages of the project MPCP would be working mostly with the UAW leadership at the plant. Later, it would bring in other unions, such as the engineers' unions that also has a large membership at the plant.

The UAW stated that its goals were to reemploy workers and rebuild its own base within the plant. It agreed to work with MPCP and the state DEBD and other parties to identify a set of alternative—or additional—products[2] that the company can produce to utilize excess capacity and create new jobs for the laid-off workers. In addition, it expressed an openness to work cooperatively with other unions, and even with management. It stated its willingness to consider more flexible wage structures and job classifications, if necessary, to create new jobs.

To initiate this process, the group (with a representative from the engineers' union who attended, unofficially, as an observer) began selecting a range of products ideas for additional products proposals.[3] First establishing a set of criteria for selecting potential new products, the group decided on the following: marketability, engineering and manufacturing viability, job transferability, profitability, social utility, quality of work, environmental impact, and local sourcing.

The group then identified and recommended products that are of social use in the civilian sector, are commercially viable (i.e., marketable, and profitable to produce), and would best match the capacity and skills at the plant and maximize employment. For ideas, it drew upon the Lucas Plan, other studies and efforts,[4] and the expertise and experience of its members. An initial list of ideas included transportation equipment, alternative energy technologies, medical technologies, capital equipment (e.g., machine tools), environmental protection equipment, and oceanic equipment.

The final list was narrowed down to light rail and rapid transit equipment, commuter aircraft, cogeneration equipment (specifically, heater-chillers), and power wheelchairs. This initial set of pilot product feasibility studies—to be carried out with the help of student interns and technical consultants—would be used to "seed" a longer term planning process of product idea generation, evaluation, selection and implementation.

Later, a small ad hoc committee of people, comprised of MPCP and DEBD staff members and experts in the areas of finance and corporate strategic planning, suggested that a number of considerations might determine the project's success or failure. For example, MDC is already having difficulty competing in one civilian market—that is, commercial jet transport. Its ability to successfully design, manufacture, and market in a new, untried commercial product area is questionable.

Although its Douglas division was once a successful independent civilian aircraft manufacturer, MDC is primarily a military firm, and military firms have been notoriously unsuccessful when attempting to diversify into civilian lines through new start-up operations.[5] Their managements, engineering work forces, and marketing operations have generally had little or no experience operating in the civilian sector, which is a completely different environment than the military market. Consequently, their failures, such as Boeing-Vertol with rail passenger cars, Grumman with buses, and both Lockheed and MDC with commercial aircraft.

In addition, even under the best of circumstances, high development costs and marketing risks are substantial barriers confronting any new product development attempt in the competitive civilian marketplace. Because of this, the original conception of a product idea in which the company would conduct all the basic engineering design, development, manufacturing, and marketing did not seem viable in all cases. Although Douglas has the capability to do both fabrication and assembly operations, its main abilities are in high-skilled assembly.

The skills and experience of the bulk of the work force represented by the UAW could easily be applied not only to a complete start-up activity for a new product idea, from design through marketing. They could also be employed in the subcontracting of manufacturing capability to another firm that has already designed and developed a new product and would carry the burden for marketing it.

In an investigation of potential markets for light rail and other mass transit rail vehicles, Jim Seal, a transportation expert and consultant with the project, learned that Sumitomo, a large Japanese bank, in conjunction with Nissan, one of Japan's largest manufacturing firms, won a contract to produce forty-two rail passenger cars from the California Department of Transportation (CALTRANS) to be used on the San Jose to San Francisco commuter run in Northern California. Because of the Surface Transportation Act of 1978,[6] they needed to find an American manufacturer to do final assembly for the vehicles. The preliminary study of Douglas's capacity showed that its facilities were near ideal for what Sumitomo/Nissan needed. Contingent of course on serious interest from MDC management, Sumitomo was approached with the idea of considering Long Beach for its assembly site. Initially enthusiastic, Sumitomo explained that they needed to make a decision about their site selection by the end of September.

The project then decided to approach the company about the potential rail car deal. Through a vice-president at the plant, the UAW made contact with the company and learned that there was, in fact, significant interest in the rail car idea, at least among some Douglas managers. They gave the project the OK to further explore and develop the Sumitomo deal.

Although, shortly after, a Northern California site was selected by Sumitomo,[7] it informed the project that they were going to bid on another mass transit contract for the Los Angeles area. This would be an even larger order than the original, involving producing forty light rail and 130 rapid transit cars for the Los Angeles County Transportation Commission (LACTC). The light rail vehicles would be used on a Los Angeles to Long Beach commuter line. They felt that McDonnell Douglas would be an excellent site for setting up assembly operations.

Douglas managers, moreover, were eager to reintroduce the rail car idea as potentially viable new business for the ailing plant. This was all the more attractive because the company would not have to bear the costs of design and development, nor the risks of marketing.

Internal differences between Douglas and corporate headquarters in St. Louis, in fact, may account for some of the receptivity of the Douglas managers to the proposal. Earlier attempts to interest the company in rapid transit vehicles by some of the managers we met with, in fact, had been rejected by St. Louis.[8] Commuter aircraft, another product idea the project is investigating, was also studied by the company in the seventies but rejected as a new product line.[9]

In the fall, however, contract negotiations between the UAW and

MDC broke down, resulting in a major strike that has lasted over three months. On 17 October 1983 nearly 7,000 workers, represented by four UAW locals, struck McDonnell Douglas at facilities in three states: Long Beach, California; Tulsa, Oklahoma; and Melbourne, Arkansas. Of these, 4,900 are members of UAW Local 148 in Long Beach. They are striking against what they feel are drastic concessions affecting wage increases, wage rates of new hired workers, the annual cost-of-living adjustment (COLA) rate, and other benefits.[10]

The wage concessions demanded by MDC follows a pattern that has been occurring in other industries in the past few years, such as in auto manufacturing. Until recently, the defense-dollar rich aerospace industry has seemed relatively immune to the concessionary wave. This year, the Pentagon has been putting pressure on its major contractors to take a harder line in bargaining to keep labor costs down.[11]

It is difficult to predict the impacts the strike situation will have on MDC's receptivity to our additional product proposals. Management attitudes appear mixed regarding the UAW. Corporate officers in St. Louis have claimed that union intransigence in the strike helped catalyze their decision to cancel the new commercial aircraft programs. In private conversation, Douglas representatives showed concern about whether the UAW's position in the strike would affect the rapid transit project. On the other hand, they continue to show willingness to participate in a labor-management committee that would oversee the development of the additional product proposal.

Nevertheless, with the support of the UAW leadership at Long Beach, MPCP set up the first face-to-face meeting with management. The outcome of this meeting was an agreement by management to participate in a cooperative process with the union and the MD Project, to pursue the rail-car production possibilities. It also showed an openness to look at other product ideas, as well, down the line. A labor-management committee is now being established.

The labor-management committee (LMC) is the principal mechanism for presenting the proposal to management. Composed of representatives from management, the unions, union consultants, and Catherine Squire (representing the state, as the impartial third party), it will oversee all aspects of information gathering, research, and predevelopment work, up through the final bidding process.

The labor-management committee is a special form of worker participation in corporate decisionmaking. Although management has exhibited suspicion, resistance, and sometimes hostility towards the concept, LMCs are particularly controversial among representatives of labor. Because LMCs operate separately from the collective bargaining process, it is difficult to enforce any decision reached by a labor-management committee. In today's political and economic environment, where trade unions are relatively weak, the LMC may be seen as the only context in which crucial issues can be discussed.

The Douglas LMC joins the company's interest in a new profitable product option with the union's desire to create new jobs. The LMC will oversee the development of all new product ideas. Items such as job classifications and initial wage rates will be discussed by the LMC. The company needs the union's cooperation concerning wage and job classifications if it wishes to present a reasonably low cost proposal for the rail vehicle assembly, for example. These agreements will undoubtedly be finalized through collective bargaining.

The McDonnell Douglas Project is now only in its earliest stages. It offers both promises and problems that should be explored. Although it began looking at additional products for the primarily civilian division of an otherwise overwhelmingly militarized corporation, its efforts may have the effect of slowing the process of a reverse conversion.

Due to its lack of success in commercial business, Douglas is being driven into greater military dependency. The company, particularly with the help of the engineers' union, has been lobbying heavily for the C-17 and other military contracts. At a recent meeting with Long Beach city officials, the prospects of new military business being brought into the ailing plant was looked upon very favorably. If it can show the viability of producing alternative products at the plant, the project may be an important step in lessening the city's and work force's current and future dependency on military production. This might eventually help them move away from political positions that support new military programs on the basis of job creation.

UNRESOLVED ISSUES AND THE CONVERSION POTENTIAL

Worker Participation

The first question concerns the extent of shop-floor worker participation in the project. A principal goal of the project is to establish a precedent of union involvement in plant level product and production planning, backed by collective bargaining, and supported by an informed and active rank and file. Unfortunately, over the last year, a combination of internal union elections, contract negotiations, and the prolonged strike has inhibited union educational and outreach activity to its members.

Up through now, only top leadership of the local has been actively involved in the project. Moreover, although the labor-management committee, once it is established, will give the union some real say in seeing its additional products proposal implemented, direct work-force involvement will be limited. On the other hand, especially in light of the strike, the union leaders will need to have the firm backing of its membership in order to maintain parity with management in the LMC process.

The willingness of management to work jointly on the project with labor derives after all from the collective bargaining power of the union. A strong union with broad rank-and-file support for the project is obviously essential for securing the integrity of the work force's position within the collaborative relationship being set up between the company and the union.

Once the strike is settled (which is imminent) the project plans to begin a serious campaign to educate and engage wide support from Douglas's work force. For example, it hopes to involve the workers more directly in identifying new product ideas they would like to see produced at the plant (such as through surveys via the union newsletter). Whether or not the local leaders are capable of generating the level of support and participation from their membership that they want and need to back the union's position in the LMC remains to be seen.

The Engineers' Role

Another important issue is the involvement of other key unions in the project—particularly SCPEA, which represents the engineers at Douglas. The engineers occupy a pivotal position in the company between management and the production work force. By definition, they must also be part of any new product development at the plant.

From the beginning, the project has sought to include SCPEA in its activities, both for its technical expertise and for political support. On the surface, the Douglas engineers have a lot to gain from the project. They, too, have suffered significant job loss. The recent cutback of 1,000 jobs—mostly engineers and managers because of MDC's decision not to product the MD-100 and MD-90 commercial aircraft—should, theoretically at least, make the engineers even more receptive.

So far the extent of SCPEA's support has been minimal. Initially, they were somewhat hesitant to be involved and even hostile towards the project. They misperceived the intent of the project as replacing existing defense work, thereby endangering their jobs. However, after a meeting with UAW president Berghoff and MPCP's Yudken, they have become much more supportive, and some members were even enthusiastic. As a significant byproduct, the project has served to bring SCPEA and the UAW into closer communication, especially regarding common contract negotiation concerns.

After the strike, SCPEA (along with perhaps some of the other unions, who represent relatively small units of workers at the plant) will be approached again to enlist their support for the project, and participation in the LMC process. Their involvement is considered very desirable, if not crucial, to the project's long-term success.

Support in the Community

A third question is what the role of the community (i.e., community-based organizations and civic groups, such as the Chamber of Commerce, Los Angeles Coalition Against Plant Shutdowns, Long Beach Labor Coalition, and so forth) should be. Up until now, community organizations have provided only endorsements and other similar forms of support for the project. In the future though, their involvement could grow in importance.

The community as a whole, of course, has a stake in new job-creating production at the plant. This means new business in the community as well. In addition, some of the products made at Douglas may even directly benefit the community, such as light rail vehicles for uses between Long Beach and Los Angeles.

The precise role of the community in the coming months will depend on how well the cooperative relationship between management and labor proceeds and what new product directions the LMC will undertake to explore. For example, a stronger community voice in the project would help encourage the company to take the joint labor-management product planning process more seriously than it might otherwise and, subsequently, be more willing to implement the recommendations of the LMC.

Community-based support could also be of great value in making some products more viable. For example, in the case of the light rail proposal, community pressure could help Douglas secure a subcontract for final assembly from the firm that wins the LACTC bid. The project intends, therefore, to broaden the involvement of community-based groups and organizations as the need arises.

The Role of the Public Sector

A fourth issue concerns the relationship of the public sector (state and local governments) to the project. The State of California administration, for example, has a stake in the project's being successful because it will create new jobs and business in an economically distressed area. The California DEBD, in the person of Catherine Squire, has been a critical actor in the project from its beginning: in its initial planning and development stages, locating and providing research interns, providing staff with technical and administrative support, and offering channels for some funding in the future. It has also helped legitimize the project, especially in our dealings with MDC management. In addition, Squire, representing the state, will act as a neutral third party intermediary in the labor-management committee.

Local communities and their governments, such as Long Beach and neighboring Lakewood, which have suffered the greatest impact on jobs and local businesses, also have a stake in the outcome of the project. McDonnell Douglas is the largest employer in Long Beach, a coastal city of over 300,000 people. As one city official has stated: "McDonnell Douglas is our benefactor."

Political support from these communities could be decisive in influencing the process by which MDC-Long Beach is chosen as a site for rail passenger car final assembly; just as pressure from northern California cities forced Sumitomo, in the CALTRANS case, to select a final assembly subcontractor in that area. City officials have already indicated a willingness to provide this kind of support.

So far, the public sector—particularly the state—has played a constructive new role as third party intermediary and a source of technical and financial resource expertise and political support in the new product development and production planning activity. The project will attempt to maintain, better define, and strengthen this relationship.

A CONVERSION MODEL?

Perhaps the most essential questions that remain unanswered concern the extent that the project will become a real model of conversion. Or will it simply be an example—albeit a productive and important one—of a union-initiated corporate diversification program?

In the first place, a number of substantial technical obstacles confront the project in achieving its conversion goals. Even under the best circumstances (i.e., with full corporate management support) major changes in engineering, management, and marketing organizations and operations might be required, in some instances, to make a transition to new product lines economically viable and profitable in national and international markets.

Such alterations, which challenge management prerogatives and power, may not be very palatable to MDC without significant offsetting advantages (such as large profitmaking potential). Management has already exhibited a reluctance to engage in expensive product design and development activity for new product ideas. Second, Douglas's marketing experience is limited to a narrow product line and overshadowed by the military orientation of its parent corporation.

Third, MDC still harbors hopes of salvaging Douglas through large new military contracts. If MDC management perceives that new product lines would compete with potential new military work for available capacity and skills, MDC is likely to balk at going along with the project.[12] Thus, only short-term production alternatives or new product lines that do not threaten the company's ability to win military contracts might find support from Douglas's management. On the other hand, if a new product idea looks profitable, management may find it difficult to reject, especially considering the substantial uncertainty surrounding the likelihood of even long-term new military contracts. In any case, only concerted pressure from the labor force, community, and government might be able to overcome management resistance, when it occurs, to convert its facilities to new forms of production. A key question, is whether the union will be able, through the LMC or some other means, to secure a lasting and effective role in determining production decisions that lead to the implementation of the project's product ideas.

One of the main sources of power and influence in this kind of situation is accessibility of information. Traditionally, management maintains an advantage in its direct access to information about its own internal workings (i.e., its financial, engineering, and marketing operations) that is rarely available to labor. It is also better equipped to do longer term financial, engineering, and marketing analyses, including that of potential new product ideas.

Some of the union's disadvantage concerning access to information and technical skill is reduced by the outside expertise provided by the MD Project and perhaps by involvement of SCPEA personnel if they participate in the LMC. In fact, in the current situation, the information imbalance between company and union is somewhat, if perhaps temporarily, reversed. The union consultants brought in by the MD Project have uncovered most of the crucial marketing and technical information for carrying out the rail passenger car deal now under consideration by the project and the evolving LMC. The union's ability to retain its information edge, however, remains to be seen.

It is likely that some degree of information parity will be able to be maintained. Nevertheless, discussions with management have suggested that there may be an unwillingness to let even an LMC have access to what management considers proprietary information, regardless if it is needed for evaluating new product ideas, if it might weaken Douglas's position relative to the union or to a competing company.

Equally important to the control of information issue is the relative strength of the union(s) in the LMC process. Aside from its own base of information and expertise, the union has two sources of influence. First, in order for the company to compete in almost any new product area, even if it is just subcontracting manufacturing capacity and skills (as in the proposed rail car idea) it will need substantial cooperation from the union concerning wage rates and job classifications.

Secondly, the bargaining power of the union is ultimately contingent on the extent of rank and file support for its position. As already noted, the union leadership's ability to muster this support, along with forging strong alliances with sympathetic community-based groups and government leaders, especially after a long, drawn-out, costly strike, is one of the crucial questions facing the project.

The outcome of this sometimes dramatic effort is uncertain. There is good reason to be optimistic that some form of new production may be attempted, if not successful, at the Douglas plant as a result of the project's activities. It must be remembered that any form of new business at the beleagured Long Beach plant that creates new jobs (and profits) will be welcomed by all parties concerned—management, labor, community, and government.

Aside from the problems discussed above, the MD Project exemplifies an even more fundamental dilemma: the basic limitation of any isolated conversion attempt, without major shifts in national industrial policies, coupled with serious reductions in military arms programs. New product ideas lack viability without growth in effective markets in many areas of social need (such as mass transit, alternative energy, health care equipment) this, in turn, requires new national investment policies. Military markets still look like the most attractive growth alternative, especially to suffering aircraft firms like Douglas, when compared to the uncertainties in the markets for nonmilitary, undersubsidized product areas.

Yet, it is clear that in the face of all these issues, the MD Project has still made a very promising beginning. It provides a real-world laboratory for examining the limits, conditions, and potentials of conversion planning. More significantly, it is establishing some of the basic elements of a viable model for change in the aerospace industry and a model for American conversion projects.

NOTES

1. Harlan S. Byrne, "New Chairman Passes Early Tests With Ease at McDonnell Douglas", *Wall Street Journal*, 25 August 1980. Douglas's commercial plan operations have been a constant corporate headache ever since McDonnell and Douglas

merged sixteen years ago. McDonnell executives considered Douglas overstaffed and loosely run. "St. Louis people, particularly those further down the management ladder, tended to regard the Douglas people as California playboys," says John Brizendine, who for many years headed the Douglas division. "It probably takes a generation to work out all the problems of two such differently run companies."

2. The terms "alternative," "new," and "additional" products are used interchangeably in this article. Nomenclature became an important issue for the UAW and SCPEA unions early on, illustrating some of the complicated political undercurrents in the project. The terms "conversion," "alternative," and even "new" were seen as potentially threatening by union leaders, because of their political connotations (conversion is associated with the peace movement and loss of defense contracts) or because they suggest challenges to management prerogatives ("alternative" or "new" connote supplanting rather than supplementing existing product lines). "Additional products" was chosen as the most acceptable terminology when we deal with the unions and management.

3. Aside from the UAW, State and MPCP representatives, and the engineers, selected outside technical experts also participated. These include Professor Lloyd J. Dumas, University of Texas, Dallas, and Sheldon Plotkin, Ph.D., and Dr. Jack Jennings, two engineers with extensive aerospace experience and members of the Southern California Federation of Scientists.

4. For example, see UAW researcher Dan Luria and economic consultant Jack Russell's *Rational Reindustrializationon: An Economic Development Agenda for Detroit,* which assesses the feasibility of energy products (e.g., deep natural gas and heavy oil production equipment, cogeneration units, mine-mouth coal gasification) as alternative products for Detroit's ailing auto industry. The International Association of Machinists (IAM) have also explored alternative product ideas in some of their programs.

5. In most cases, diversification has occurred through acquisitions rather than by investing in retooling existing facilities or start-ups of new production divisions in a new product area. For example, MDC diversified into commercial aircraft through its absorption of Douglas. Although, in a rare case of successful in-house development of new business, MDC's automation and computer services division has expanded and diversified through acquisition of other firms.

6. This bill legislates that whenever urban rail vehicles destined for U.S. markets and procured with Urban Mass Transit Administration (UMTA) funds (over 90% of them) are manufactured on foreign soil, final assembly is distinct from primary manufacture and must be performed in the United States by a domestic labor force. Final assembly of rail passenger vehicles entails gathering components and systems, stationing them at worksites, attaching them to vehicle shells, testing equipment, and preparing completed vehicles for transport to purchasers or performance test sites. Taken from the pilot product feasibility study of light-rail vehicles, prepared for the McDonnell Douglas Project by Dwight Johnson, under the guidance of Jim Seal.

7. Despite their interest in the Southern California location, Sumitomo had been submitted to intense political pressure by several Northern California communities vieing for the new production and jobs.

8. Some of the management people we are dealing with, in fact, had been proponents for producing mass transit vehicles at Douglas several years earlier. James McDonnell had killed that idea arguing that their business was aircraft, not rail cars, and it should stay that way.

9. Donald E. Fink, "Market Needs in 1980–94 Defined", *Aviation Week & Space Technology,* 31 March 1975. The article describes a year-long MDC study of the market

potential for 30–70 passenger commuter aircraft. It also completed a preliminary design of a small twin-turbofan aircraft of this size. The $300,000 study was done under a National Aeronautics and Space Administration (NASA) contract.

10. MDC points to Douglas's poor performance as one factor in its concession demand to the union. The union counters by noting MDC's overall strong financial condition. MDC had reported earnings of $121.4 million on sales of just over $4 billion during the first six months of this year. This is considerably higher than the previous year's first-half performance, which was $98.3 million on sales of $3.5 billion – "Aerospace Union Officers Continue Labor Negotiations," *San Jose Mercury-News*, 17 October 1983.

11. The Machinists union at Boeing in Seattle made the first major concessionary agreement just prior to the UAW walkout – Jane Slaughter, "Aerospace: Boeing Wins Concessions While UAW Strikes McDonnell Douglas," *Labor Notes*, 26 October 1983. According to one newspaper account the outcome of the MDC-UAW debacle is considered vital by both sides, because it would set the tone for other settlements that could affect 55,000 aerospace workers nationwide – *San Jose Mercury-News*, 17 October 1983.

12. According to a reliable internal source, Douglas purposely has been keeping some of its capacity idle to enhance its chances of winning the C-17 military cargo aircraft contract from the Pentagon.

PART IV

How To Make It Happen

10

Undoing the Iron Triangle: Conversion and the "Black Box" of Politics

Gordon Adams

The Defense Department plans to spend more money in fiscal year 1985, in constant dollars, than in any year since the end of World War II. The rapid increase in American military spending since 1981 has given rise to growing criticism of the role of military spending in American foreign policy and the American economy. Three-fourths of the American people support the call for a bilateral nuclear weapons freeze, once an issue with appeal only to a small peace movement. Specific weapons such as the MX missile and the B-1 bomber, which are central elements in the next generation of strategic nuclear weapons, are the targets of criticism and debate. American deployment of new intermediate-range nuclear missiles in Europe has caused deep and enduring fissures in the Atlantic Alliance.

There is also growing evidence that the Defense Department spends money in wasteful and inefficient ways. The M-1 tank, investigations show, has frequent breakdowns; the Bradley infantry fighting vehicle is too small and highly vulnerable; the Air Force has bought Allen wrenches for $9,600.[1] The dramatic growth in spending for new weapons, moreover, is putting pressure on the entire defense budget. Rapid purchases of weapons could actually reduce military readiness, since the cost of the weapons is forcing the Defense Department to slow down spending for operations, maintenance, and personnel.[2]

The criticism of runaway defense spending comes from all corners. Conservatives (Heritage Foundation), Defense Department officials (Franklin C. Spinney), and liberals (Brookings Institution) all warn that the spending process is out of control with a fearsome bill coming due.[3] Congress, gradually realizing that these problems are real, has begun to tackle—and slow—the growth of the defense budget.

The economic consequences of such spending remain real, however, and the spending process is difficult to reverse, so entrenched has

147

the military economy become in America. Defense budgets are having a direct impact on soaring federal budget deficits, high interest rates, and low supplies of investment capital, impeding future investment and the opportunity to create new jobs for working Americans.[4]

Ironically, in a country that fears the concept of economic planning, the Defense Department carries out the only seriously planned economic and industrial policy in existence. The Defense Department owns billions of dollars' worth of industrial plants and equipment that are provided, in most cases, rent free for the use of defense contractors. On Long Ísland, for example, over 40 percent of the floor space used by the Grumman Corporation is owned by the Department of the Navy.[5] In addition, the Defense Department has undertaken a $500 million program to introduce new manufacturing technologies—computer-aided design and manufacturing and industrial robots—into defense factories.[6] In late 1983, the Department announced another $1 billion program to design and build a high-volume, sophisticated computer circuit. According to Robert E. Kahn, director of the Information Processing Techniques Office at the Defense Advanced Research Projects Agency, the Defense Department's goal is to "use this program as a mechanism for building a technology base within industry." In addition to these investments, the Defense Department employs or provides contract dollars for private firms to employ nearly six million American workers. In government, the Defense Department sets wages for its workers. In the defense industry, the Defense Department determines, through its contracts, the level of wages it will support and the degree to which it will encourage or discourage corporate resistance to union wage demands—in effect, a more planned and coherent labor policy than the Department of Labor itself.[7] The defense economy, linking government, and industry and labor, remains one of the most entrenched and coherent pieces of the entire national economy.

Americans have never before been so deeply involved in the politics of national security policymaking, with the possible exception of the Vietnam War debate. National security and defense spending issues were once left to the experts. Today, religious denominations, schools, civic groups, professional societies, and many others are engaged in this debate. The continued growth of defense spending, persistent waste in that spending, Congress's difficulty in reducing defense budgets or halting weapons systems, and the enduring presence of defense money in the American economy all suggest that the rising volume of criticism has still not penetrated the American political system in such a way as to have a real impact on public policy, forcing budget reductions and weapons cuts.

The MX missile is a prime example. When the rationale for this cumbersome, expensive system lost credibility in 1982, the President appointed a commission to examine strategic nuclear weapons policy—the so-called "Scowcroft Commission." Although the commission acknowledged that the MX missile had little justification, it recommended proceeding with production and deployment of the MX and called, at the same time, for the production and deployment of another missile, dubbed "Midgetman," that would replace the MX and make its construction unnecessary.[8] Liberal members of Congress known as critics of the administration's strategic policies, such as Rep. Les Aspin (D–WI) and Albert Gore, Jr. (D–TN), urged the Congress to accept the commission's policy. For example, the call for a bilateral nuclear weapons freeze, passed by the House of Representatives after exhaustive debate in the spring of 1983, was followed by a crucial vote on the MX missile, which a freeze would halt. Of the members of the House who endorsed a freeze, ninety-seven also voted for the MX program.

To cite another example, although Congress did reduce the President's defense budget request in 1983, cutting the rate of real growth in defense budget authority from 10 percent to 5 percent, this action proved to be largely a paper exercise. Although the level of budget authority (the right to begin spending money) for 1984 was reduced by over $15 billion from the administration's request, actual outlays (the money to be spent in 1984) were expected to be only $5 billion less than what the administration had sought.

The politics of defense spending and national security are clearly difficult and frustrating. Critics of major weapons decisions, of levels of defense spending, of nuclear and nonnuclear military policy choices seem to go unheard. Behind a veil of national security, bureaucratic and industry participants in the process exercise significant power. The pressure to maintain high levels of military spending is reinforced by the perception that economic well-being and jobs are dependent on that spending.

Advocates of arms control and spending reductions have begun to focus on these political and economic realities frustrating their efforts. Economic adjustment planning, or conversion, is seen as a key policy to deal with the dilemma. Smoothing the transition from a defense-dependent to a more healthy economy, critics reason, will help make it easier to break up the coalition that provides political support for persistently high defense spending.

Despite the logical appeal of this approach, however, conversion planning bills have languished in the Congress, virtually untouched, for decades. Conversion planning alone is a technical solution to making the transition from an economy dependent on high rates of military spending to one with lower defense budgets. It is not, however, a political approach to this problem of transition. The politics of defense spending have been treated as a "black box" — something poorly understood and not challenged directly. Yet conversion, like successful arms control and real reductions in defense spending, ultimately depends on understanding and changing the politics of defense spending in America.

This political process takes place behind a rhetoric of national security and involves real, intimate, and constant interaction, over time, between bureaucrats in the Defense Department anxious to continue their authority and business firms anxious to continue their contracting activity. Congress plays a crucial role in mediating between the other two players. National security policy is made inside this "iron triangle"; opening the triangle and introducing new alternative policies is crucial to the success of such efforts as conversion.

THE VEIL OF NATIONAL SECURITY

The first obstacle to a truly successful alternative policy is the rhetoric of national security. Defense spending is traditionally justified by this rhetoric. Myths or assumptions about national security are important elements in isolating the reality of defense politics from public and Congressional efforts to hold defense decisions up to greater public scrutiny and accountability.

These myths begin with the simple assertion that the defense budget is the logical result of a process in which threats to the United States are assessed, the forces needed to meet these threats are defined, their missions clearly stated, and weapons the troops require are designed. Theoretically, national security needs, then, define the size and contents of the defense budget.[9]

For most Americans, national security is the most common and comfortable arena of debate about defense. Yet, cloaked in secrecy, "national security" arguments legitimate existing policymakers and their plans, since they have exclusive access to the "secrets." Critics in Congress and the public lack the requisite expertise and credibility, and cannot be seen as major actors in the policy process.

The arms control and freeze debates have helped change this myth by bringing the public into this hitherto closed arena. Critics of the current policy argued, with growing credibility and legitimacy, that the "threats" to the United States have been exaggerated and that the Reagan defense buildup was based on a series of myths: the myth that the Soviet Union outspent the United States on defense in the 1970s; that U.S. forces are, as a result, "vulnerable"; and that the Warsaw Pact dramatically dominates the forces of NATO.[10]

Moreover, it is less and less clear to the public that the expansion of spending for new weapons actually provides military security. New intermediate and strategic nuclear weapons appear to be fueling the arms race, leading to expanded Soviet nuclear spending. Expanding military intervention capabilities have led to the use of troops in the Caribbean, Central America, and the Middle East. Funds for new weapons seem to be reducing the Defense Department's ability to maintain the military readiness of the forces already in existence.

THE DEFENSE BUREAUCRACY

Behind the national security rationale lies a second obstacle to change: the bureaucratic policymaking processes of the Defense Department. Defense budgets, spending decisions, runaway costs, and politically entrenched weapons systems are all linked, in part, to the way the Pentagon does its business. These bureaucratic phenomena include the tendency of Pentagon officials to defend and promote their interests, the fascination inside the military services with the next generation of military technology, the rivalry among services that leads to wasteful duplication and higher budgets, and the contracting process that builds in high rates of spending on weapons.[11]

The Army, Navy, and Air Force, for example, compete for defense budget funds and often seek duplicate weapons systems. The Air Force buys an F-15 and F-16 fighter while the Navy buys an entirely separate pair, the F-14 and F-18. Common programs, such as the effort to make the F-111 a joint program, are usually abortive.

Inside each military service, moreover, officials become attached to a weapon system, in part because the next weapon will ensure that the service continues to have a specific military mission in the future. Although the B-52 bomber could survive until the year 2000 as a carrier for the new cruise missiles, for example, the Strategic Air Command (SAC) insists on having a new bomber—the B-1. Without the B-1, SAC's only significant mission after 2000 would be to manage land-based strategic missiles.[12]

The way the defense bureaucracy negotiates and administers its contracts has a direct impact on costs, on the defense budget, and on the close ties between the Defense Department and weapons manufacturers. David Stockman, Director of the Office of Management and Budget, has described the Department of Defense as a "swamp of waste" containing some $10–$30 billion in excessive spending that could be eliminated with no risks for American national security.[13] In 1983, the President's Grace Commission, appointed to explore waste in federal spending, also pointed to roughly $30 billion a year in unnecessary Pentagon spending.[14]

Bureaucratic in-fighting, self-protection, and inefficiency keep defense spending levels high, have a direct effect on procurement choices, and make doing defense business attractive to private sector companies.[15] The federal government's largest "buying" bureaucracy is committed, moreover, to defending itself from outside criticism and penetration.[16]

THE POLITICS OF DEFENSE

Once national security and bureaucratic barriers are crossed, however, the major obstacle to conversion planning remains: the political "black box." The activities that keep defense spending high, that protect new weapons, and that inhibit policy alternatives are all played out in a highly political arena.

The black box of politics is built on a deep-rooted and historical intimacy linking the Defense Department and its corporate suppliers of weapons and services. Intimacy between government and business, of course, is anathema to the traditional American political ideology, which suggests that business and government are antagonistic.[17] In reality, a cooperative set of relations has developed between business and government in the twentieth century, especially where defense spending is involved. This relationship began during World War I, when business executives planned virtually all sectors of U.S. industrial production for the war and a new military industry began to grow in America.[18] The relationship developed into a permanent one during and after World War II. The Defense Department, which subsidized construction of a vast military production base during the war, continued a clear policy of maintaining that base in the private sector.[19]

The U.S. commitment to a global foreign policy provided a justification and focus for continuous defense planning, a large military force, and massive arms procurement. The American economy seemed capable of containing the expense, absorbing guns and butter in a constant expansion of both. Service bureaucracies and private sector officials interacted regularly, as the defense industry self-consciously developed a capacity to penetrate and influence the policy process.

This constant interaction has expanded and deepened since the 1950s. It satisfies both participants: Defense Department officials, defending their missions, find useful allies among contractors committed to remaining in defense business. Both sides require the active participation of a third major actor—the Congress. Through Congress, the Defense Department acquires the funding that enables the relationship to continue; therefore, the Congress must be brought into the relationship as an active participant. The resulting political configuration is a familiar one:

a close intimacy among the Pentagon, its defense industry client, and members of Congress with a special interest in the defense section of the federal budget (the Armed Services Committees, the Defense Appropriations Subcommittees, and members from districts and states that have military bases or defense contractors within their boundaries).

This relationship can be described as an "iron triangle," linking the major interested parties and isolating them from other areas of government policymaking.[20] It has several key features.

First, there is a *close working relationship* among the three key participants. Second, there is an *intimate interpenetration* between the corners of the triangle. Policymakers and administrators move freely between industry and government. Policy issues tend to be discussed and resolved among the participants, who develop and share common values, interests, and perceptions.[21] As the industry and government officials interact, they share policymaking authority; often private sector participants become policymakers and administrators without ever entering public service. Defense Department power and private industry power become indistinguishable.[22]

Third, the triangle has *emerged slowly* over time. It was not willfully created in a single moment but came into being as a result of constant interaction among its participants. Defense Department bureaucrats help nurture and maintain the industry. Industry has pursued policies and procedures it desires from the Defense Department and works to maintain the triangle as circumstances change. Both work hard to build and maintain support in Congress. Shared interests develop between bureaucrats and industry, and disagreements must be reconciled over time through constant interaction.

Fourth, the triangle has become "iron." Through the years, it has become isolated from other areas of policy, from many in the Congress and especially from the public. Strenuous efforts have been exerted by the participants to keep it isolated and protected.[23] As a result of this isolation, outsiders and their perspectives on policy alternatives are shut out and have no credibility inside the triangle. Defense Department officials and industry planners share the assumption that they act not only in their own interests but in the public interest as well. Behind the veil of national security, the triangle has developed unique political power. As Philip Hughes, former Deputy Director of the Budget Bureau described it:

> The most relevant consideration is, in blunt terms, sheer power—where the muscle is—and this a very power-conscious town, and the Secretary of Defense and the defense establishment are a different group to deal with, whether Congress is dealing with them or whether the Budget Bureau is dealing with them.[24]

The continued existence and success of this iron triangle depends on a steady flow of information, access, influence, and money. Defense contractors are the most crucial actors in this process. Defense contractors are highly self-conscious about the link between the political arena and their business success. Defense is big business: The Defense Department contract market amounts to over $100 billion per year. It is also a concentrated and stable business: Most of the top twenty-five contractors to the Defense Department have been in the business for over thirty years and receive 50 percent of all of the contract dollars the Defense Department awards. Finally, it is important business: Many of the leading contracting companies do well over 50 percent of their sales with the federal government.[25]

THE IRON TRIANGLE IN OPERATION

Close ties with the Pentagon have led defense contractors to become innovative in finding ways to influence public policy. As a result, contractors exercise an unusually high degree of influence over an arena of federal policy. Moreover, contractor influence is unusually difficult to detect because it begins at the earliest and least visible level of the weapons planning process—research and development.

At this crucial stage, ideas move freely between industry and government officials, giving contractors ample opportunity to influence future decisions. Contractors participate in roughly fifty advisory committees (and hundreds of subcommittees) of the Defense Department and NASA— most notably, the Defense Science Board and the scientific advisory groups of each branch of the military. Membership on these key committees gives the contractors a further opportunity to affect new weapons policies long before the public or Congress is aware of them.[26]

The constant interaction of government and contractor researchers means that new weapons ultimately bought by the Department of Defense are often created by the firms that stand to gain if these weapons are produced. As one defense industry official described it in the late 1960s: "Your ultimate goal is actually to write the R.F.P. [Request for Proposal], and this happens more often than you might think."[27]

The nation's eight leading military research and development contractors—Boeing, General Dynamics, Grumman, Lockheed, McDonnell Douglas, Northrop, Rockwell International, and United Technologies— received a total of over $20 billion in research and development contracts alone in the 1970s. In addition, these same companies were reimbursed roughly $2 billion for their own direct corporate investment in research work, through the "Independent Research and Develoment/Bids and Proposals" (IR&D) program.[28]

The close ties between industry and government are reinforced by a steady flow of employees between the two sectors. In the 1950s, more than 1,000 retired military personnel took jobs in the defense industry, according to Congressional studies. In the 1960s, this number rose to about 2,000. Between 1969 and 1974, the figure reached 2,000 for the top 100 contractors alone. An examination of the eight leading defense contractors noted above showed that during the 1970s, 2,000 of their employees transferred either from industry to government or from government to industry. Of the nearly 500 civilians in this group, 34 percent had worked in the key research and development offices of the Army, Navy, Air Force, and the Office of the Secretary of Defense.[29]

There are many examples of the revolving door. General Alexander Haig, for example, moved from the Army to the presidency of United Technologies, to Secretary of State, and back to an advisory committee with United Technologies. United Technologies employs other government alumni. Clark MacGregor, head of the company's Washington, D.C. office, is a former Congressman. Hugh Witt, a government relations specialist in the same office, previously worked in the Office of the Secretary of the Air Force and subsequently as director of the Office of Federal Procurement Policy in the Office of Management and Budget.[30]

This revolving door provides unique access to the defense policy-making process. The *Wall Street Journal* reported, for example, that the Boeing company had obtained information about future land-based missile plans from a Boeing employee "on leave to work in the Pentagon's Weapons Research and Development Office." Once this employee had read the relevant report, he telexed its substance to a former Defense Department employee working at Boeing's headquarters in Seattle. The *Journal* concluded: "The movement of weaponry experts between industry and government jobs, frequently on the same project, facilitates the easy flow of information and tends to blur the distinction between national security and corporate goals."[31]

Special access at the level of research and development and the "revolving door" of personnel help get a weapons project started. Once underway, it acquires an increasingly powerful constituency, making the project hard to cancel. Defense contractors' Washington offices are frequently the nerve centers in developing and focusing this constituency. From 1977 through 1979, the eight leading defense companies employed 200 people in their Washington offices, along with forty-eight registered lobbyists. According to audits conducted by the Defense Contract Audit Agency, Boeing, General Dynamics, Grumman, Lockheed, and Rockwell International together spent $16.8 million on their Washington offices in 1974 and 1975, an average of $1.6 million each per year. Rockwell alone spent $7 million from 1973 through 1975.[32]

These Washington offices track developments in the Pentagon and

NASA, follow legislation and lobby on Capitol Hill, conduct public relations activities, funnel information to the company, and negotiate with weapons buyers from other countries. Virtually all of the nonentertainment expenditures of these offices, including lobbying, have been billed to the government as administrative expenses related to defense contracts.[33]

The third active participant in this triangle is Congress, the body that appropriates the money if the triangle is to continue functioning.[34] Because of its role in the budget, Congress is a prime target for lobbying, both by Defense Department bureaucrats and by the contracting industry. Curiously, despite its potentially great influence, Congress plays only a secondary role in the defense policy process. Weapons budgets and the information justifying them are produced by the Defense Department, not by Congress. Congress reacts with less information in hand.[35] Moreover, since many weapons contracts are already underway, with strong bureaucratic commitment and corporate involvement, Congress has limited room to make changes.

As a result, Congressional oversight, though extensive, appears to have little impact on the defense policy process. Hearings on defense procurement waste in the late 1960s, for example, did little to change the way the Defense Department procured weapons. The same issues have been raised in the 1980s; their effect on the Pentagon procurement process is still unclear.

From the industry's point of view, however, it is crucial to influence Congress, especially members of the Armed Services and Defense Appropriations Committees and members who represent districts where defense contracting business is done. Inside the Congress, these key committee members jealously guard authority over the defense budget, while members from key districts must protect their constituents to ensure reelection.

Contractors also reach members of Congress through campaign contributions and grass roots mobilizations. Defense contractor Political Action Committees (PACs) are among the largest corporate PACs in the country. These PACs concentrate their campaign contributions on the key members of Congress. While a campaign contribution does not necessarily mean the member will always vote with the company, it does bring access. Access, in turn, speeds the flow of information and influence.[36]

Defense contractors also organize grass roots lobbying campaigns to influence Congress. Company employees, the communities in which they are located, stockholders, and subcontractors depend on defense contracting for their survival. Trade unions, such as the United Auto Workers and the International Association of Machinists, have many members in defense firms; their locals often follow a company's call for support of its weapons systems in Washington.

In the mid-1970s, for example, Rockwell International mounted a grass roots effort on behalf of the B-1 bomber program, then on the brink of cancellation. The company urged its 115,000 employees and the holders of its 35 million shares of stock to write to their Congressmen. More than 3,000 subcontractors and suppliers in forty-eight states were also asked to tell their Congressmen about the adverse impact scrapping the B-1 would have in their districts. Rockwell acknowledged that it spent $1.35 million on such efforts from 1975 through 1977, an amount that opponents of the B-1 could not have hoped to match.[37]

UNDOING THE TRIANGLE

The only constituency left out of the political processes of the iron triangle are those who foot the bill—the public. The iron triangle is the crucial political obstacle to successful arms reductions and conversion planning. Overcoming national security myths is an important first step. Gaining control over a runaway bureaucratic process will also be crucial in order to permit planning to take place. The political process, however, is key. This process must be opened up and changed in order to provide the political space and legitimacy conversion advocates need to begin making conversion policy. In turn, a conversion element in all defense policy positions taken by arms reduction advocates is essential lest those harmed by reduced arms spending see no advantage to slowing the arms race. Opening up the iron triangle and conversion planning go hand-in-hand. Without an open, accountable defense policy process, no conversion planning of any kind will be possible. Conversion planning is one important element in a strategy for opening up the process.

Dealing with defense contractors, who have a great stake in high levels of defense spending, is a first step. Such large companies as Lockheed, McDonnell Douglas, Grumman, Northrop, and General Dynamics, as well as many smaller contractors, do more than two-thirds of their business with the Defense Department and argue, honestly, that they know how to do little else. As already noted, these firms work hard to perpetuate their contracting work. Their actions as contractors and their involvement with the policy process, however, are usually beyond public scrutiny, since they operate behind the double barrier of national security and "proprietary" corporate information.

Legislation is needed to make this highly intimate relationship more publicly accountable. Since they are wards of the public purse, such dependent companies could be required to disclose the activities through which they knit the iron triangle together and close it off from the public: their subcontracting arrangements, stockholding patterns, lobbying expenditures, and hiring of government personnel, among other things.

A case can be made that companies whose very existence depends directly on public tax expenditures have a duty to be more than normally forthcoming about the way they spend those funds. Moreover, since the subcontracting, stockholding, lobbying, and personnel characteristics of these companies are part of the process by which the iron triangle is reinforced, greater public information would provide the groundwork for greater public accountability.

A number of changes can be made in the way defense contractors do business to ensure that the political process cannot become so dependent on their spending:

- Defense contractors can be prohibited from forming PACs and making campaign contributions, breaking their link with the electoral process. Alternatively, public financing of Congressional elections would sever this tie.
- Contractors could be prohibited from organizing grass roots lobbying campaigns in favor of defense contracts. Such lobbying itself might not be prohibited, but corporate participation and sponsorship would be.
- Contractors could be required to compete for all subcontracts through public bidding, reducing the temptation to award such subcontracts in a way that would increase political support for their programs.
- Contractors could be prohibited from hiring former Defense Department employees who worked, in any way, on systems or policies that affected their defense business. Retiring or departing employees would not be prohibited from defense industry jobs, but they would not be allowed to work with companies over whose defense contracts they had had some authority.
- Advisory committees on weapons plans should include public representation to leaven the effect of early, closed-door planning on perpetuating defense spending.
- Research and development subsidies for private defense contractors (the IR&D program) should end. Like other companies, defense contractors should take their own business risks.
- Stricter limits are needed on lobbying practices by defense contractors, including clear limits on the amount of allowed activities and expenditures and stricter enforcement of existing lobbying statutes.

Ultimately, public ownership of some defense production facilities might be considered. The precedent exists for such a change. Before World War II, public ownership of defense production facilities was common, especially in shipbuilding and ammunition. While some might argue that public ownership is not greater guarantee of production efficiency, such a structural change would make company performance with tax funds more directly accountable to the source of those funds—the Congress and the public.

There is also a need for dramatic changes in the way the Defense Department does business in order to open up the iron triangle and permit policy and conversion planning alternatives to enter the debate:

- Far greater competition for defense contracts than now exists is urgently needed. The fact that contracts can be lost should provide contractors with the incentive to diversify and convert some of their business.
- Profit margins on defense contracts should be low and carefully scrutinized. Profits should not be used as an incentive to do the public's essential business—the provision of weapons. This policy change, too, would encourage corporate diversification and conversion.
- Cost control, testing, and auditing procedures can all be reformed and tightened. This includes real, independent evaluation of contractor cost proposals and independent tests of weapons and close scrutiny of contractor claims of incurred costs. Without such strict, independent Defense Department attention to costs, the defense budget becomes an attractive pork barrel for contracting companies, reducing the incentive for conversion planning.
- The Defense Department should provide the Congress with clear, detailed, up-to-date, usable data on contracting costs. Current reporting requirements are inadequate; the data disclosed are confusing and late. Intimate contracting relations and runaway cost problems emerge late, long after Congress or the public can get them under control or define alternatives.

The Congress, too, can be reformed in the way it relates to the rest of the iron triangle. Members who are less lobbied and who no longer receive campaign contributions will be less subject to the pressures of the Defense Department and contractors. In addition, jurisdiction over defense spending issues should be expanded, with a wider variety of Congressional committees scrutinizing defense practices. Given the wide impact of defense spending on the economy and on national priorities, a number of committees can reasonably explore defense issues as they relate to labor, education, commerce, and human services, among others.

Ultimately, conversion processes themselves will help open up the political process. Legislation providing for alternate use planning and federal assistance for job retraining, relocation, and interim benefits such as the Weiss and Mavroules bills provide weaken the link that makes communities, unions, and work forces dependent on defense contracting. Federal assistance for economic investment and diversification, in the framework of a national industrial policy, would encourage corporations and communities to convert and diversify away from defense production.

It will also be politically crucial for conversion advocates to understand and deal with the wider range of issues within which adjustment planning falls. Major sectors of the American public now live without adequate social services and with little or no federal assistance for the community economy development and job training that ensure their economic future. A restructuring of American economic priorities is a crucial ingredient of conversion planning and suggests the need for new political coalitions.

This wider coalition of support for a healthy, peacetime economy will have to address the political black box to succeed. Elegant technical solutions to conversion problems will fail endlessly without some serious attention to the political process whose closed nature has made conversion such an urgent necessity. Once the veil of national security is lifted, the role of bureaucratic and political elements in defense planning becomes clear.

It will not be easy to change the politics of the iron triangle. Defense Department and industry resources are large, and past efforts have foundered, thanks to a narrow program and strong resistance. Addressing the political issue, however, will help draw in the larger coalition needed to make the defense spending process accountable and to put conversion planning on the American political agenda.

NOTES

1.   On the M-1 tank, see contributions by Patrick Oster, Bruce Ingersoll, and John Fialka, in Dina Rasor, ed., *More Bucks, Less Bang: How the Pentagon Buys Ineffective Weapons* (Washington, D.C., Fund for Constitutional Government, 1983), pp. 34–50. On the Bradley Infantry Fighting Vehicle, see William Boly, "The $13 Billion Dud," in Diná Rasor, *More Bucks*, pp. 13–28.
2.   House Armed Services Committee, "Staff Briefing on the FY 1984 DoD O&M Request," Washington, D.C., March 1983, speech by Walter F. Mondale to the American Newspaper Publishers Association, 26 April 1983, p. 4.
3.   See, George Kuhn, "Department of Defense: Ending Defense Stagnation," *Agenda '83* (Washington, D.C., Heritage Foundation), pp. 69–114; Franklin C. Spinney, *The Plans/Reality Mismatch and Why We Need Realistic Budgeting*, Defense Department Briefing Paper, December 1982; U.S. Air Force Systems Command, *The Affordable Acquisition Approach Study*, Washington, D.C., U.S. Air Force Briefing, February

1983; William Kaufmann, "The Defense Budget," in Joseph A. Pechman, ed., *Setting National Priorities* (Washington, D.C.: Brookings Institution, 1983), pp. 39–79.

4. See, for example, the statement of The Bipartisan Appeal to Resolve the Budget Crisis, a business group for slower growth in defense spending, in a letter to William C. Clark, 25 March 1983.

5. See Gordon Adams, *The Politics of Defense Contracting: The Iron Triangle* (New Brunswick, NJ: Transaction Press, 1982), p. 286.

6. See House Committee on Armed Services, *Capability of U.S. Defense Industrial Base*, Hearings before the Committee on Armed Services and the Panel on Defense Industrial Base, 1980; and Air Force, Wright Aeronautical Laboratories, Manufacturing Technology Division, Materials Laboratory, *Air Force Manufacturing Technology Program: Annual Report, FY 1982*, 1 May 1983.

7. Dave Elsila, "The Pentagon's War on the Workers," *Solidarity* (August 1983): 11–13.

8. *Report of the President's Commission on Strategic Forces*, April 1983.

9. Each Defense Department annual report by Secretary of Defense Caspar Weinberger has had this tone. See Department of Defense, *Report of the Secretary of Defense*, Fiscal Years 1983 and 1984.

10. See, for background, Franklyn Holzman, "Are the Soviets Really Outspending the U.S. on Defense?" *International Security* 4: 4 (Spring 1980): 86–104; Holzman, "Soviet Military Spending: Assessing the Numbers Game," *International Security* 6: 4 (Spring 1982): 78–101; Holzman, "Are We Falling Behind the Soviets?" *Atlantic* (July 1983): 10–18; Richard Stubbing, "The Imaginary Defense Gap: We Already Outspend Them," *Washington Post*, 14 February 1982; Federation of American Scientists, *Public Interest Report*, September 1982; John Collins, *U.S.–Soviet Military Balance: Concepts and Capabilities, 1960–1980* (New York: McGraw-Hill, 1980); and Senator Carl Levin, *The Other Side of the Story*, monograph, May 1983.

11. See Morton J. Peck and Frederick M. Scherer, *The Weapons Acquisition Process: An Economic Analysis* (Boston: Harvard School of Business Administration, 1962); J. Ronald Fox, *Arming America: How the U.S. Buys Weapons* (Boston: Harvard School of Business Administration, 1974); Harvey M. Sapolsky, *The Polaris System Development: Bureaucratic and Programmatic Success in Government* (Boston: Harvard University Press, 1972); A. Ernest Fitzgerald, *The High Priests of Waste* (New York: Norton, 1972).

12. Gordon Adams, *The B-1 Bomber: An Analysis of Its Strategic Utility, Cost, Constituency and Economic Impact;* (New York: Council on Economic Priorities, 1976); Adams, "A Bomber for All Seasons," *Newsletter* (New York: Council on Economic Priorities, February 1982).

13. Quoted in an article by William Grieder, *Atlantic* (December 1981).

14. President's Private Sector Survey on Cost Control ("Grace Commission"), *Task Force Report on the Office of the Secretary of Defense, Task Force Report on the Department of the Army, Task Force Report on the Department of the Air Force*, Washington, D.C., July 1983.

15. See Fox, *Arming America*; Fitzgerald, *High Priests of Waste*; Peck and Scherer, *Weapons Acquisition Process*, for examples of this process, and Richard Kaufmann, *The War Profiteers* (Garden City, NY: Doubleday/Anchor Books, 1972).

16. See, for example, the major effort mounted by the Defense Department and the defense industry to resist the idea that contractor lobbying costs should not be reimbursed by their defense contracts.

17. See Arthur Bentley, *The Process of Government: A Study of Social Pressure* (Evanston, IL: Principia Press, 1945); E.E. Schattschneider, *The Semi-Sovereign People* (Hinsdale, IL: Dryden Press, 1975); David Truman, *The Governmental Process: Political Interests*

and Public Opinion (New York: Knopf, 1975); E. Pendleton Herring, *Group Representation Before Congress* (Baltimore, MD: Johns Hopkins Press, 1929).

18.   See Robert D. Cuff, *The War Industries Board: Business–Government Relations During World War I* (Baltimore, MD: Johns Hopkins Press, 1973); Paul A.C. Koistinen, *The Military–Industrial Complex: A Historical Perspective* (New York: Praeger Publishers, 1980); Gordon Adams, "Defense Policy-Making, Weapons Procurement, and the Reproduction of State–Industry Relations" (Paper for the American Political Science Association, Washington, D.C., 28 August 1980).

19.   See Kaufmann, *War Profiteers;* Fox, *Arming America;* Peck and Scherer, *Weapons Acquisition Process;* and James Kurth, "The Political Economy of Weapons Procurement: The Follow-On Imperative," *American Economic Review* 62: 2 (May 1972): 304–11.

20.   Among other writers who have explored this and similar concepts, see Gordon Adams, "Disarming the Military Subgovernment," *Harvard Journal on Legislation* 14: 3 (April 1977): 459–503; Lester Salamon and John Siegfried, "Economic Power and Political Influence: The Impact of Industry Structure on Public Policy," *American Political Science Review* 71: 3 (September 1977): 1026–43; Joel D. Auerbach and Burt Rockmen, "Bureaucrats and Clientele Groups: A View from Capitol Hill," *American Journal of Political Science* 22: 4 (November 1978); Grant McConnell, *Private Power and American Democracy* (New York: Knopf, 1967); John Lieper Freeman, *The Political Process* (Garden City, NY: Doubleday, 1955); Douglas Cater, *Power in Washington* (New York: Random House, 1964); and Michael T. Hayes, "The Semi-Sovereign Pressure Groups: A Critique of Current Theory and Alternative Typology," *Journal of Politics* 40: 1 (1978): 134–61.

21.   Harmon Zeigler and Wayne G. Peak, *Interest Groups in American Society* (Englewood Cliffs, NJ: Prentice Hall, 1972). The authors point out (p. 180) that in such a relationship

> agencies and their clientele tend to develop coincident values and perceptions to the point where neither needs to manipulate the other overtly. The confident relationships that develop uniquely favor the interest groups involved. They need only exchange persuasive resources for instrumental policy benefits within administrative markets to satisfy many of their material demands.

22.   Harold Seidman, *Politics, Position and Power* (New York: Oxford University Press, 1970). The author points out (p. 18) that "private bureaucracies in Washington now almost completely parallel the public bureaucracies in those program areas where the federal government contracts for services, regulates private enterprise, or provides some form of financial assistance." Grant McConnell, (*Private Power*, p. 244), describes this interpretation as the process of "privatizing" the state, while James O'Connor uses the term "appropriateness of a sector of state power by private interests" to describe the same phenomenon in *The Fiscal Crisis of the State* (New York: Saint Martin's Press, 1973), p. 66.

23.   See Adams, *Harvard Journal;* Schattschneider, *Semi-Sovereign People;* and Hayes, "Semi-Sovereign Pressure Groups" for examples. See also Richard Neustadt, *Presidential Power* (New York: Wiley, 1976).

24.   Quoted in Kaufmann, *War Profiteers,* p. 248.

25.   This is particularly true of General Dynamics, Grumman, Lockheed, McDonnell Douglas, and Northrop, who are usually among the top ten contractors with the Defense Department.

26.   See Adams, *Politics of Defense Contracting,* ch. 11. See also the report of the Defense Department Inspector General's office, 1983, on the interrelationship of industry and the Defense Department in the Defense Science Board, as reprinted in the *Congressional Record,* 22 July 1983, p. S 10663–S 10677.

27. A North American Aviation official quoted in David Sims, "Spoon Feeding the Military: How New Weapons Come to Be," in Leonard Rodberg and Derek Sherer, *The Pentagon Watchers* (Garden City, NY: Doubleday, 1970), p. 249.

28. See Christopher Paine and Gordon Adams, "The R&D Slush Fund," *Nation* (26 January 1980); and Adams, *Politics of Defense Contracting*, ch. 7.

29. See Adams, *Politics of Defense Contracting*, ch. 6.

30. Ibid., ch. 6 and Company Profiles.

31. *Wall Street Journal*, 29 February 1980.

32. See Adams, *Politics of Defense Contracting*, ch. 9.

33. Ibid.

34. See Adams, *Harvard Journal*.

35. Now retired Senator Thomas McIntyre (D–NY) described the problem he faced as chair of the Senate Armed Services subcommittee on research and development in the face of thousands of Defense Department projects for research and development: "We spend an awful lot of time, but we are lucky if we can take a look at or have a briefing or hearing on, say, 15 percent of those projects." (Quoted by Louis Fischer, "Senate Procedures for Authorizing Military Research and Development," in Joint Economic Committee, Subcommittee on Priorities and Economy in Government, *Priorities and Efficiency in Federal Research and Development: A Compendium of Papers*, 94th Cong., 2d sess., 1976, p. 26.)

36. See Adams, *Politics of Defense Contracting*, ch. 13.

37. Ibid.

11

Can Business Become a Participant?

John E. Ullmann

Economic conversion has long ceased to be a moral good. From the economic point of view, it is a necessity. The arms race and corporate practice has produced such intensive dysfunctions in industrial operations that the whole business process—indeed, the very survival of the industrial system and the basic economic and political arrangements that prevail in American society—have been called into question.

Although many have welcomed the so-called recovery of 1983 and have sited reductions in unemployment statistics, the fact that so many uncertainties cloud this statistical measurement indicates that it has become unreliable in itself and useless as a standard against which to measure our economic well-being. Just as uncertainty about economic well-being characterizes the labor force, so too it is pervasive throughout the business community. Business failures continue at record rates, and even enterprises in the forefront of high technology, like Texas Instruments, Atari, and Commodore are having considerable competitive, organizational, and financial problems. Manufacturing continues its decline, and its rate of purchase of new equipment is nowhere near that needed to maintain itself.

Most immediately and directly, the still high interest rates are expected to rise even more. Even at their current levels they impede industrial investment, for managers are loathe to take risks on developing new products when they can make safe investments at such high rates.

Some might argue that these conditions make conversion more difficult, but in a sense the very same conditions increase the opportunities for beneficial change—provided, that is, there are sharp reductions in military expenditures and that business can be convinced to alter some of its unproductive habits.

Everyone who has read the business and trade press is familiar with the long list of once prosperous and viable American industries that are now in serious trouble. Shipbuilding, shoes, and automobiles are only some of the more prominent ones that have come to public attention. The problem is far broader, however.

Several analyses are possible to demonstrate the current difficulties. One useful approach is to look at the changing relationships between imports and exports of selected products and commodities. Table 14–1 provides the ratio of exports to imports (EIR) for 1967 and 1980 for key categories of products and commodities that are relevant to an analysis of the more technically oriented industries. A third column gives the ratio of the EIRs for 1980 to those for 1967. Thus, if that ratio has a value greater than unity it indicates a relative improvement in the export/import balance, and if it is less, a relative decline. With two exceptions in the major groupings—that is, food (which includes beverages and tobacco, animal and vegetable oils and fats) and crude materials exclusive of fuels— all the final ratios are less than one.

When crude materials exclusive of fuels are added to fuels where a combination of enormous price rise and increased dependency has put the United States at a most serious and increasing disadvantage, the total shows a final EIR ratio of 0.42. Therefore, with respect to the aggregate raw materials of an industrial society, the United States has experienced a drastic deterioration in its position.

The chemical industry, where American product development has often been sophisticated, sustained, and competent, has lost ground overall. Table 14–1 shows the major components of the industry, and it is quite clear that even within its parts there is very little from which to draw comfort. Essential oils, a small (4%) portion of the total, explosives (a still smaller item, which excludes military shipments) and fertilizers, a volatile and quasi-raw material industry, are the only ones in which the EIR ratio exceeds one. Such industries as organic chemicals and synthetic resins in which American pioneering work, especially with respect to petrochemicals, was a leading ingredient of early success have fared worse than the industry as a whole.

The statistics for machinery are also presented in some detail because the industry provides the sinews for the nation's industrial establishment. Here the individual portions all show substantial declines. Of special note is metalworking machinery in which the United States turned from net exporter to net importer for the first time in this century. General and special machinery that between them furnish a good deal of equipment to chemical processing industries have likewise lost ground.

Even office machinery, which includes computers, has lost overall. There is a substantial Japanese entry into the next generation of computer memories and prospective dominance of later developments. Telecommunications, which includes radio and TV sets, also shows a very poor ratio, little better than that of machinery as a whole. The data reflect such

TABLE 11–1.   Export-Import Ratios for Selected Items, 1965, 1967, and 1980.

Item	Ratio of Exports to Imports (EIR)			Ratio	
				EIR(1980)	EIR(1980)
	1965	1967	1980	EIR(1967)	EIR(1965)
Chemicals, total	3.12	2.91	2.42	0.83	0.77
Organics		3.42	2.24	0.65	
Inorganics		1.51	1.27	0.84	
Dyes, etc.		2.10	1.73	0.82	
Medical, pharmaceutical	4.41	4.00	3.80	0.95	0.86
Essential oils		2.04	2.16	1.06	
Fertilizers	1.37	1.63	2.05	1.26	1.50
Explosives		0.44	1.47	3.34	
Synthetic resins, etc.		7.88	6.01	0.76	
Other chemicals		6.21	3.48	0.56	
Food (inc. beverages, tobacco, animal and vegetable oils and fats)	1.21	1.05	1.70	1.62	1.40
Machinery and transport equipment	3.44	2.17	1.40	0.65	0.41
Power generation		2.74	2.20	0.80	
Special machinery		5.87	2.72	0.46	
Metalworking machinery		1.67	0.97	0.58	
General industrial machinery		3.21	2.64	0.82	
Office machines, computers	3.47	3.14	2.97	0.95	0.86
Telecommunications	1.10	0.89	0.51	0.57	0.46
Electrical machinery		1.84	1.30	0.71	
Road vehicles	1.46	1.12	0.57	0.51	0.39
Other transport		5.69	5.56	0.98	
Steel mill products	0.58	0.49	0.45	0.92	0.77
Crude materials, exc. fuels	0.92	1.10	2.27	2.06	2.46
Fuels	0.43	0.49	0.10	0.20	0.24
Total raw materials	0.71	0.84	0.35	0.42	0.50

SOURCES: U.S. Department of Commerce, *U.S. Exports, Annual 1967*, FT/450, Table 1; *U.S. Exports, Annual 1980*, FT/455, Table 1; *U.S. Imports, Annual 1967*, FT/155, Table 1; *U.S. Imports, Annual 1980*, FT/155, Table 1; 1981 *Statistical Abstract of the United States*, pp. 850–53.

changes as the total eclipse of manufacture of TV and radio sets in the United States, the virtual end of stereophonic systems production and the U.S. nonentry into home TV recording. In the allied field of photography, U.S. products have, in effect, been reduced to photogenic materials and a few of the cheaper cameras, in spite of a long pioneering history.

In steel there has been little change; note, however, that the United States became a net importer of steel after 1962, a year in which exports and imports were directly in balance, and that for a considerable time stringent quota restrictions have protected the American industry. Similar rules in other industries would certainly produce the trade wars which are now such a clear danger.

The extreme right of Table 11-1 shows EIR ratios for the period 1965-1980. They were available in consistent form for only a few categories but for chemicals and machinery they show a further decline which suggests that in 1967 the decline noted here was already well on its way. These changes took place while the U.S. dollar declined sharply. Even its rise since 1980, which has served as a welcome excuse for continuing trade losses, leaves it way below its 1971 levels in relation to the strong currencies. By all rights, one would have expected imports to fall and exports to rise—not the opposite.

These melancholy statistics therefore show a profound decline of American technology. They explain, for example, why, if one travels abroad, one seldom sees products made in the United States for sale. They also explain, inter alia, the bizarre vicissitudes of public transit equipment for American communities; the debacle of the Grumman buses in New York in January 1984 is one example. Another, equally far-reaching one is that of electric traction that was practically invented in the United States but has gone into a terminally troubled state, compounded by wrong designs, high costs, poor performance, and bad maintenance.

As a result, recent major orders for rapid transit rolling stock for the United States have all been placed abroad—in Germany, Japan, France and Canada. After an electric locomotive designed by General Electric proved too heavy and otherwise unsatisfactory in the Northeast Corridor rail service between New York and Washington, General Motors had to step in with a model produced under license from ASEA of Sweden. To be sure, these orders will all have U.S.-made parts, but increasingly these consist of heavy structures, weldments, and other simple details, with the more sophisticated driving units and other parts all imported. The United States, in short, is being treated like a developing country that wants in on some of the industrial action.

In the case of subway cars for New York City, built by Kawasaki of Japan, this procedure had to be changed, for political reasons, increasing the U.S. content to 43 percent of their value. In February 1984, the cars began to be delivered on time from Japan, but defective, U.S.-made door switches and brakes caused the cars to fail their tests and led to a delay of at least six months in their introduction. The company making the defective brakes was none other than Westinghouse Air Brake Co., which had developed the original standard railroad brakes in the 1880s.[1]

Almost daily, the business and technical press brings news of further disasters. For instance, in the great construction projects done abroad American participation, if any, is increasingly limited to a few special jobs and even those tend to be done by foreign subsidiaries or licensees of American firms, as in the Russian gas pipeline to Western Europe.

Not only have businesses suffered but the entire infrastructure of the country has deteriorated. The Council of State Planning Agencies in 1981 published a bill of particulars eloquently entitled "America in Ruins."[2] This organization of the planning and policy staffs of the nation's governors found extensive deterioration of vital services such as clean water, reliable transportation, efficient ports, and waste disposal that are the indispensable underpinnings of an industrial system. In an even more pessimistic review, "The Decaying of America," *Newsweek* suggested that the nation may be faced before long with a $3 trillion repair job, including some reequipment for industry.[3] Another estimate, in *U.S. News and World Report,* came up with a total of $2.5 trillion for the infrastructure as such and a further $1.9 trillion for making U.S. industry competitive again, for a total of $4.4 trillion.[4]

The enormous progress of Japan is perhaps the leading economic development of the last generation. Yet, certain things are quite clear. When the capital fund of defense spending—and it is a capital fund—is added to new (producers') fixed capital formation, the United States spends 31.5 percent of that total on the military, Japan 3.6 percent.[5] Since this comparison was made in 1977, the gap has widened further. The crucial role of military spending in all this is no secret to policymakers. William Brock, Mr. Reagan's Special Trade Representative has said, "If the United States spent as little as Japan does on defense, we could balance the budget, cut taxes, and have 8 percent interest rates."[6] Therein lies the difference—not in Japanese management secrets that would be hard to transfer to the United States for cultural and historical reasons and are, in any event, under increasing attack in Japan itself.

Japan graduates approximately 75,000 engineers a year, which is somewhat but not decisively more than the 61,000 or so in the United States; however, while at least a third of the latter go into military-oriented research, virtually all the Japanese engineers work to provide more power to Japanese industrial progress.

The diversion of American engineers has a very simple reason: Engineers only work when someone wishes to invest in their products and provides them with the requisite expensive and sophisticated equipment. In the absence of these tools and of employment opportunities, the rationing of engineering talent for American technical industry necessarily goes on. When industry itself is starved of investment funds the problem is compounded; in particular, the stream of innovation dries up.

The decline of innovation is demonstrated by such objective measures as the so-called patent balance. After decades of American advantage, American patents taken out by foreigners have come to exceed substantially the number of patents taken out abroad by Americans. More evidence is provided by simple comparison between the periods of 1945–60 and 1961–76. Since about 1960, there has been a hiatus in technical innovation that contrasts painfully with the enormously productive period between 1945 and 1960 when antibiotics, steroids, television (black and white, and color), new plastics and fabrics, insecticides, computers, and so forth all made their debut, as did more star-crossed developments like nuclear power. After 1960, this stream of innovation largely dried up, and then promising leads such as those in solar and other energy, transportation, and sea water desalination were no longer followed up. When some of them were taken up again following the energy problems of the early 1970s it was almost as if everyone had gone to sleep for a good decade.[7] Many of them lag badly even now.

The beginning of this fallow period coincided quite precisely with the sharp expansion of American military research and the concentration of effort in those areas, following President Kennedy's alleged missile gap, the escalation of the Vietnam War, and the moon shot. Countering this view, it has been asserted that the fifteen years from 1945 to 1960 were something of a historical freak. However, consider 1920–35: It brought plastics, synthetic fabrics, radio broadcasting, diesel traction for the railroads, and passenger aircraft, and witnessed the growth of mass merchandising of capital products of all sorts for personal consumption. Or, consider 1895–1910: One need only mention a few names: Westinghouse, Edison, the Wright brothers, Henry Ford, and Marconi—all but the latter having been Americans.

The importance of innovation is crucial. It is, among other things, the only way of coming up with true quantum jumps in the improvement of productivity. Whenever new equipment is being considered, rational technical-economic analysis dictates that its rate of return shall be adequate to justify the new investment; in MAPI parlance, the challenger must be substantially better than the incumbent equipment.[8] Only in that way can increased wage costs provide real wage increases and enable the product to be turned out more cheaply. The alternative is to pass along the increased cost, thus adding to inflation and making the firm and industry concerned ever less competitive. If there is no innovation, no renewal is possible, unless the old plant has irremediably collapsed or new capacity must be added. But there is a limit to that.

In a study of economy of scale in relation to productivity change, we concluded that, in most industries, making production units bigger rather than better has been the principal way of improvement and the principal source of whatever productivity improvement still took place. There are, however, limits to that process set not only by the theory of economy of scale itself[9] but by technical developments that change the character of whole industries. The replacement of large central computers by smaller ones and the impending cost and market breakthrough of small scale devices for the production of electricity are examples.

WHAT IS TO BE DONE?

The reconstruction of American industry is clearly a complex task. The experience of the United States shows that industrial development does not exhibit the comforting monotonic increase that proponents of inevitable progress have long espoused. Rather, current trends will inevitably lead not merely to an inability to recreate an industrial sector but rather will call into question the ability to maintain whatever is left now. In this way, a country is gradually "deindustrialized."

In order to arrest this decline, business will have to change many of its deeply ingrained habits; thus, leaving the job to those presently managing (or mismanaging) industry is not the ideal solution. What is needed, first of all, is a significant infusion of capital so that support allocations are not distributed by lottery. Moreover, substantial funds would also assure the necessary degree of diversification so that impossibly high standards of acceptance are not imposed. Without a substantial commitment, there is little chance of success.

There are essentially two aspects to building support within the business community for conversion: one concerns the military industrial firms; the other, firms engaged in civilian production. Military industrial firms are obviously the ones the most in need of conversion, but there is also a need to involve those outside. They too would be affected by any conversion to civilian commercial work which would increase competition in the market place. In general, of course, the health of the entire business community would be improved by such benefits as lower interest rates and more technical innovation in the nonmilitary sector.

The military industrial firms have the advantage of large facilities and sizable technical resources. These, however, are more than counterbalanced by some severe obstacles. First, there is Pentagon pressure against conversion initiatives. Contractors that seem to want out are treated as the undeserving poor and may risk not getting further military contracts. This attitude is designed to assure true dependency, for workers no less than managements, and this is what generates those broadbased protests that invariably follow contract cancellations.

As to the managers themselves, they not only tend to be politically conservative and therefore attuned to cold war permanence but are also used to having to justify their activities on what they perceive to be patriotic grounds. Many of them therefore take the view that conversion neither can nor should happen and that therefore the issue is largely moot. Moreover, they unfortunately share the sentiment that whatever ails the economy can be solved by blaming it on unions, workers, and consumers.

When one gets down to details, however, other and more personal matters begin to surface. Although the so-called universality of management—if you can manage one thing, you can manage anything—is a treasured article of faith of management theory as taught in business schools, it is widely and correctly disbelieved. To be a manager of a given industry requires, or should require, excellence rather than mere competence. The belief in the above universality is a prominent reason why it frequently receives neither.

Even though it complicates matters further, therefore, it is probably not the most fruitful approach to expect that major contractors can be persuaded to espouse enterprise-wide conversion. Nevertheless the outlook is not entirely grim. For one thing there is enough work ethic (of whatever provenance) left in workers and professionals to be often frustrated by the bureaucracy, waste, and restrictions of military work. Even scientists and engineers, supposedly attracted to the field by work at the so-called frontier, feel frustrated by the "paper factories" of which they often become part, by the interminable reports, delays, and special brand of politicking that goes on. It takes very little probing to elicit responses along these lines among aerospace or military electronics engineers. Not infrequently they themselves have product ideas, either as concepts or as breadboard or other experimental work, that could lead to true spin-offs several miles down the road. That road, of course, has been predominantly traveled by the Japanese in recent history.

The inability to proceed further with such developments frustrates many engineers and has led some of them in the past to break with their employers and strike out on their own. However, given the current economic crunch, many good ideas simply lead to part-time attempts to get off the ground (if that far) and continued dependence of their authors on military work with an employer that either refuses to see the potential or is constrained in some way from exploring it.

What is required then is a decentralized scheme that would encourage individuals to break with established practice and established employers. Although the alternate ideas may come from the military work itself, they will often result from nonmilitary applications of new technologies designed by engineers who have had prior training in civilian production. These engineers and designers therefore deserve to be granted a sympathetic hearing and to be backed accordingly. Mere skills in proposal preparation might even give rather direct opportunities to a few of those now engaged in the interminable clerical minutiae of military work.

A more direct approach that might work in a few cases is to encourage companies with military and commercial divisions to make transferring from the military to the commercial departments easier. There is now some reluctance to do so, not only because firing people is considered these days as the highest virtue of American managements, but because military-industrial work habits are at least widely reputed to be unsuitable among the managers of the commercial divisions. In several large mixed firms, therefore, it appears to be quite difficult to make the transfer, at least at a comparable rank or position. How to devise such encouragement is not easy, given these impediments, but pressures might properly come from within, *provided* an alternative set of products can be proposed along with the transfers.

We now turn to the rest of the business community. There, the evidence that they are being damaged by *somebody* is pervasive enough, but again, the reluctance to blame military spending and, in extenso, the cold war, is likewise profound. It is easier to blame the Japanese, for instance. A second difficulty lies in the practice of managements to prefer short-term results to long-term chances; even where there still is a commitment to a given industry the enterprise may have reached a stage of just trying to survive from one quarter to the next. Again, in such an environment, the pickings are likely to be slim. However, once more the situation is not hopeless. Especially among smaller technologically oriented firms one is amazed by the variety of new products, materials, and systems that are constantly being proposed. If the job is done right, there is an enormous potential here for speeding up what has otherwise become a rather glacial pace of development.

To tap this reservoir, the first requirement is an adequate development fund and, very importantly, lower interest rates. For as long as coupon-clipping is a viable and widely preferred alternative to creative development, and so-called safe interest rates are available at high levels, venture capital of the right kind will not materialize. At present, venture capital is much given to fashion, so much so that one observer of the scene recently remarked that, software being currently "in," some firms were there mainly "to fulfill the need for venture capitalists to participate in the marketplace."[10] It is necessary, therefore, to direct effort, and try to encourage the best in each field. It cannot be too strongly emphasized that individual projects must be evaluated rather than rendering lofty judgments that industry X was good while Y was on its way out. If this is done, there will not be any shortage of applicants, nor of creative ideas for finding people and facilities something viable to do.

In some nonmilitary areas it would, in fact, help for government to stop supporting its present pets. This is so, for instance, in the field of energy where the Reagan administration put its might behind two evident losers—nuclear power and synthetic fuels—while cutting back on other, more promising sources as well as conservation. It did this in the face of the obvious fact that the clearest security threat to the United States is dependence on oil imports, especially those from the Middle East and Mediterranean areas.

Such considerations reinforce the point that there is important public business to be done of positive national value when conversion plans are put in hand. It also suggests, however, that the market by itself is not enough and that some governmental judgment should be exercised. How does one reach the business community? There is obviously no clear general answer, any more than with other groups.

Both within the business community and the general populace, one must rely on broader political reevaluations. There is little that can be done, in the last analysis, for people who will not try to save their own lives, who will not even try to develop fallback positions in a country like the United States in which the capriciousness with which one can lose one's job in most occupations is quite notorious. To assume that all such fears and concerns will yield to simple persuasion is clearly an illusion; one must hope and assume that there are enough people with good new ideas or ideas for doing existing things better to make a difference. But the above-mentioned horses cannot drink when there is not enough water.

There is, therefore, no very great difficulty in devising a set of plans and actions that would improve security, give opportunities beyond measure to a wide variety of distressed industries, and would give employment to precisely the broad spectrum of skills that are now so badly served by the current distortions. We would then leave to posterity a well-functioning national structure, rather than the bankrupt one now in clear prospect. Conversion is not merely a relief measure for military overspending. Rather, it is the alternative to a downward spiral of the United States to a condition of economic-industrial deterioration that cannot fail to affect adversely every other aspect of its well-being.

NOTES

1. S. Daley, "First Cars for IRT Made By Japanese Fail 30-Day Test," *New York Times*, 18 February 1984.
2. S. Walter and P. Choate, "America in Ruins," Council of State Planning Agencies, Washington, D.C.
3. "The Decaying of America," *Newsweek*, 2 August 1982, p. 12.
4. "The Rebuilding of America—A $2.5 Trillion Job," *U.S. News and World Report*, 27 September 1982, p. 57.

5.   Quoted in D. Shribman, "Trade Official's Message: Start Competing," *New York Times,* 22 March 1982.

6.   S. Melman, "Looting the Means of Production," *New York Times,* 16 July 1981.

7.   For an extended discussion of innovation and its managerial implications, see J.E. Ullmann, "Tides and Shallows," in L.R. Benton, ed., *Management for the Future* (New York: McGraw-Hill, 1978), ch. 23.

8.   The original MAPI method is from G. Terborgh, *Business Investment Policy* (Washington, D.C.: Machinery and Allied Products Institute, 1958); similar methods are found in all texts on engineering or managerial economics.

9.   J.E. Ullmann, *The Improvement of Productivity* (New York: Praeger, 1980).

10. "Software: The New Driving Force," *Business Week,* 27 February 1984, p. 96.

12

Converting Economic Conversion: An Argument for Building Broader Coalitions

Kenneth Geiser

Senator George McGovern first presented the term "economic conversion" to American audiences during his 1972 campaign for the U.S. presidency. Economic conversion was part of the McGovern plan for redirecting the national economy following the close of the Vietnam War. A decade later the concept still offers an unrealized vision for building and uniting a broad movement for change.

Economic conversion is a code term for the orderly reduction of resources from military production to production meeting basic social needs. The term is used to describe macroeconomic proposals advocating the conversion of national economic policies.[1] More often, however, it refers to plans for converting specific plants to domestic production, such as General Dynamic's Quincy shipyard, where the South Shore Conversion Committee is preparing specific alternative use production. Although economic conversion is commonly considered in relation to military production, the concept has applications well beyond the military to domestic transformation. Economic conversion could well serve as a guide for preventing plant closings in general or for transforming industrial production wherever the processes do not meet broader social objectives.

While there were many efforts to formulate product conversion schemes for transforming production facilities prior to the struggles to save the Lucas Aerospace Combine in Great Britain, the Lucas struggles there marked the emergence of the current definition of economic conversion. Having recognized the inevitability and desirability of the defense cuts prepared by the Labour government after 1970 the Lucas shop stewards sought in their corporate plan to demonstrate how such cuts need not lead to layoffs if Lucas simply shifted its production to alternative products manufactured for new markets. Central to the effort was a planning agreement that would protect jobs, maintain plants, and

175

manufacture socially useful products. Rebuffed by corporate management, the effort failed at Lucas, but the idea spread. Soon the efforts led to a series of conversion experiments, including the Greater London Enterprise Board's encouragement of socially useful product conversion and the offshore wind power plant proposals for the shipyards at Bremen, Germany.

Developed as a response to plant closings, the argument for economic conversion was soon grafted on to the peace and disarmament movements. As tentative as this adoption has been, the opportunity for growth in the larger movement has proved great. The adoption of economic conversion into the peace and disarmament movement raises interest in its potential for diffusion into other movements. Could economic conversion, which has served as an important link between peace activists and labor leaders, not also attract activists in the environmental movement, the consumer movement, the community development movement, and others as well? Could the concept bring to other such movements opportunities to consider directly questions of industrial production? Could economic conversion provide a base for larger coalitions of activists and working people? The answer is a clear yes.

Ideas are accepted into movements when they have the capacity to propel action forward, when they resolve current contradictions, and when they have little cost. Economic conversion meets these conditions. Today, both the peace and disarmament movement and the labor movement regard it as a potentially powerful idea, but each movement views it as a product of the other movement. Peace activists tend to view economic conversion as a labor initiative demonstrating how military dependent plants can be converted to peaceful production. Labor activists view economic conversion as a peace initiative to court labor's support for disarmament. Neither movement fully embraces the concept, yet there are active proponents in both movements.

The entrepreneurs of the economic conversion argument are, instead, a collection of economic planners, church leaders, worker democracy advocates, and trade union activists who are struggling to push economic conversion onto peace platforms and woo trade unionists concerned about economic stability. This struggle might appear futile if there were not such compelling reasons for grafting economic conversion onto the two movements.

THE POTENTIAL OF ECONOMIC CONVERSION

There are at least two compelling reasons why economic conversion can serve as a vehicle for positively advancing ·current progressive struggles. First, the concept counters negativism in organizing. Second, the concept links progressive social change to the needs and interests of working people.

Every organizer knows that it is easier to mobilize people to stop something undesirable than to start something desirable. Organizers learn to attract activists by framing issues negatively. People are engaged against condominiums, nuclear power plants, nuclear bombs, or the threat of war. While such a conceptualization is often useful in early phases of organizing, many participants soon grow restless with a continually negative approach. They need to buttress their opposition with some vision of positive alternatives. Thus antiwar movements transform into pro-peace movements, and antipollution movements become pro-environmental movements. The peace movement has long sought positive constructions for advancing organizing. It has been a matter of necessity.

Because increased militarization is thought to advance economic development, the apparent trade-off between peace and development seemed to imply that to be against war meant also to be against local economic growth. Economic conversion offers a conceptual way out of this seeming paradox. In advancing economic conversion one can be at once for peace and a strong economy. Converting current plants from war production to peace production is the vehicle that adds a positive credibility to the peace position. Alternative use plans and economic transition training become positive development weapons in the antiwar campaigner's arsenal.

A second compelling argument for advancing economic conversion is that it links progressive social change directly to the economic well-being of working people. Many peace activists are frustrated when they discover the depth of support among the working class for the military and successful military enterprises. Middle-class activists dominate the U.S. peace movement, which American workers believe is hostile to working-class organizations and working-class leadership. While already wide, this gulf becomes almost unbridgeable when disarmament advocates target military contractors that provide respectable jobs for working people or when peace activists suggest that workers in military plants should quit their jobs for moral reasons. Because it focuses so centrally on the preservation of jobs and the stabilization and enhancement of production plants, economic conversion reduces the economic quarrels between activists and workers who might otherwise share the same moral objectives. Worker participation in plant conversion planning offers a central role for working people in the conversion to peace.

Even with such compelling justification, economic conversion has crept into the peace and disarmament movement by the back door. Rather than an immediate adoption on face value, the broad international movement first arrived at economic conversion via an argument about the tremendous social and then economic costs of an expanding military budget. The American Nuclear Weapons Freeze Campaign and the Jobs with Peace organizations first argued that military spending was not a long-term investment for revitalizing and stabilizing the economy. The argument aimed to challenge the idea that military spending and economic recovery were positively linked, but for most local organizations the argument was too abstract and macroeconomic. Economic conversion of specific plants is more concrete. It is becoming the microeconomic argument to those sensitive to local job loss or business decline.

With these values, the concept of economic conversion needs to be considered more broadly. What economic conversion has done for the peace and disarmament movements in Europe, it can also do for other locally based movements—provide a positive mechanism that counters negative organizing and provide a link between progressive change and worker support. Furthermore, economic conversion expanded to this larger vision offers a significant opportunity for linking together a series of currently disparate movements into a common approach to industrial restructuring.

While economic conversion may serve a useful role among many different local campaigns, three are suggested here to illustrate the potential for further diffusion. The emerging movements around plant closings, around worker rights, and around toxic chemicals all offer opportunities for economic conversion.

ECONOMIC CONVERSION AND PLANT CLOSING STRUGGLES

The struggle around public policy responses to plant shutdowns in the United States and Europe is little more than a decade old. The search for governmental involvement grew with increasing public awareness of the number of plant shutdowns caused by corporate disinvestments. Economists Barry Bluestone and Bennett Harrison in their pivotal work on the subject have estimated that during the 1970s between 450,000 and 650,000 American jobs were lost directly to plant shutdowns and relocations.[2]

Relying on the work of MIT researcher David Birch, Bluestone and Harrison estimate that while twenty-five million jobs were created between 1969 and 1976, 39 percent of those jobs existing in 1969 were wiped out due to plant closings by 1976.[3] In fact, during this period private industry destroyed more jobs through plant closings in the Northeast states than it created through new plant openings.

The personal and social costs of plant closings are high. Workers terminated due to plant shutdowns suffer from lost wages and benefits. Plant closings also disrupt family life and local affective ties, particularly where employees must relocate to find new jobs. Where workers do not move, prolonged unemployment and various physical and psychological problems may ensue. A recent Cornell University study surveyed workers terminated by a plant shutdown in upstate New York. Of the 2,800 affected employees over one-quarter were left unemployed for a year or more while 10 percent remained unemployed two years after the closing.[4] The study went on to review health consequences of such job loss, noting increased hypertension, ulcers, respiratory diseases, and conditions leading toward diabetes and gout. Other studies have documented severe depressions, increased alcohol abuse, and a heightened suicide rate in laid-off workers.[5]

Economic conversion is a perfect strategy for plant closing struggles. In Europe, it developed out of the Lucas Aerospace plant closing furor. Indeed, economic conversion is a central feature of the more sophisticated plant closing movement of Europe. Efforts to fight plant closings at Lucas, Rolls Royce, and Massey Ferguson in England and Lip Watch in France have been paralleled by broader struggles in national and international forums.

Several countries have passed financial disclosure laws that require corporations periodically to provide designated works councils the right to information and consultation concerning corporate investment decisions. Plant closing provisions in the form of advanced notification is often included, but is seldom timely (anywhere from ten to sixty days) with the exception of the twelve-month requirement in Germany. In many cases compliance remains voluntary.[6] During the late 1970s the Organization for Economic Cooperation and Development, the International Labor Organization, and the United Nations each issued calls for increased accountability of corporations, particularly transnational corporations, to governments and workers. While these efforts have provided useful model planning agreements and codes of practice, each referring to policies on plant shutdowns, corporations have strenuously resisted anything but voluntary guidelines.

In 1980 the European Economic Community (EEC) took up a draft directive—referred to as the Vredeling plan after its author—that would legally require corporations operating in the EEC to provide information and consultation rights to employee representatives on matters of key importance to the life of the plant such as reorganization plans, introduction of new technology, and planned layoffs or shutdowns. Not only have European employer associations attacked the proposal, but three bills have been introduced in the U.S. Congress to limit the impact of the Vredeling Plan on U.S.-based transnational corporations.

During the mid-1970s a movement emerged in the United States in various Northeastern states to pass so-called plant closing legislation. The model for many of these legislative struggles was a bill drafted in 1977 for the Ohio legislature by the Ohio Public Interest Campaign. Many of the early bills called for advanced notification of impending plant closings (anywhere from a year to a month), severance pay provisions, and job training and relocation. While bills were introduced in at least twenty states and at least twice into Congress, the only state legislatures that passed even simple advanced notification provisions were Maine and Wisconsin. Since 1978 opposition by industry has been significant and well organized. Only a sixty-day prenotification ordinance passed in Philadelphia has been enacted in recent years.

The movement emerging around plant closings is diverse but firmly based in working-class and trade union organizations. Much of its support has come from the largest international unions. The United Auto Workers and the International Association of Machinists funded plant closing research with special tours of Sweden, Germany, and other European countries in the late 1970s and strongly supported prenotification, job search allowances, transferable pensions, and health insurance coverage for workers laid off by plant closings.[7] Locally, unions, neighborhood organizations, citizen action groups, and church groups make up the many state coalitions. Nor has the movement declined because of its poor legislative record. This year some fourteen states are considering some kind of plant closing legislation. In November 1981 the Western International Conference on Economic Dislocation was held at Los Angeles to consider new directions for plant closing struggles. Three of these directions open opportunities for considering economic conversion: union contract negotiations, local community planning agreements, and worker buy-outs.

Bennett Harrison in his recent review of the European plant closing movement notes that while American trade unions focus most on severance pay and the length of prenotification time, their European counterparts want the right to consult with management over the necessity of closure.[8] Consultation rights open the door to considerations of plant conversions. Consultation over product conversion lay at the heart of the long struggle at Lucas Aerospace and became the basis of many of the future successes at the Greater London Enterprise Board and Sheffield. Such consultation was lost in the long struggle at Massey Ferguson where a workers' alternative product plan was resisted by management eager to close the plant and demonstrate fiscal responsibility. Yet union-sponsored product conversion plans have not always been so thoroughly resisted. The plan put forth by the United Auto Worker's Research Division for the "reindustrialization" of Detroit has become a focus for city and state initiatives. The plan stems from the work of Dan Luria and Jack Russell, who have attempted to look at the special industrial facilities, labor force, and market position of Detroit and plan for product manufacture that would be specifically adapted to Detroit's closed plants and laid-off workers.[9]

A second entry point for economic conversion in plant closing discussions is during negotiations over community planning agreements. Local governments eager for new industrial development often provide significant incentives to location-shopping corporate developers. To ask for some corporate agreement in return is increasingly considered responsible community development practice. Often such agreements may require firms to provide some land use amenities or a certain number of job openings for local residents. But, equally, communities could negotiate for prenotification of planned closures and the ability to work with management in formulating new product lines or funding potential plant purchases. This is not as extreme as it sounds. A recent agreement signed between the United Electrical, Radio and Machine Workers (UE), the Oakland Plant Closing Project, and the City of Vaccaville, California, requires that future corporations locating in Vaccaville must sign affirmative action agreements, must recognize the UE if the plant was relocated from previously unionized location, and must provide a one-year prenotification on a future closure plus a willingness to negotiate with the city and the workers over the future of the plant.[10]

Finally, economic conversion arguments in plant closing struggles are useful in advancing experiments in worker buy-outs. Hyatt-Clark Industries in Clark, New Jersey, provides a recent example. A General Motors (GM) facility since 1938, the plant made only roller bearings for the parent company. Contemplating a limited future in rear-wheel-drive roller bearings, General Motors announced in 1980 its intention to sell or close the plant. Local management, equally surprised as the workers, soon joined with representatives of the strong United Auto Workers Local 736 to consider new orders or products for the plant. This joint labor–management committee served as a vehicle for advocating an employee purchase plan when in 1981 General Motors did finally announce its decision to close. Convinced that there was sufficient viability in the market for continued success, the joint committee sought local support a union loan of $5 million, and federal grants. Failure to secure the loan or grants led the committee back to General Motors to cut a deal. The deal reduced wages and assumed liability for the pension fund but gained from General Motors a $23 million loan and an agreement to purchase up to 80 percent of the corporation's previous roller bearing orders. Employees voluntarily contributed $100 each for a feasibility study, and in a testy vote in 1982 they approved an employee stock ownership plan. Today Hyatt-Clark employs some 1,100 worker-owners, productivity is up 80 percent, and grievances have dropped from a high of 2,000 pending to about three a month.[11]

At Hyatt-Clark, there was no product conversion, hardly even a market conversion—only an ownership conversion. So far the new firm is a reported success. Still, worker buy-outs remain difficult. Seldom is a parent corporation so cooperative, and frequently the sale is reported only after serious disinvestment—"milking"—has diminished the viability of the plant. Yet the concept of ownership conversion is important to arguments for reasonable advanced notification. Time is often a primary determinant in avoiding plant closings.

ECONOMIC CONVERSION AND WORKPLACE RIGHTS

The struggle around workplace rights is a second rich area for introducing the concept of economic conversion. From its early inception at Lucas through the shipyards at Bremen, economic conversion has engaged shopfloor workers and trade unionists in considering alternative products and in alternative methods of production.

The workplace struggle for control of work conditions, schedules and timing, discipline and protocol, and health and safety reflect a conflict over the rights of workers and managers. Grievances and contract negotiations under collective bargaining agreements often clash over such rights. Contract language and legal precedent stemming from the Wagner Act in U.S. law relegate a large proportion or work condition discretion to management rights. Yet workers, who enjoy basic democratic rights outside the plant gates, are not surprisingly resentful of their diminished rights inside the plant.

Indeed, there is increasing argument that expanding worker rights in plants is good for business. The growth of concern about worker productivity in the United States and Europe has led to various experiments in "worker participation" and limited expansion of worker rights. Springing from early experiments begun in the 1960s in "quality circles" and "quality of work life" reforms, the movement was advanced rapidly by management following the 1973 wildcat strikes at General Motor's Lordstown plant. At this highly automated plant a relatively young, well-trained and well-paid work force rebelled against the alienation of their work through a series of extensive acts of sabotage. Today, it is estimated that somewhere between one-third and one-half of the Fortune 500 corporations are sponsoring some kind of worker participation scheme.[12]

Most worker participation schemes have relied on small discussion groups for offering workers participation in management problem solving or in autonomous work groups that set their own work schedules and quotas. Studies of worker participation programs at Saab and Volvo do suggest that some expansion of worker rights does improve worker performance and job satisfaction.[13] Yet most of these participation schemes do little to change basic patterns of management control. The problems to be solved are only those determined by management, and the autonomy of work groups is undercut by the manipulation, coercion, and individualizing of the group supervisors.[14] Indeed, these worker participation schemes are often challenged on the basis that they are directly intended as antiunion strategies, either by replacing union functions or inhibiting union organizing. Yet, the idea has lingered that worker participation leads to improved production.

Recent business theorists in the United States have fed more fuel to this fire by questioning the effectiveness of American management. Robert Hayes and William Abernathy of Harvard argue that American managers focus too heavily on short-term financial returns, portfolio expansion, and product markets and too little on innovation, risk, and customer satisfaction.[15] Finally, there is the growing worker ownership movement advancing producer cooperatives where workplace democracy is central to production policy.

Increased productivity through worker participation and the failure of modern management are tenets of a proposition that fits neatly into the economic conversion argument. Where advancing worker rights is extended to considerations of the products produced or the processes by which products are produced, the potential for plant conversion is clear.

A further struggle around democratic rights in industrial production has centered around worker involvement in determining health and safety conditions in the plant. The long history of union efforts to effectively establish worker controlled health and safety committees laid the foundation for the activism of the past decade. The passage of the U.S. Occupational Safety and Health Act (OSHA) in 1970 created a central place for government standards and inspections but did not abrogate the need for local shopfloor monitoring and advocacy. In fact, OSHA simply provided an enforcement vehicle for employees willing to demand better and safer working conditions.

Few health and safety campaigns have been more thoroughly engaged by strong management opposition than the struggle around labeling of toxic chemicals in the workplace—a struggle over workers' so-called "right to know." Serious efforts to mandate labeling of chemical hazards in the workplace originated shortly after the passage of OSHA when trade unionists and occupational health advocates joined together to support rigorous federal chemical labeling standards. Throughout the 1970s, industry vigorously fought such efforts on the grounds that such standards would be costly and cumbersome to effect and that in many cases these standards would force firms to reveal trade secrets that would damage their competitive position. Unable to win federal standards, worker advocates turned to the state level where right-to-know bills were submitted and won in several key industrial state legislatures. By 1980 California, Connecticut, Maine, Michigan, and New York had all passed right-to-know laws. Because these early laws were all the product of labor lobbying coalitions they were restricted to labeling, record access, and training for workers only.[16]

Granting employees the right to know about chemical hazards in their workplaces is a significant step in advancing their democratic rights to workplace self-determination. Yet the struggle has been long and adversarial and, if it ceases with the right-to-know alone, it is incomplete. Knowledge about toxic chemical exposure can only be the first step in a several step process that permits workers the right to reduce their exposure through effective labor-management negotiations. The opposition of management to worker right-to-know laws is certainly based on a recognition that once workers know of their exposure they will want to change their working conditions. Such changes could be called economic conversion if they involve actual changes in the industrial production process. Such changes—whether involving the chemicals used, the machines employed, the composition of the product itself, or the type of product made—all involve basic economic questions of production. Economic conversion of an industrial process could become the step beyond right-to-know in advancing workers' rights.

ECONOMIC CONVERSION AND THE ENVIRONMENTAL MOVEMENT

The tragedy at Love Canal in the United States marked the commencement of a new environmental movement focused around toxic chemicals. The relocation of families away from the Hooker Chemical waste dump site was soon followed by the discovery of hazardous waste dump sites across the nation. Today the Environmental Protection Agency estimates there may be as many as 180,000 potential hazardous waste dump sites in the nation, and of those nearly 2,000 may pose a significant threat to human health.[17] Around many of these sites local citizens have organized into local advocacy groups. The initial issue may be a specific dumpsite or a chemical accident in a nearby plant or a proposed hazardous waste treatment facility. Once formed, these neighborhood organizations are continued and matured, promoting now national conferences and national newsletters, and becoming a growing component of the larger environmental movement. In February 1984 a national conference was held in New Hampshire to kick off a National Campaign Against Toxics. This new movement, like the plant closings movement, differs from the mainstream environmental movement in its class composition. Based in working-class communities and in factories, its actions are often more militant and media-oriented than the older environmental groups' bureaucratic and legal approaches to regulations and standards.

The European toxic chemical movement that emerged from an equally tragic toxic chemical spill at Seveso, Italy, is not as broad based in local community organizations nor as militant as its U.S. counterpart. But because of the closer ties between environmentalists and other activists, particularly peace activists, in countries like Great Britain, the Netherlands, and Germany, toxic chemical concerns are more commonly accepted into party politics and broader movements for change.

Dump cleanup, drinking water protection, and toxic chemical containment are often the first demands of citizens organizing around hazardous waste sites. People concerned about their own health and safety or that of their families look for remedial and compensatory action. But as organizations persist and as campaigns emerge at the national level the demands are more focused on preventive actions with a particular focus on processes of industrial production that require toxic chemicals and produce hazardous waste. Such a focus is known as source reduction, because it attacks the toxic chemical problems by reducing chemical pollution at its source in the production process. Source reduction can include substitution practices that substitute less toxic for more toxic chemicals, conservation practices that reduce the volume of chemicals required by more careful management, recycling practices that cleanse and reuse chemicals, on-site treatment practices that detoxify chemicals before they leave the plant, or exchange practices that sell wastes to other firms for reuse. Where source reduction involves production changes or, particularly, changes in products it can be seen as a form of economic conversion.

Examples of source reduction abound. In 1979 Ian Heath Ltd., a silver plating firm in Birmingham, England, took advantage of the inflated price of silver to install an electrolytic cell to recover plating silver from spent solvents. The unit paid for itself in eight weeks.[18] Allied Metal Finishing of Baltimore installed an electrolytic cadmium recovery unit in 1978 that reduced its cadmium effluent level well below the EPA standard. According to a company vice-president, "With the money I don't have to spend on chemicals to create a sludge and on shipping and land fill fees to dispose of it, I can pay back the cost of the reactor in a year and a half. Maybe less."[19]

Union Carbide, a corporation that owns a ferro-alloy plant in West

Virginia, once labeled "the smokiest factory in the world," spent years in court battles over pollution abatement. Then, in the late 1970s, as the corporate director of environmental affairs put it, "we got tired of always being the bad guys." Union Carbide instituted a source reduction program that included a materials balance audit of each plant and an aggressive pollution control program. In one plant that was discovered to be losing 20,000 pounds of materials a day, simple conservation measures led to a savings of $2,000 per day.[20]

Perhaps the most outstanding example of source reduction is the "Pollution Prevention Pays" program instituted at 3M in 1975. The "3P" program used product reformulation, process modification, the redesign of equipment, and the recovery of materials through recycling throughout its plants in the United States and Europe. The result in five years was elimination of 75,000 tons of air pollutants, 1,325 tons of water pollutants, 500 million gallons of polluted waste water, and 2,900 tons of sludge per year, resulting in an estimated annual cost savings of $2.4 million.[21]

These examples have not gone unnoticed. In 1981, California Governor Jerry Brown appointed a special toxic waste group to examine alternatives to the 1.3 million tons of hazardous waste disposed annually in the state's landfills. The report prepared by representatives of industry, government, universities, and environmental groups concluded that up to 75 percent of California's toxic wastes could be recycled, treated, or destroyed. The potential lay in simply converting current industrial practices.[22]

The environmental movement can pave the way for economic conversion campaigns in at least three ways. The first, source reduction programs in industrial production as a form of economic conversion, has just been considered. The second is the conversion of existing plant production to products that improve or protect the environment, and the third is the use of environmental policy as a stimulant for economic revitalization.

When new products are developed for environmental cleanup or protection, industrial plant conversion is often required. Environmental regulations create new markets and even new industries. The Environmental Industry Council estimates that the pollution control equipment industry, largely developed due to environmental regulations, is made up of nearly 600 new companies.[23] Michael Royston notes that between 1972 and 1976 the market for equipment and services to combat pollution expanded by 86 percent.[24] Many of the suppliers of this market are firms that have themselves undergone industrial conversion. For instance Boeing, the famous aircraft company, now manufactures silencers for motors, equipment for the recycling of industrial wastes, and a system for drying sewage sludge. Oil companies such as Exxon and Shell make the chemicals that help to eliminate oil spills at sea. The FMC Corporation, which has been in the courts for its pollution of the Ohio River, now markets equipment to treat the waste waters from steel plants.[25]

The third opportunity for economic conversion into environmental advocacy is where it advances macroeconomic policy. National environmental legislation and federal regulation can be used to spur economic development or to create jobs. During the economic recession of 1970, the Swedish government promulgated strict new environmental protection laws but also set up subsidy programs to provide 50 to 75 percent of the cost of pollution control equipment for older plants to enable them to meet the new standards. These programs created a significant new demand on process equipment and the chemical and construction industries. Because of the key role of such industries in the Swedish economy, these environmental protection programs were credited with up to 9 percent of the economy's recovery.[26] Japan launched an even more significant program in 1973, when a combination of stiff environmental regulations and broad government investment and incentive programs provided up to 20 percent of the post–oil crisis recovery.[27]

While the common conception is that environmental regulations destroy jobs by forcing closures of polluting plants, the aggregate effect of environmental policies is just the opposite. The U.S. Environmental Protection Agency keeps tabulation of such plant closures. In ten years the EPA has reported 153 plant closings due to environmental regulations. It is estimated this resulted in 32,000 lost jobs.[28] At the same time the EPA through its construction grants for sewage treatment plants directly contributed 46,000 on site construction jobs and indirectly an estimated 46,000 jobs off site during one year—1976—alone.[29]

A 1981 Data Resources estimate covering economic impact of federal pollution control since 1970 estimates that the annual U.S. unemployment rate is 0.3 percent lower due directly to environmental regulations.[30]

Where such environmental regulations have led to increased investments in pollution control equipment, in new products for environmental protection or energy conservation or in production process changes that yield the same products with reduced pollution, the outcome can be considered economic conversion. Industries that develop new products for new environmentally conscious markets provide a rich opportunity for the conversion of plants in declining industries. Luria and Russel in their plans for "reindustrializing" Detroit note several retooling opportunities in new energy industries.[31] The Green party in Germany is advocating the development of off-shore wind generation plants in the partially closed shipyards at Bremen.

THE SEARCH FOR COALITIONS

Many movements are searching for a national agenda and an electoral platform. The newer movements — movements around the environment, women's rights, consumer protection, nuclear power, and citizen action — seek in political party structures niches for their own issues. It is an ambivalent search, for many of these movement activists do not trust electoral politics or existing parties. Where in Europe the parliamentary structure permits new party formations such as the Green Party in Germany, in the United States new party formation is not a likely agenda, at least not now. Faced then with existing parties, many choose to play on a tricky tight rope, working with existing parties but not in them.

Yet there remain well-recognized limits of "single issue" movements. Political weakness and marginality form one pole, while the serious potentials for cooptation and continued disaffection of participants provides the other. For those concerned with broader structural change in the economy, single issue movements produce a fragmented political base and a tendency for myopic self-interest amongst activists. In forms reminiscent of the political climate of the 1930s, the emerging resolution of these conditions is found in experiments with coalitions and alliances.

In the United States coalitions are becoming a common feature of the political landscape. Often put together around specific legislative struggles or special events, coalitions link organizations and movements around common goals. Such coalitions have emerged around utility reform, condominium conversion, civil rights, wilderness protection, federal block grants, so-called right to know campaigns, and plant closing bills. Both the nuclear freeze and the antiwar movements are spearheaded by coalition structures. Coalitions make for strange bedfellows, but the real problem is that even such coalitions have limited longevity and provide little common ground beyond the immediate legislative campaign or demonstration.

The limits of these coalitions reveal the fragmented character of the current movement for change. Where the power people yearn for comes from united and common action, the most prominent ongoing campaigns offer only isolated avenues of struggle. The peace movement emerges separated from the labor movement. Environmental campaigns advance isolated from the civil rights movement.

Missing are the common themes that not only attract single issue organizations into coalitions but also unite coalition participants into common support for each other's struggles. Coalitions move forward and deepen political base when they emerge into united alliances of interorganizational solidarity. Such alliances require the discovery of common themes that transcend specific issues. Central to such alliances must be common targets and shared metaphors upon which to base demands. The common target that is emerging is the crisis in the economy. Thus economic conversion, as presented above, is a ready candidate for a common metaphor of action. Conversion connotes transcendence and redirection. Modified by the term "economic," it takes on a special meaning about changing the conditions under which power and wealth are distributed. Applying economic conversion to plant closings, environmental quality, or workplace rights suggests changing the way in which industrial production decisions are made.

The demand for economic conversion thus links progressive goals to struggles in the workplace and unites the workplace and the community. Economic conversion propelled by community organizations and trade unions advances ideas of greater democracy and increased working-class participation in economic policy. Whether economic conversion affects products, processes, or ownership, it offers an opportunity for shifting the balance of rights in plant management. Finally, as noted, economic conversion presents a positive and constructive approach to otherwise defensive and obstructionist struggles.

This conception of economic conversion draws common attention to industrial production facilities. This converted industrial production is to produce socially useful products. It is to do so without polluting the environment or endangering the health of workers. It is to be developed to support the economic stability of its community. It is to be conducted so as to engender pride, respect, and a sense of self-determination in its work force. This vision of economic conversion could unite many now separate movements. It suggests a common goal for many experiments in social transformation, and it suggests a real basis for a new industrial policy.

NOTES

1. Several exciting definitions of economic conversion are identified in *Economic Conversion: What Should be The Government's Role?: A Special Study*, U.S. Congressional Budget Office, Washington, D.C., January 1980.
2. Barry Bluestone and Bennett Harrison, *The Deindustrialization of America* (New York: Basic Books, 1982), p. 29.
3. Ibid., p. 31.
4. Robert Aronson and Robert McKersie, *Economic Consequences of Plant Shut Downs in New York State* (Ithaca, NY: Cornell University School of Industrial and Labor Relations, May 1980).
5. Sidney Cobb and Stanislaw Kasl, *Termination: The Consequences of Job Loss*, U.S. Public Health Service, Department of Health, Education and Welfare, Washington, D.C., June 1977.
6. Bennett Harrison, "Coping with Structural Unemployment by Anticipating It: The International Movement for Corporate Disclosure and Advanced Notification of

Business Shutdowns" (Unpublished paper for the Industrial Relations Research Association Conference, San Francisco, California, 28 December 1983), p. 10.

7.   *Economic Dislocation: Plant Closings, Plant Relocations and Plant Conversion*, Joint Report of a Labor Union Study Tour Participants, United Auto Workers, International Association of Machinists, May 1979.

8.   Harrison, "Coping with Structural Unemployment," p. 34.

9.   Dan Luria and Jack Russell, *Rational Reindustrialization: An Economic Development Agenda for Detroit* (Detroit: Widgetripper Press, 1981).

10.   Newsletter of the Coalition Against Plant Shutdowns, Los Angeles, CA, 1: 2 (August 1983).

11.   "An Experiment in Jersey, Workers Buy a Factory," New York Times, 27 April 1982.

12.   Charles Hecksher, "Worker Participation and Management Control," *Journal of Social Reconstruction* 1: 2 (January–March 1980): 79.

13.   See essays in Alan F. Westin and Stephen Salisbury, eds., *Industrial Rights in the Corporation* (New York: Pantheon, 1980).

14.   Leonard A. Schlesinger, "Supervisory Roles in Productive Work Systems," quoted in Hecksher, "Worker Participation": 95.

15.   Robert Hayes and William Abernathy, "Managing Our Way to Economic Decline," *Harvard Business Review* 58: 4 (July–August 1980).

16.   Caron Chess, *Winning The Right To Know: A Handbook for Toxics Activists*, Philadelphia, PA: Delaware Valley Toxics Coalition, 1983).

17.   U.S. Environmental Protection Agency, *Environmental Remedial Response System List*, Washington, D.C., 1981.

18.   Monica Campbell and William Glenn, *Profit from Pollution Prevention* (Toronto: Pollution Probe Foundation, 1982).

19.   Ibid., p. 48.

20.   Michael Royston, *Pollution Prevention Pays* (New York: Pergamon Press, 1979), p. 88.

21.   Toxic Waste Assessment Group, *Alternatives to the Land Disposal of Hazardous Waste: An Assessment for California*. Governor's Office of Appropriate Technology, Sacramento, CA, 1981.

22.   Environmental Industry Council material quoted in Richard Kazis and Richard Grossman, *Fear at Work: Job Blackmail, Labor and the Environment* (New York: Pilgrim Press, 1982), p. 24.

23.   Royston, *Pollution Prevention Pays*, p. 67.

24.   Ibid.

25.   Ibid., p. 81.

26.   Ibid., p. 82.

27.   U.S. Environmental Protection Agency. *Economic Dislocation, Early Warning System*, 2nd Quarterly Report, Washington, D.C., 1981.

28.   Quoted in Kazis and Grossman, *Fear at Work*, p. 24.

29.   Data Resources, Inc., *The Macroeconomic Impact of Federal Pollution Control Programs*, U.S. Environmental Protection Agency, Washington, D.C., 1981.

30.   Luria and Russell, *Rational Reindustrialization*, p. 22.

13

Conversion and Industrial Policy

David Gold

Industrial policy has become a popular term in recent years, although one with almost as many meanings as there are proponents. As the U.S. economy deteriorated in the 1970s, more and more people began to see that other nations, especially Japan, were successful with more government intervention into the economy, and greater government management of investment, finance, technology, and foreign trade.

The industrial policy debate has focused on whether government involvement in investment decisions, and in managing the transition from declining to expanding industries, would be more effective than existing arrangements, or would become a captive of the interest-group-dominated political process.

Two points have been lost in the debate up to now. Economic policy, whether in its liberal demand-side version or conservative supply-side manifestation, has fallen short in part because it has left investment decisions to the market and to the leaders of industry and finance. The social and economic costs of many of these investment decisions are only too painfully apparent.

Moreover, most economic policy schemes, including most versions of industrial policy, either ignore the negative economic consequences of military spending, or support the continuation of high levels of military outlays as a means of economic stimulation.

In order for economic policy to become more effective, it must confront both the issue of investment allocation, and the issue of converting from military to civilian production.

MACROECONOMICS FROM THE SUPPLY SIDE

Supply-side economics was supposed to cure the problem of stagflation by attacking both inflation and slow economic growth. The centerpiece of supply side economics was large reductions in income tax rates. With lower tax rates, people would work harder and realize more income from saving and investing. These greater incentives would promote the kind of productive effort and higher rates of capital formation that are needed to stimulate economic growth. At the same time, a reduction in the role of government, both through cutting expenditure and removing much of the burden of regulation from business, would improve the income prospects of both individuals and business. Added to the mixture, albeit for noneconomic reasons, was a third element—a major military buildup.

The recession and recovery of the Reagan years cannot, however, be attributed to supply-side economics. The recession was primarily the result of the Federal Reserve's tight money policies, while the recovery followed as monetary policy eased and consumer and government spending grew, the latter financed by large deficits. Typical of business cycle patterns, the recession was severe because of the degree of restraint needed to bring down double digit inflation while the early vigor of the recovery was a response to how far the economy fell during the recession. Despite all the fuss about tax incentives and deregulation, the Reagan program has operated via now traditional demand-side channels. As Nobel laureate James Tobin recently remarked, "the beginnings of the recovery...can be credited to Keynesian policies, however reluctant, belated, or inadvertant."[1]

The supply side tax cuts and deregulation program represent an attempt to stimulate production by first providing greater benefits for the wealthy and for business. This approach is consistent with previous economic policy in the United States. The Kennedy–Johnson program, for example, began with the investment tax credit and the acceleration of depreciation allowances in 1962, and the formulation of wage-price guidelines, designed to restrain the growth of wages. Only after these measures were in place was it possible to pass the famous large personal income tax cut in 1964.[2]

Economic policy in the United States has given primacy to the stimulation of investment via changing incentives. The government has shied away from policies that would have more direct influence on the timing and industrial and geographic distribution of new investment. While government has assumed responsibility for regulating demand by adjusting monetary and fiscal policy, it has left investment, production, and the entire supply side of the economy in private hands.

The Reagan policy is also consistent with past U.S. policy in its emphasis on an expanding military budget. There is substantial precedent for the military program to be used for economic stimulation. In the 1940s, in the debate over U.S. foreign policy, it was argued that substantially higher levels of military outlays would not only permit a more aggressive foreign policy, they would also provide economic stimulation by giving a boost to total purchasing power. During the 1950s, with military spending over 80 percent of all federal government purchases of goods and services, an increase in government spending that was designed to stimulate the economy would almost automatically be an increase in military spending.

The large proportion of government outlays devoted to the military has imposed costs on the U.S. economy, costs that become more apparent when military spending is analyzed in relation to the supply side of the economy. Outlays for the military can impart stimulation by providing a boost to purchasing power. Military spending, however, absorbs a substantial portion of investment and research and development resources. Because of such diversions, military expenditures tend to hamper a nation's potential for new investment and its innovation in new production technology. The demand-side impact is felt immediately while the supply-side effect becomes more important over time. The degree to which an economy benefits from military outlays may depend on its own pattern of development and whether alternative sources of demand stimulation are available. But the supply-side impact will show up eventually.[3]

INDUSTRIAL POLICY

While conservatives were formulating supply-side economics, many liberals began advocating industrial policy—a catch-all term referring to attempts to influence important segments of the economy, especially those concerned with investment, research and development, and international trade. The United States has long flirted with industrial policy, at least since Alexander Hamilton's Report on Manufacturers and the Gallatin Plan of the early 19th century. But this flirtation has been piecemeal, focusing on the problems of individual sectors and often with industry representatives dominating the decision-making process. The New Deal contained the last attempt at a coordinated industrial policy, and it was replaced by macroeconomic management.[4]

Today's version of industrial policy is an addition to, not a replacement for, macroeconomic stimulation. In effect, industrial policy recognizes that macroeconomic policy is incomplete and cannot effectively influence investment.

Advocates of industrial policy have been primarily concerned with two problems, the "deindustrialization" of the United States economy, and the decline in the ability of U.S. industries to compete in world markets. Barry Bluestone and Bennett Harrison refer to deindustrialization as the decline in investment in the economy's basic production industries, and the resulting loss of employment and disruption of communities. According to this view, the fall in investment is not due to any overall capital shortage, but to the fact that investment funds are misallocated— shifted away from basic industries and toward speculative investments, mergers, and investment abroad.[5]

Even the growth of high technology industries cannot produce enough to compensate for the loss in output and employment resulting from deindustrialization. High tech has been notably poor as a job creator.[6] The decline in basic production industries and the shift to high tech, moreover, have created economic and social disruptions. The shift to high technology industries has drained resources away from older communities, turning many of them into the modern equivalent of ghost towns. And it has created the phenomenon of the boom town, where social structures and economic resources are strained by a rapid expansion of production. Although most people prefer the boom town to the ghost town, both present problems of adjustment, and impose costs on some while others reap benefits.[7]

Industrial policy advocates attribute the decline in the ability of U.S. companies to compete internationally to a number of sources. Some argue for a shortage of capital; others that capital has been misallocated. Some claim that management has been too oriented toward short term profits while others, Robert Reich for example, have emphasized that U.S. management practices are oriented toward an older industrial structure, and needs to be more flexible in the coming age of high technology production. For others, the problem is the misallocation of research and development money. Finally, some industrial policy advocates argue that foreign companies have gained a competitive advantage from the industrial policies employed by their governments. Thus, the United States needs an industrial policy to be competitive.[8]

Industrial policy is designed to improve the performance of the U.S. economy by easing needed adjustments and improving competitiveness. The specific policies and institutions that have been proposed cover a wide range, and not all proponents of industrial policy have the same list of what needs to be done. One important theme is the need to improve financial mechanisms in order to increase the amount of money available to finance new, productive activity. Investment banker Felix Rohatyn has proposed that the government establish a financial institution along the lines of the Reconstruction Finance Corporation of the 1920s, 1930s, and 1940s.[9] Such an institution would be capable of lending large sums to companies in need of adjustment assistance, such as was the case with the Chrysler Corporation, and provide loans and direct investments for companies starting anew or entering new areas. A permanent government-supported financial institution would have the resources and the flexibility to move quickly when needed, and to seek out those areas that have the greatest long-term potential.

Chief among the areas thought to need government financial assistance is research and development. R&D is a classic externality—many of the benefits go to society as a whole, not the company or individual undertaking the expenditure, so there is a tendency for a private enterprise economy to spend less on R&D than is economically justified. The federal government has supported R&D, but federal spending in this area is dominated by the military and space programs. The weakness of civilian oriented R&D is one of the major problems industrial policy advocates seek to solve. In his recent book, Robert Reich pointed to the distortions produced by military R&D as a reason for needing industrial policy in this area.[10]

Beyond financial assistance, some people have advocated that the government develop institutions that can play a coordinating role in the economy. This could be largely advisory, in the form of disseminating information or exploring the basis for economywide consensus on policy issues. Or it could be more of a planning agency, with authority to influence how firms allocate their resources. The model most frequently referred to is the Japanese Ministry of International Trade and Industry (MITI), which combines advisory, planning and financial functions.

One of the key issues in the debate over financial and planning schemes involves who is going to do the planning. Many industrial policy schemes emphasize top-down planning. Key decisions would be made by small groups of people representing the primary power groups in society, with little or no input from democratically elected representatives. In the past, government programs have often been captured by the interests they were supposed to be regulating. If industrial policy formulation becomes the province of dominant political interests, it will not be successful.

A second key issue, but one which has not entered the industrial policy debate, is military spending. The growth of military spending in the 1980s will make it more difficult to institute effective industrial policy. This is largely because the military buildup is absorbing a high portion of the economy's current savings, and because military firms are using the same skilled labor, scarce inputs, and productive capacity that are needed for revitalizing U.S. manufacturing and generating the new industries and management structures needed for increased competitiveness.

Ironically, the Department of Defense is accomplishing its own objectives using many of the same industrial policy programs that are being advocated for the private sector.[11] The Pentagon has programs to subsidize company research and development, provide advance funding to help companies start up production, support research into new production technologies, subsidize new industries that are not yet competitive in private markets, and aid in the export of military equipment, among other policies. Such policies have helped the Pentagon attract the resources it needs for its buildup, and have given the Department of Defense substantial influence in shaping developments in key industries, such as aircraft, machine tools, and electronics.

The Pentagon's industrial policy has helped shift resources from the private economy, and is one of the forces behind the distortion of technology, and loss of competitiveness, in a number of industries. Moreover, the Pentagon's industrial policy has failed in many of its internal management tasks; cost growth, for example, continues at a rapid pace. The United States has highly sophisticated weaponry with high failure rates, unacceptable amounts of "down time," and extremely costly repair and maintenance. If cost and reliability is a criteria for measuring industrial success, the Pentagon has failed.

DOD industrial policy has been predicated on the continued expansion of the military economy. The Pentagon has shown little interest in aiding firms, communities, and workers who suffer when contracts are not renewed or military bases are closed. The Pentagon manages its industrial policy with a bloated bureaucracy, little success at instilling principles of efficiency, and hardly any concern for keeping costs down on a long-term basis. This is partly because the product, national security, is defined in a politically charged atmosphere and objectives often cannot be met without throwing efficiency out the window. But the defense bureaucracy has shown no interest in real reform. The Pentagon is a poor model for industrial policy.

CONVERSION AND ECONOMIC POLICY

Conversion planning provides a better model to work with. Converting a significant portion of military industry to producing for civilian markets would benefit the economy as a whole.[12] If history is any guide, the end of the Reagan buildup will be followed by cutbacks in military procurement and disruptions within military industries.

The last time military spending was cut substantially, at the end of the Vietnam War, there was also a recession. Unemployment in heavily defense dependent areas skyrocketed and with a national recession, unemployed military workers had few places to turn. Similarly, companies without new military contracts had few alternative markets.

The economic instability generated by sharp swings in military outlays is often added to the instability generated by the economy. This was certainly true in Vietnam. The burst of military spending occurred just as inflationary pressures were beginning to emerge in the economy. When the war ended, the sharp decline in military outlays came on top of a weakening economy. While the Reagan buildup provided some stimulation when the economy was in recession, the use of deficits to finance the buildup is putting strains on financial markets. Record high deficits threaten to cut short the expansion and create another recession.

If military budgets were reduced, there would be substantial disruptions, and the need for public action to aid in the transition. Many individuals who work in defense industries would need to be retrained and their skills applied elsewhere. Unemployment has been drifting upward in the postwar period, to the point where a 6 percent unemployment rate is now effectively defined as full employment by U.S. policymakers, and the upward drift has probably been understated. While it is theoretically possible for many individuals to move from military to civilian pursuits, it is practically quite difficult, as civilian jobs are in short supply.

Many people within military industries with skills and experience do not find their training useful in the civilian sector. The skills, and more important, the culture engendered within military industries is highly specific; engineers and managers work in an environment where achieving performance specifications is far more important than producing to cost. The ease with which cost growth is accepted by the buyer, the Pentagon, reinforces this style of work. Inefficiency is not only unpunished, it is frequently rewarded. While people experienced in this environment can be retrained, civilian firms have shown a reluctance to recruit such people, reflecting their assessment of the costs.

The people whose skills are more easily transferable, production and office workers, face a barrier in the form of high civilian unemployment. The people in more skilled occupations, who presumably should have an easier time since they face lower unemployment, confront a civilian economy that has become wary of their skills.

When military industries decline, it is usually the result of defense and foreign policy decisions. The need for conversion planning would emerge from a political decision to reduce military procurement. In the past, such actions have been taken with little prior notification for workers and communities and with no planning for alternatives to replace the income generated by the defense business. Similarly, military base closings have usually been disruptive for the community in question. Again, the social costs created by the government action suggest that there are benefits to be gained from a more rational approach to the problem.

In the context of possible military spending cuts, there would be a choice between restructuring military industry producers, or managing their demise: can new processes and products be found to utilize existing facilities and labor skills, or should there be a fresh start?

The emphasis in conversion planning has been on alternative use—finding economically viable substitutes for military production. In some cases, finding alternative uses for military production facilities and for the existing skills of military industry workers may be possible. In many instances, however, since military production is so highly specialized, retraining of workers and reconstruction of facilities needs to be the primary objective.

Conversion planning is best seen as a means of dealing with declining industries in the defense sector. Thus, conversion is a special case of the more general industrial policy concerned with declining industries and communities, allocating investment, retraining labor, and fostering long-term competitiveness.

The postVietnam experience and prospectively substantial cuts in military budgets raise a basic dilemma. Reducing military outlays may be healthy for an economy over time as civilian activities grow. Initially, however, the loss of purchasing power is very damaging. Policies designed to ease the adjustment are needed, as are monetary and fiscal policies that are aimed at keeping demand and employment as high as possible.

As discussed above, economic policy in the United States has favored programs that place investment stimulation at the head of the list. This was the policy of Kennedy, Johnson, and Carter, as well as of Nixon, Ford, and Reagan. In addition to direct aid for investment, this approach has included policies for keeping costs down, such as wage-price guidelines (Kennedy), wage-price controls (Nixon), and deregulation (Carter and Reagan). The problem with trying to keep costs down, especially labor costs, is that payments to labor represent both costs of doing business for the individual firm, and income for a majority of the population. Keeping labor costs down slows the growth of income and since income is the primary determinant of consumption, it slows the growth of total demand. Thus, a macroeconomic policy that places investment incentives and wage restraints at the head of the list is a macroeconomic policy that is going to run out of demand. Increasingly, the economy would have to use higher deficits and easier credit to stimulate purchasing power, and run the risk of rapid inflation.

There is an alternative. A stimulative macroeconomic policy emphasizing growing wages is one that would be less likely to run out of steam on the demand side. There can be no doubt that investment is needed to sustain growth since it is through investment that we expand productive capacity, increase productivity, and generate more employment. But the record of the United States since World War II indicates that demand growth precedes new investment; as demand grows, businesses see the need to expand capacity, and plan for greater investment.

The scenario which has consumption leading investment is borne out in the present recovery. This is a recovery stimulated by high levels of government spending with record high deficits and a monetary policy that turned easier in 1982, while the recession was still severe. Consumer spending began to grow early in 1983, but it was not until late in 1983 and early in 1984 that businesses increased investment in new plants and equipment. The tax cuts, new tax incentives, and further deregulation pushed by the Reagan administration were not sufficient to stimulate an increase in investment; it was high consumption fueled by budget deficits and easier money that was the catalyst.

Stimulative monetary and fiscal policies have, in the past, contributed to inflation. Inflation occurs when production is unable to keep pace with the growth of demand. Shocks on the supply side, such as the oil price hikes of the 1970s, also generate inflation. But since the economy adjusts to such shocks, they are not likely to generate the same type of ongoing inflationary pressure as arises from excess demand.

There are several ways to moderate the inflationary pressure that can result when demand stimulation exceeds supply growth. One is to adopt policies aimed at increasing capacity and productivity, in order to expand production in pace with expansions in demand. Second, it should be recognized that a stimulative demand-oriented policy has its limits and no attempt should be made to push beyond those limits. Finally, an incomes policy should be adopted to keep growth in wages and other incomes in line with real growth in real output. A number of recent proposals for tax-based incomes policies are promising. Tax-based policies impose tax penalties in those instances where prices grow faster than targeted levels, thereby reducing the incentive to push for excessive price growth. They would be easier and cheaper to manage than the kinds of wage-price policies we have tried in the past.[13]

Industrial policy can be an important addition to monetary and fiscal policy. Among the problems that make monetary and fiscal policy less effective than they could be are the excessive reliance upon military spending for economic stimulation, the instability generated by fluctuations in investment spending, and the uneven pace of economic change, where some sectors experience wage and price increases while other sectors are still in the throes of substantial unemployment. An industrial policy that eases conversion from military to civilian activity, helps channel investment and R&D resources, provides relocation assistance, and so on, would make it easier to maintain stimulative monetary and fiscal policies. At the same time, a stimulative monetary and fiscal policy would make it easier to establish industrial policy, since it would help generate growing demand for products.

Conversion and industrial policy also go together. The problems that would be faced by an attempt to convert defense industries are similar to problems that have been identified in the industrial policy debate, and the solutions may also be similar. Conversion may be a necessary precondition for a successful industrial policy. At the same time, it may not be possible to have conversion without an industrial policy.

Conversion is usually seen as the relocation of economic activities away from the military and toward the civilian economy. In fact, conversion from one kind of economic activity to another occurs all the time, and much of the industrial policy debate is about how to manage conversion from declining to expanding industries. When we talk about conversion, we are in effect treating the defense sector as a declining industry. Many of the policies being advocated for declining industries in general may be applicable to conversion, and vice versa.

Conversion needs to be planned for; it needs to be funded; and it needs the participatioin of all who are affected. Planning occurs at several levels. There needs to be planning at regional and local levels for new activities, including infrastructure. There needs to be planning for skill transfer, retraining of workers, and programs to help workers move to new locations, if necessary. There needs to be technical planning for the reconstruction of factories, the redesign of machinery, and other aspects of changing the defense workplace into a civilian workplace.

Some of this planning can occur well before conversion begins; indeed planning should occur early since its absence will make it even harder to actually convert. It is not difficult to begin early, since planning is relatively inexpensive. For example, a modest program to foster research in engineering schools on technical aspects of plant conversion would cost very little, but would be extremely important in providing a basis for deciding what could be done with any given military production facility.

Advocates of conversion planning have long argued that planning should involve all affected groups. When a company has to close or reduce operations due to a loss of a contract, for example, planning for alternative uses could bring together representatives of the company, the union, and the affected community. Additional groups, either those that are affected or those with useful expertise, could also be included. Thus, in emphasizing that conversion planning needs to involve all affected parties, the conversion movement has explicitly raised the issue of how decisions will be made.

This is an extremely important issue, both for conversion and for industrial policy. If one wants to use conversion in the defense sector, one comes up against a closed system characterized by long-standing links between the Pentagon, Congress, and the defense industry. This is the "iron triangle" that Gordon Adams speaks of, that determines broad policy choices as well as specific decisions regarding weapons acquisition, and new research directions.[14]

Such closed decisionmaking practices also prevail in nonmilitary industries and make it hard for more than a narrow elite to shape economic decisions. Business leaders and financial institutions dominate investment decisions, and while they are subject to constraints determined by competition and the world market, they are under little obligation to consider the effects of their actions on workers and communities. For example, industries moving from the frostbelt to the sunbelt, or from the United States to other countries, are often given incentives to move by governments, but there is little planning or financial assistance for those left behind. Companies have fought such measures in the past, and have even refused the seemingly reasonable request for prior consultation or even notification to workers and communities, on the grounds that prior consultation would interfere with managerial prerogatives.

Democratizing both national security and the economy is desirable as the extension of a fundamental American value. It is also essential if more democratic results—greater equality within the economy, policies that can achieve growth without inflation, growth policies that can also address environmental issues, and a substantial reduction in the reliance upon military power—are to be obtained.

Democratization can begin with relatively modest steps: rank-and-file union representation on the boards of pension funds; community and regional planning agencies with elected representation; conversion working groups with representation from communities, workers, and companies. New economic development legislation can include provisions for greater public participation, and can emphasize decentralization of authority. There is already precedent for some of these changes, and these precedents can be extended.[15]

Conversion can only emerge out of a political process. Defense will become a declining industry only if we cut military spending, and reorient U.S. foreign and military policy. And democratization of industrial policy will only occur if there is greater acceptance of the idea that workers and communities should have some say in the investment and production decisions that effect their lives.

At the national level, groups concerned primarily with nuclear weapons and foreign policy issues, and groups working on economic and social justice issues, have a common interest in reducing military spending and shifting resources to the civilian economy. Military expansions are frequently justified, especially at local levels, as economic development programs—they bring jobs and money to communities that would have less in their absence. The reality is that communities would be far better off with less military and more civilian economic activity. The peace movement needs to sell economic redevelopment as part of its program.[16]

Similarly, while the need for reduced inequality and improved economic performance is recognized by many, not all see the detrimental link between the economy and the military. Transferring resources from the military to civilian economies requires changing our approach both to economic policy and to national security. The economic justice movement needs to confront the issues of national security as part of its program.

Both business and labor would benefit from conversion. In the short term, business would benefit as reduced federal deficits would allow lower interest rates, while the greater job creating potential of civilian production would benefit labor. In the long term, the freeing up of military-dominated technological resources would help generate greater innovation and improve economic growth prospects. The planning mechanisms that have been suggested to deal with conversion explicitly recognize this commonality of interest; they recommend joint labor, management, and community representation on planning agencies dealing with conversion.

Conversion occurs at a local level, in specific factories and offices, and communities. Yet changing military priorities and military budget is a national decision, and it has impacts upon the national economy. Planning mechanisms need to be coordinated, and planning needs to be linked to national budgetary and monetary policies. This suggests the need for greater coordination among those political groups working primarily at state and local levels around issues of economic development, and those whose focus is primarily in Washington.

A key issue in the formulation of all economic policies is the issue of who is in control. Both economic policy and military policy have suffered by being dominated by a narrow range of political interests. Some industrial policy schemes suffer from the same problem—they are top-down, elitist proposals which do little more than replace a corporate-dominated economy with a corporate-dominated government agency.

Conversion and industrial policy are part of the same political and economic fabric. Both seek to use government mechanisms to manage the transition from declining to expanding economic activities. Both seek to expand people's options, but both can only work if people are more actively involved in the process of change. The only way to change the priorities of the economy is to change the decisionmaking process, and the only way to do that is to get the people involved.

NOTES

1. James Tobin, "Keynes' Policies in Theory and Practice," *Challenge*, (November/December 1983): p. 5.
2. David Gold, "The Rise and Decline of the Keynesian Coalition," *Kapitalistate*, 1977; Alan Wolfe, *America's Impasse: The Rise and Fall of the Politics of Growth*, (New York: Pantheon Books, 1981, Boston, South End Press, 1983).
3. Seymour Melman, *Profits Without Production*, (New York: Alfred A. Knopf, 1983); Mary Kaldor, *The Baroque Arsenal*, (New York: Hill and Wang, 1981); Robert DeGrasse

Jr., *Military Expansion, Economic Decline,* (Armonk, N.Y.: M.E. Sharpe, Inc., 1983); Dan Smith and Ron Smith, *The Economics of Militarism,* (London: Pluto Press, 1983).

4.   Congressional Budget Office, *The Industrial Policy Debate,* (Washington: U.S. Government Printing Office, December 1983), summarizes the debate.

5.   Barry Bluestone and Bennet Harrison, *The Deindustrialization of America,* (New York: Basic Books, 1982).

6.   Henry Levin and Russell Rumberger, "The Low-Skill Future of High Tech," *Technology Review,* (August/September, 1983).

7.   Bluestone and Harrison, *The Deindustrialization of America,* Part II; George Sternlieb and James W. Hughes, *The Atlantic City Gamble,* (Cambridge, Mass.: Harvard University Press, 1984), analyze a recent boom town.

8.   Ira Magaziner and Robert Reich, *Minding America's Business,* (New York: Harcourt, Brace, Jovanovich, 1982); Robert Reich, *The Next American Frontier,* (New York Times Books, 1983); Felix Rohatyn, *The Twenty-Year Century,* (New York: Random House, 1984).

9.   Rohatyn, *The Twenty-Year Century,* ch. 7.

10.   Reich, *The Next American Frontier,* pp. 189–193.

11.   See David P. Leech, "The Bridge to War," *Inquiry,* (December 1983) and Jacques S. Gansler, "Defense: A 'Demonstration Case' for Industrial Strategy," *Challenge,* (January/February 1984) for two views on Defense Department industrial policy.

12.   Lloyd J. Dumas, ed., *The Political Economy of Arms Reduction,* (Boulder, Colorado: Westview Press, 1982).

13.   Samuel Bowles, David M. Gordon, Thomas E. Weisskopf, *Beyond The Wasteland: A Democratic Alternative to Economic Decline,* (Garden City, New York: Anchor Press/ Doubleday, 1983), pp. 295–303.

14.   Gordon Adams, *The Politics of Defense Spending: The Iron Triangle,* (New Brunswick, N.J.: Transaction Books, 1982).

15.   Bowles, Gordon and Weisskopf, *Beyond the Wasteland,* present a program for a democratic economy. See also, Martin Carnoy and Derek Shearer, *Economic Democracy: The Challenge of the 1980s,* (Armonk, N.Y.: M.E. Sharpe, Inc., 1980).

16.   William Hartung, *The Economic Consequences of a Nuclear Freeze,* (New York: Council on Economic Priorities, 1984).

14

Trade Unions and Paths toward Economic Conversion: European and American Contrasts

Christopher S. Allen

When conversion activists meet at conferences and seminars, in conversion groups within their unions, and at peace gatherings most of their discussions begin at the bottom of the economic pyramid—that is, at the plant level—and rarely move up. How, conversion activists ask, can groups use existing facilities and move away from military and toward civilian production? What can be produced, and how can workers at each factory best utilize their skills? Although this is a critical discussion, its approach is not sufficient: To be ultimately successful, economic conversion must go beyond the "one firm–one union" plant level and grapple with sector-wide, region-wide, and/or nationwide issues.

Whether in the form of extended unemployment compensation for dislocated workers, retraining and job matching programs for deskilled workers, research and development studies to determine feasible non-military products, or targeting investment capital to create socially needed and job producing employment, programmatic and coordinated government response is crucial. In mapping ways of moving from one sector to another active state involvement is key—especially when conversion activists counter the criticism of those who claim that conversion is "anti-jobs."

Despite this clear mandate for explicit public sector involvement many officials of American labor unions are reluctant to embrace government interference on the subject of conversion, not to mention on the more general issue of industrial policy. In spite of the increasing enthusiasm by some of the AFL-CIO leadership for increased business-labor-government cooperation, rank and file American unionists have shown considerable antipathy toward a strong government role in any restructuring of the American economy. When compared to their European union counterparts, this absence of pressure for strong state involvement is quite striking. The organized European working class has shown a much more forthright endorsement of the concept of public sector participation on both industrial policy and, in some cases, conversion.

In their relationships with employers in the workplace, American unions also have achieved fewer collective bargaining successes than have their European counterparts. To be sure, American labor has strongly challenged the positions of its employers at various times during its history, particularly in achieving wage and fringe benefit increases. Yet not only has European labor used a similar type of "defensive militance" to protect its previously won gains, it has also used innovative militance to go much further in challenging the management prerogatives of European employers.

What is responsible for this fundamental difference between European and American unions? What is its manifestation in the political and labor market arenas? And given this difference, what obstacles does it present as industrial dislocation may force American unions to give greater consideration to conversion as a possible avenue for economic regeneration?

COMPARATIVE PERSPECTIVES

The European "Rule"

Although both the United States and Western Europe share similar levels of economic development, their respective union movements have historically had very different views of the state's role in the economy and of what they, as trade unions, could expect from it. In the simplest of terms, the European working class has always seen the state as *potentially* "us" whereas the organized American working class has shown a much greater propensity to view the state as "them."[1] Two interrelated elements help explain this difference: European trade unions draw their more interventionist perspective from both the distinctive patterns of European industrialization and from the socialist ideology that underlay the formation of the organized labor movement.

Industrialization in continental Europe took place within a framework very different from the American context. The persistence of feudal elements in most European countries (Britain excepted) well into the nineteenth century dramatically retarded the emergence of the individual entrepreneur as a major economic actor.[2] Moreover, the traditional fusion of both political and economic power in the hands of feudal lords created a familiarity with (if not an acceptance of) the state's role in economic growth.³ Secondly, slower economic development at that time in most of Europe meant that any attempts to follow the laissez-faire model of a multifirm and gradually evolving textile industry would run directly up against a mature British sector that was already established on world markets.⁴ Thirdly, by the middle of the nineteenth century it seemed increasingly unlikely that spontaneous industrial growth would generate sufficient capital for continental European economic development.⁵ In short, if continental Europe wished to compete with the leaders of the world economy—Britain and, later, the United States—it could not afford to wait for the free market to extend a helping unseen hand.

These European countries required a different path of development. First, growth could not evolve in a leisurely or haphazard fashion. Careful evaluation and planning that determined which sectors offered the best opportunity for rapid economic development was needed. Secondly, if individual entrepreneurs were unable to generate the massive amounts of needed capital, they would have to find other investment sources. This, then, explains why European states became so involved in generating investment capital both through public funds and through close cooperation between the state and, in some cases, increasingly powerful investment banks.⁶

In order to industrialize rapidly European capitalists and political leaders in the late nineteenth century also needed one other crucial factor of production—namely, a working class. In some countries this required the movement of, within one or two generations, a substantial portion of the population from an agriculturally based economy to an industrially based one. This rapid dislocation of centuries-old patterns of life, combined with the lack of any substantial political democracy for most of the nineteenth century, helped produce a socialist movement and offered it the opportunity of mobilizing working-class support for an ideology that combined both economic and political goals.⁷

Not surprisingly, European workers also formed trade unions that were much more ideologically based than their American counterparts. Strengthened in part by a much more strategic ideological perspective, by unions organized more along industrial rather than craft lines, and by deflecting efforts at cooptation through the social insurance schemes of political leaders like Bismarck, the organized European working class developed a greater sense of its own strength. More importantly, it also realized that the use of state power was not just a one-way street. If, by controlling state power, capital could achieve its goals, so too the European left saw the state as a prize to be captured and thereby to attain its objectives.⁸

As the political franchise was extended from the bourgeois to the working classes during the early twentieth century (largely prodded by the socialist left), the European trade unions and their political party allies realized that the state was just one more arena for struggle with the industrialists and their allies. If the "proper" party could gain control of political institutions, they could then combine their power in the workplace with their newly attained political power and create a much more just and humane world for the working class.[9]

As the post-1975 years have challenged the European working class in the form of structural unemployment, technological change, and capital flight, the labor movement has not turned against the state in principle. It may think that the "wrong" party may be in power, but it does not reject the possibility of the state (in the "correct" hands) creating the industrial policies that will help overcome these economic obstacles. Among the most significant proposals from the European unions during the past ten years have been initiatives that would combine a "humanized" work environment with controls on private capital investment (in some cases using union-controlled wage earner funds) thereby attempting to create both growth and equity. The European working class carries on the legacy of the state as "us" because it still reinforces the public, collectivist viewpoint that has imbued the European left for over a century.

The American "Exception"

The development of capitalism in the United States has taken place in an entirely different context. In America there was no feudalism, no titled nobility to monopolize its control over small parcels of territory.[10] Instead, land was easily available (often given to "freemen" in the form of king's grants). In contrast to Europe, American responses to the satisfaction of economic needs took place on individualistic terms. If land was to be settled, if food was to be grown, if game was to be hunted, the yeoman farmer had to do it himself.[11] In addition, these economic arrangements did not create the impression of a fusion of economic and political power. In fact, the American colonial experience and subsequent revolution were expressly a revolution *against* centralized political power. The revolution, moreover, conferred on the American citizen democratic rights that Europeans were not to attain for over a century.[12]

Thus, from the late eighteenth century, the development of American capitalism was characterized by the prominent role of the individual entrepreneur, small firms in highly competitive markets, the formation of capital almost exclusively via retained earnings, and a trial and error style of capitalism. In America, the role of the free market thereby determined which sectors would be developed, and at what pace. Concentrating on the individual satisfaction of domestic consumer needs via such industries as textiles and leather generated the profits that then served as the base for future investment in more capital intensive sectors such as coal and steel. Most importantly, because this process took place gradually, it seemed governed more by a Smithian "unseen hand" rather than by the "intrusive" intervention of the state.[13]

As industrialization took off[14] during the mid- and late nineteenth century, the legacy of an individualistic and free market-dominated society reinforced the notion that defined who were—and who were not—considered appropriate economic actors. Moreover, individual mobility, which continued well after the official closing of the Western frontier in 1900, bountiful natural resources, and a domestic market largely isolated from competitive economic pressures until the twentieth century all gave American capitalists great comparative advantage.[15] Unlike their European counterparts, American entrepreneurs were never forced to rely on the government to stimulate economic growth openly and programmatically.

The contrasting strategic views between Europeans and Americans regarding state involvement in the economy can be seen concretely in the respective responses to the formation of monopolies and cartels at the turn of the century. Many Europeans argued that concentrated economic power should be nationalized in order that growing private power could be brought under public control, thereby benefiting the entire society. The American position was generally one of antitrust, that the state should break up these powerful economic forces and return to a simpler age of competitive market capitalism.[16] It is a telling example of the strength of the individualistic, free market conception of society that many in the United States failed to see that the very process of growth and development of capitalism led to the formation of these monopolies and cartels.

Conventional wisdom in America then considers the state a mere "night watchman". Yet in sharp contradiction to this view, the American government has, for at least 150 years, repeatedly intervened in the economic arena. Nineteenth-century government support for the building of the canal and railroad networks, funding of the land grant universities located in the country's heartland, and tax policies that supported and reinforced the tradition of individually held private property are all examples of the public sector's influence on economic affairs.[17]

Partially sanctioned state involvement also continued during the twentieth century. Again examples abound—the Progressive movement, the War Industries Board during World War I, the New Deal, the interstate highway system, the Great Society, and even Ronald Reagan's non-industrial policy of tax breaks for the rich. The state's active participation, however, is consistently unacknowledged. Even when political leaders openly admit they are using the state to achieve particular economic ends, they insist that they are only temporary measures and for limited and specific purposes.

In America, as in Europe, capitalists also needed a working class to industrialize rapidly during the nineteenth century. Rather than recruiting culturally homogeneous ex-peasants, American employers relied primarily on successive waves of ethnically diverse immigrants, as well as on the exploitation of both blacks and native Americans. The open immigration pattern of the nineteenth century (itself a form of industrial policy) proved a tremendous boon to American industry since it guaranteed both an abundant work force as well as growing markets for the goods that this system produced.

While necessary for U.S. capitalists, these and other developments presented major obstacles to the formation of a cohesive organized labor movement.[18] Employers used ethnic differences as a barrier to working-class solidarity at the most basic level. The more gradual American industrialization process also created a trade union structure organized along smaller, craft lines rather than on a larger, industrial basis. These earlier craft workers often had real control over the process of production but tended to see this control in individualistic terms. It was much more common, for example, for some of these skilled craft workers to rise from their class and become entrepreneurs themselves than to rise with their class and band together to establish cooperatives. Large firms replaced smaller ones as the dominant actors in the American economy in the early twentieth century, however, and undermined much of this craft tradition (individualistic as it was). Prior to industrialization, the existence of political suffrage for white males (the core of the working class) denied the American labor movement the opportunity to link economic oppression with political nonrepresentation as the Europeans had so successfully done.[19] The pursuit of goals in both the political and economic arenas proved mutually reinforcing for European unions and thereby allowed them to focus their attention much more explicitly on the state as a locus of real power.

The continued impact of individualism and geographical mobility are perhaps the most significant reasons that explain the lack of a unified U.S. labor movement and the great unwillingness of American workers to rely explicitly on the state for collective, public goods. During the late nineteenth and early twentieth century Easterners flocked West in search of the frontier, rural inhabitants streamed to the cities as the structure of both agriculture and industry rapidly changed, waves of European and Asian immigrants arrived in search of work, and many earlier European arrivals found that the streets were not, in fact, all paved with gold and repatriated.[20] Thus, turn of the century American society was in a state of constant flux and turmoil. Most American unions found that this process destroyed the social continuity European unions had used to create a vibrant and permanent working-class culture. Studies done of New England factory towns at the turn of the century that matched census data from one decade to the next showed turnover rates in working-class neighborhoods between 65 percent and 75 percent.[21]

In America the escape route of individual mobility undercut fragmentary attempts by some unions and socialist political parties to develop collective responses in either the labor market or political arenas. What little collective radicalism that did emerge was overshadowed by the individual radicalism personified by the character Mac in the first volume of Dos Passos's trilogy, *U.S.A.*[22] When confronted with oppression, this character neither showed sufficient patience nor received adequate support from other workers for comprehensive collective solutions. Continually on the move, in search of "revolution," he never remained in one place long enough to undertake the hard and necessary struggle.

This individualism also adversely affected the pre-New Deal performance of the craft-based AFL unions. Because they were not forced to work for voting rights in the political arena, American unions—encouraged by American capitalism's apparent ability to continue to deliver the goods—tended to concentrate on wage issues in the economic arena.[23] And because their organizational tradition emphasized the individual, specialized skills of the craftsman, many American unions merely considered themselves an assembly of individuals who could attain higher wages by bargaining with their employer at the same time. Unions, in fact, often viewed each other—not their employer—as the opposition, and several unions in one plant might try to outbid each other to see which would receive the highest settlement.

However, the emergence at the same time of a mass production-based form of capitalism, increasing union militance, and the arrival of the New Deal in the United States partially changed the framework of American industrial relations. By the 1930s, employers wanted to "Taylorize" their production process by standardizing operations in a way that broke down all manufacturing operations to their simplest form.[24] The employers' goal was larger production runs, which meant both lower costs and higher profits. They used these economies of scale at first to fulfill World War II production needs and later to satisfy the booming postwar domestic market.

Yet in order to achieve this fundamental restructuring of the labor process, American capitalists required a work force that was both adequately large and sufficiently dependable. At a time when the labor movement showed its greatest degree of militance, as evidenced by the CIO organizing drives of the 1930s, this challenge represented a substantial threat to industrialists' ability to operationalize their new pattern of production.[25] A deal was struck however in the 1930s between labor and capital in the United States: In return for the labor movement's surrendering to the employers its craft skill input into the manufacturing process and its embracing of the new regime of mass production, American industry gave certain benefits to its work force. Among these were union recognition by some employers of labor's right to bargain collectively (encouraged by the New Deal's Wagner Act), increased wages, and a growing package of fringe benefits.

The militant union organizing of the 1930s had at last provided the labor movement with a certain collective identity that it had always lacked, although most of the American union movement still saw itself primarily as an organization whose primary function was to attain higher wages and benefits. At the time, however, given the depths of the depression, such union strategies made great sense. In fact, of great strength for the union movement then was the fact that their specific material interest (higher wages) connected with the nation's larger economic need (Keynesian demand stimulus).

This confluence between the unions' needs and more overreaching social goals, however, lasted only as long as Keynesianism was the medicine for what ailed the economy, and this condition did not last forever. Yet while these characteristics were beneficial in the short run, in the long run they set the labor movement back by surrendering any interest in challenging industrial leaders' organization of the production process. Whatever collective militance it had acquired was directed toward wage bargaining. And as long as American labor movement leaders were able to bask in their "success" during the postwar years (due to American capitalism's providing increased union wages), such strategies made great sense.[26]

At the electoral level, major unions did not push for the creation of a labor or a socialist party either before or after the New Deal. Instead they "rewarded their friends and punished their enemies," and chose between individual Democrats and Republicans. The unions therefore had no institutional lever through which they could have major influence on political power. Without this formal link to the public sector, unions had far fewer possibilities to shape events than did their European counterparts. When the state did intervene in union affairs, organized labor often saw such action favoring the employers ("them") rather than the working class ("us"). For Europeans, state action more often than not brought such benefits as social insurance and public sector jobs. For Americans, state action often produced a squad of National Guardsmen or Pinkertons moving in to break a strike.[27]

The unions thus never developed a strategic conception of how the state could be seen as "us." For most of this century (with the possible exception of the increased political activism of the unions in the Democratic Party during the 1930s), American unions came to see actions by the state in the economic arena as primarily representing the interests of the employers far more than their own. In part, organized labor's view of the state became a self-fulfilling prophecy. By ceding the terrain of the public sector to the capitalists, the labor movement guaranteed that most public policy would tend to reflect the former's interests. In part though, this union perspective was taken with good reason. For despite the qualitative gains which the labor movement was able to achieve from the state during the 1930s, it still paled by comparison to those that European labor obtained.

Because action by the American public sector in economic affairs was not seen to be strategically legitimate no matter who made the demands, the unions knew that they had to rely more on their own strength than on action by the public sector.[28] This quality has certainly been visible in the many militant and courageous instances of opposition to repressive action by both the employers and the state. Yet because of the structural obstacle of a nonactivist state, the American labor movement has never developed a viewpoint that sees the public sector as a major strategic actor on its behalf. We have yet to see the American trade unions refer to the public sector as West German workers do to theirs by saying, "This state is *our* state."[29] And because the American unions never developed anything equivalent to the socialist philosophy of public control over the production process, they were never able to help "legitimize" the state as a major actor in American society.

CONTEMPORARY AMERICAN TRADE UNION RESPONSES

These two obstacles to concerted collective action—the fear of centralized political power and the strong strain of individualism that permeated the society—were not altered drastically when the 1930s ushered in both the New Deal and the hegemony of mass production industries over the previously dominant craft-based ones. Consequently, the way these obstacles get played out in the political and labor market arenas now require that union responses be seen in a more nuanced and differentiated way.

The Political Arena

In the past fifty years, support for such measures as social security, the Wagner Act package of labor law reforms, and some social welfare spending—particularly since this last item represented a source of jobs—would indicate that the American labor movement has begun to have greater enthusiasm for government involvement. Nevertheless, organized American labor (as a whole, and with some significant exceptions) has yet to see the state as a potential force for innovative and programmatic action—one that could possibly transform society and give the labor movement genuine control of its own destiny. At best most trade unions see the state as a service provider, one that can soften the rough edges of working-class life in an otherwise acceptable capitalist society. At worst the state is depicted negatively—what it does is "limit the damage" caused by particularly adverse instances of structural adjustment.

A comparative view of the steel industries in Europe and in the United States provides an example of this latter instance. When increased competition from lower cost Third World steel producers began to threaten the European steel industry, both the employers and the unions (at least on this point) shared a common vision: they would either increase government subsidies or nationalize the industry. Such intervention, trade unionists felt, would save jobs, maintain a sector that has been for many the definition of industrial capitalism, and perhaps help the industry and its workers make a transition to more marketable production.[30] Even if the two had different viewpoints as to what the precise form of this public sector support would look like, both the employers and the unions saw the state as a potential force for positive action.

Faced with the same crisis, management and unions representing the American steel industry joined to demand that the government establish barriers to the import of foreign steel that other governments were "unfairly" subsidizing. Given American management's official position on government involvement, it is not surprising that the steel executives were not pressing for either explicit subsidies or nationalization. What is surprising, however, is that the steelworkers' union also chose to join management in leading the charge for foreign import restriction and did not call for either job-saving subsidies or explicit government action to help them transform the industry, not to mention nationalization. The United Steelworkers of America union simply could not imagine that a fair response might include the same demands on the public sector made by their European counterparts.[31]

Since the onset of sharp structural dislocation in many industries from the mid-1970s on and the coming to power of Ronald Reagan in 1980, there have been signs of greater enthusiasm by the labor movement for more innovative action in the political arena. One has been the more active political role of the AFL-CIO. From the Solidarity Day demonstration in Washington of some 400,000 in 1981 to the formation of solidarity coalitions in various states to push for more labor-oriented legislation, to the early endorsement of Walter Mondale as the Democratic Party presidential candidate, the labor confederation has begun to move some distance from its George Meany-era posture. Another has been labor's participation in some states (Michigan and Massachusetts, for example) in government-sponsored programs to deal with the problems caused by deindustrialization. A third has been efforts by such unions as the International Association of Machinists (IAM) to sponsor legislation that raises conversion issues.

Although these examples show some movement by American organized labor to increase their activity in the political arena—trying to make the state more "us" than "them"—the dominant intellectual current still conceives of public sector power in an incremental and derivative sense. Following a well-established tradition, most in the union movement have yet to demand the kinds of innovative political action that would make organized labor's political responses a much more positive force for fundamental social change.

The Labor Market Arena

Perhaps the most serious obstacle that prevents American unions from progressively transforming the economy via conversion is their view of appropriate labor market action. Whereas American labor has always shown reluctance to confront the employer's legitimacy at the point of production, its individualistic craft traditions in the nineteenth and early twentieth centuries at least gave it a sense of pride in its creation of manufactured goods. Yet organized labor's post-World War II attitude in a society dominated by mass production had become almost totally oriented around its function as a consumer and thereby had lost what little sense it had of its function as a producer.[32] In so doing, the labor movement no longer acted for any larger social goal. Thus, people outside the labor movement could easily come to agree with management's castigation: that the labor movement had become a "special" interest group concerned with protecting the rights of a small group of organized workers at the expense of the unorganized and the society at large. Despite a similar embrace of demand-based policies in Europe, most of organized labor there also continued to challenge the principles of capitalism in both the work place and in the macroeconomy. Europe trade unions thereby spoke for the poor and the working class as they sought to protect the rights of all workers.[33]

To be sure, the same process of economic crisis was beseting the European trade union movement, but their response was much better targeted to the shortcomings of the employers. From "Humanization of Work" programs to increased attempts at worker control in the factory and on the boards of directors, to demands that investment be directed in ways that would create employment, to the use of pension fund capital to create more jobs, the European unions were far more willing to challenge the prerogatives of capital as the crisis hit during the mid-1970s.[34] They may have been much less successful in attaining these goals than they had hoped, but they at least realized that if something was wrong with the way that capitalists were directing the economy, then unions had just as much right and knowledge (if not more) to offer potential solutions.

American unions' inability and unwillingness to speak for all workers and all disenfranchised citizens proved most problematic, of course, from the mid-1970s on when American capitalism was no longer able to deliver the goods. Because it had ceded the workplace terrain to the employers it could not address their mismanagement of the economy. Some attempts at more innovative workplace solutions have been visible in unions such as the UAW and the IAM in the form of the unions' proposing solutions. And even the unionized employees at Eastern Airlines, who traded concessions for a large (if only a minority) block of shares in the company, tried to develop innovations in the face of management's failure to do so. However, most American unions in the early 1980s seemed to be spending more time in deciding what to give employers in the way of concessions and in fighting decertification elections due to the efforts of union-busting "consulting" firms than in proposing new innovations.

OVERCOMING STRUCTURAL OBSTACLES TO CONVERSION

What will help the American labor movement to overcome its antipathy toward the public sector and its unwillingness to challenge management's total control over the process of work—a challenge that is, after all, at the heart of conversion? If the labor movement is to overcome these obstacles and move toward conversion, mobilizing at both the political and labor market arenas, then it needs to undertake three fundamental tasks.

First, it has to learn that its problems do not stem from some imperfections in the market system. Rather they come from the essence of capitalism itself. Specifically, the labor movement must grasp that its present situation is not due to a short-lived cyclical downturn in an otherwise smoothly functioning economy. Labor's current problems instead are a clear-cut result of employer-led drives to deprive workers of those gains accorded labor during more prosperous times. Labor also has to accept that the crisis will not solve itself nor will it be alleviated by more of the same demands for higher wages.

American capitalism is changing dramatically. In the coming years we will see a new mix of industries, one that is being shaped by a heightened process of struggle both in the workplace and at the political level. American unions need to understand the dynamics of this system, and this will perhaps lead to the realization that, without a direct challenge to management prerogatives, their position will only become worse.

Second, it must create a producer consciousness to overcome its post-New Deal strategy of doing little more than demand higher wages. Based on the assumption that employer control over the process of work was the best and only possible arrangement, this perspective was deemed appropriate due to the years of long postwar growth. It now seems clear, however, that those "golden years" were the exception rather than the rule.

As evidenced by their failure to produce smaller cars after the oil crisis, their continued attempts to create a nuclear power industry, and their woeful record in systematically failing to modernize the steel industry, American capitalists do not, in fact, have a monopoly on all of the ideas for economic growth. If workers are not encouraged to feel that they often know far more about how to improve the production process than do the employers, they will continue to ignore the fact that long years on the job have created a huge reservoir of expertise that can be mobilized to serve society. Workers can indeed use their strength in both the workplace and in the political arena to propose solutions to economic crisis themselves.

Third, workers have to combine a renewed understanding of the dynamics of capitalism with a new producer consciousness to design and produce socially useful and marketable commodities. Using their own and outside expertise in both the private and public sectors they can help determine what possibilities exist for successful conversion efforts.

American workers have a great opportunity for shaping fundamental structural change. They still need, however, to address the formidable obstacles that remain in their way.

NOTES

1.　For a discussion of the "us" versus "them" theme as articulated by an American union, see James Matles and James Higgins, *Them and Us* (Boston: Beacon Press, 1975). Their account is of the struggles of the United Electrical (UE) workers during the 1940s and 1950s.
2.　See Tom Kemp, *Industrialization in 19th Century Europe* (London: Longmans, 1970).
3.　See Charles Tilly, ed., *The Formation of National States in Western Europe* (Princeton: Princeton University Press, 1975).

4.   See F. Fishwick, *A Study of the Evolution and Concentration in the United Kingdom of the Textile Industry* (Luxembourg: Office for Official Publications of the European Commission, 1975).

5.   See Geoff Eley, *Reshaping the German Right* (New Haven, CT: Yale University Press, 1980).

6.   See Fritz Stern, *Gold and Iron: Bismarck, Bleichroeder and the Building of the German Reich* (New York: Alfred A. Knopf, 1977).

7.   See Wolfgang Abendroth, *A Short History of the European Working Class* (New York: Monthly Review Press, 1973).

8.   See Maurice Duverger, *Political Parties and Pressure Groups* (New York: Thomas A. Crowell, 1972).

9.   See Carl E. Schorske, *German Social Democracy, 1905–1917* (New York: Harper and Row, 1972).

10. See Louis Hartz, *The Liberal Tradition in America* (New York: Harcourt Brace, 1955).

11. See James Oliver Robertson, *American Myth–American Reality* (New York: Hill and Wang, 1980).

12. See J.R. Pole, *Political Representation in England and the Origins of the American Republic* (Berkeley: University of California Press, 1971).

13. See Robert Green McCloskey, *American Conservatism in the Age of Enterprise, 1865–1910* (Cambridge: Harvard University Press, 1951).

14. See Joseph Schumpeter, *Capitalism, Socialism and Democracy* (New York: Harper and Row, 1975).

15. On the "frontier thesis," see Frederick Jackson Truner, *The Frontier in American History* (New York: Columbia University Press, 1921).

16. See Richard Hofstadter, *The Age of Reform* (New York: Vintage, 1955).

17. For an excellent treatment of this issue during the early twentieth century, see James Weinstein, *The Corporate Ideal in the Liberal State* (Boston: Beacon Press, 1968).

18. For the most concise treatment of this issue, see Jerome Karabel, "The Failure of American Socialism Reconsidered," in Ralph Miliband and John Saville, eds., *The Socialist Register 1979* (London: Merlin Press, 1979).

19. For a treatment of how "pluralism" undercut these possibilities in the United States, see Theodore J. Lowi, *The End of Liberalism* (New York: W.W. Norton, 1969), particularly chapter 2.

20. See Stephan Thernstrom, "Urbanization, Migration and Social Mobility in Late Nineteenth-Century America," in Barton J. Bernstein, ed., *Towards a New Past: Dissenting Essays in American History* (New York: Vintage, 1968), 158–75.

21. Ibid.

22. John Dos Passos, *The 42nd Parallel* (New York: Signet, 1969).

23. See Melvyn Dubofsky, *Industrialization and the American Worker, 1865–1910* (Arlington Heights, IL: AHM, 1975).

24. See Charles Sabel and Michael Piore, *The Second Industrial Divide* (forthcoming).

25. See Irving Bernstein, *The Turbulent Years* (New York: Pelican, 1967).

26. See Derek Bok and John Dunlop, *Labor and the American Community* (Cambridge, MA: Harvard University Press, 1968).

27. See Jeremy Brecher, *Strike!* (Greenwich, CT: Fawcett, 1972).

28. See Margaret Weir and Theda Skocpol, "State Structures and Social Keynesianism: Responses to the Great Depression in Sweden and the United States," in *International Journal of Comparative Sociology* (December 1983).

29. See Andrei S. Markovits and Christopher S. Allen, "Power and Dissent: the Trade Unions in the Federal Republic of Germany Re-examined," *West European Politics* 3: 1 (January 1980): 68–86.

30.   See United Nations—Economic Commission for Europe, *The Steel Market* (1969).

31.   See United Steelworkers of America, "The Administration Must Act Now to Save America's Basic Steel Industry," (Advertisement), *New York Times*, 7 June 1983.

32.   Sabel and Piore, *The Second Industrial Divide*.

33.   See Klaus von Beyme, *Challenge to Power* (Los Angeles: Sage, 1980).

34.   See Peter Gourevitch, Andrew Martin, George Ross, Steven Bornstein, Andrei Markovits, and Christopher Allen, *Unions and Economic Crisis: Britain, West Germany and Sweden* (London: Allen and Unwin, 1984).

15

How To Get Labor Involved

Gene Carroll

Over the past few years, labor's attitude toward military spending and the military economy has changed dramatically. As America's economic crisis has intensified, a growing number of rank and file union members from a wide range of industrial and public sector unions have become more skeptical about prevailing national security arguments and the idea that enormous economic benefits will automatically follow unbridled military growth. When the AFL-CIO surveyed its state and local leadership in 1983, 60 percent of those polled would not support any increase in military spending. Eighty percent of the respondents thought the Reagan administration was spending too much on the military. Even the traditionally hawkish federation executive council had to agree to support a military budget proposal smaller than that proposed by the President.

Twenty national unions (representing a majority of American union members) have gone on record endorsing the proposal for a nuclear weapons freeze, and eight have endorsed the National Jobs with Peace campaign. An increasing number of unions have begun to distance themselves from the AFL-CIO's positions on foreign policy issues. When the federation lobbied in support of the MX missile, some of the largest unions—the American Federation of State, County and Municipal Employees (AFSCME), the United Food and Commercial Workers (UFCW), and the International Association of Machinists and Aerospace Workers (IAM)—opposed the MX. The UFCW, the largest union in the AFL-CIO, sent a delegation to West Germany to meet with representatives of the DGB (the West German trade union federation) to discuss common trade union concerns and the role of West German unions in the peace movement opposing deployment of Pershing II and cruise missiles and Soviet SS-20s. Shortly after the delegation returned, the UFCW international executive board voted to oppose deployment.

On military intervention issues, opinion is equally divided. The National Labor Committee in Support of Democracy and Human Rights in El Salvador, supported by the Amalgamated Clothing and Textile

Workers Union (ACTWU), the United Auto Workers (UAW), the IAM, and the International Union of Electrical Workers (IUE), opposes military aid to that Central American nation as well as the conclusions of the Kissinger Report.

It is clear that this shift from traditional support for military intervention and high military budgets represents an opportunity to build the new coalition necessary to achieve both peace and full employment. Economic conversion is a key ingredient in helping forge such an alliance. Without conversion any successful nuclear freeze campaign would put 300,000 workers on the unemployment lines and would make passage of the nuclear freeze difficult if not impossible. Without a significant commitment to the kind of investment in new, socially useful production that would renew the economy, there is no concrete vehicle for economic reconstruction.

To create a real mass movement for economic conversion, labor–all of labor–must be a key actor. The questions then are, How do we get labor on board? How do we overcome the obstacles that stand in the way of organized labor's participation in the conversion movement, and how do we heal the breach between the American labor movement and the growing American peace movement? We can begin to answer these questions by looking closely at the conversion activities sponsored by a number of different unions.

Over the past two decades, several American unions have promoted conversion among their staff and rank and file members. One of the first unions to discuss conversion was the United Auto Workers. In 1969, Walter Reuther–then the union's president–testified before a committee where he gave an address entitled "Swords into Ploughshares: A Proposal to Promote Orderly Conversion from Defense to Civilian Production." Over the years, the UAW has reprinted his article and has also promoted conversion legislation. In 1977, the UAW worked with other unions–including the IAM, United Electrical Workers, and Oil, Chemical and Atomic Workers Union–to draft what was to become the McGovern-Mathias bill on economic conversion. It supported the Dodd-McKinney amendments to the public works bill in 1979. These amendments provided the necessary components of conversion–prenotification for impending contract cutbacks, income and health benefit relief for impacted workers, and money for local enterprise and local community plans for alternative production. (Although these amendments passed the House, they were not enacted because the House, that year, failed to pass a public works bill.) The UAW now supports the Mavroules bill for national conversion legislation.

The United Electrical, Radio and Machine Workers have also been very active in advocating conversion. The UE has conducted educational drives within its membership and has also actively supported all conversion legislation. The union is working with state legislators in Pennsylvania and Ohio on the Mid-West Rail Compact—an effort to develop a regional program for a railroad and mass transit system—and is also working to lobby Congress to create a program, on the scale of the space program, to rebuild the nation's rail and mass transit system.

On the individual plant level, UE members in the layoff-ridden railroad manufacturing industry are pressuring management at the General Electric's Locomotives Works, the Westinghouse (a subsidiary of the American Standard Corporation) Air Brake and Union Switch and Signal plants to produce equipment for a new high speed rail passenger system similar to those of Europe and Japan. Such systems would link Midwest cities and other potential high speed corridors and would push American producers into a market dominated by foreign manufacturers.

UE members at those three plants are also asking management to use their knowledge of rail technology and electronic control systems, as well as their good relations with the railroad industry, to take advantage of the natural paths created by railroad rights of way. The union wants management to make their plants new centers for the development and production of ancillary networks providing cable transmission, electronic mail, and other telecommunications links that would run along railroad rights of way. In educating members about the need to develop such technology, the UE has emphasized the necessity of increasing production competence in transportation systems. Ten years ago, for example, the United States led the world in the development of advanced passenger rail technology—magnetic levitation systems that run high speed trains a fraction of an inch above the track. But federal funding cuts forced MIT scientists to abandon Mag-Lev and switch to missile guidance research. Thus American workers lost jobs, and foreign competitors entered the domestic market. This trend, the UE says, must be reversed.

The union most closely associated with an active, ongoing conversion program is the International Association of Machinists and Aerospace Workers (IAM). The IAM began its conversion work in 1977 with a two-stage educational program. Before jumping into the nuts and bolts of conversion planning, President William W. Winpisinger and other union leaders recognized that they had to launch a campaign to win their members to the concept of economic conversion itself. This meant clearing up a great many misunderstandings. Misunderstanding number one was the defense worker's perception that conversion would immediately lead to a wholesale abandonment of any and all defense work and thus result in massive job losses. To explain that conversion was, in fact, a job-creating strategy that threatened neither national nor employment security, the IAM decided to poll its membership to find out exactly where its members worked so that it could then commission studies investigating the impact of the military budget on regional employment.

After discovering these basic employment facts and commissioning several convincing studies on regional employment impact of military spending, the union constructed an alternative program to demonstrate that more jobs are created from certain nonmilitary production than military production. Cautioning their members that they were not asking them to protest or revolt against military production immediately, the union suggested that *"whenever and for whatever reason* military production ceases (due to budget cuts, congressional cancellation of contracts, contract cancellations due to political events like the deposing of the Shah of Iran, or a corporate contractor's decision to move a production facility) a previously prepared plan for alternative production be immediately brought into play."

In spite of resistance from some IAM members (for example, military workers in nuclear defense factories who simply do not believe that there is any way to convert a radioactively contaminated, or "hot" plant, to alternative production and current increases in military buildup that take the pressure off many military workers), the union's educational and organizing efforts have produced a membership that supports the concept of conversion. Indeed, the union points out that its nonmilitary members who have been adversely effected by skewed national budget priorities have formed a strong lobby to urge military production workers to work toward more balanced protection options.

Although many engineering professionals traditionally scorn their unionized coworkers, the union has also encouraged the formation of alliances with engineers and designers within the companies it represents. The union asks designers and engineers if they have submitted product ideas that management has rejected and urges them to share these ideas with union conversion advocates. In May 1983 the union took the first steps in establishing a series of pilot alternative production projects. In the May issue of its newspaper, the IAM published an extensive questionnaire seeking product ideas and suggestions from shopfloor members. Designed to survey conditions in various production facilities as well as workers' interest in the conversion process, the questionnaire targeted shopfloor workers who consider themselves inventors and designers and who constantly use their skills to alter equipment and work processes on the shopfloor. After asking a series of questions about plant, equipment, and skills, the survey got to the heart of the matter:

1.   Do you think it is a good idea if each local union has an alternative production planning committee that might come to the rescue if the company closes, shuts down, runs away to another

       community or country, mismanages, goes broke, or installs new equipment and technology that puts large numbers of people out of work?

2.   Would you be willing to help your local union set up an alternative product planning committee?
3.   If the place where you work should close or shut down, would you be willing to share your expertise or ideas for alternative or new products with your local union's alternative production planning committee if it had one?

The union reported that preliminary results indicated wide support for the idea of conversion and that many union members were willing to share their product ideas. Building, then, on real shopfloor knowledge, the IAM plans to hold a meeting of its best designers and inventors. These union members will select several product options and will explore how best to develop them. These, in turn, will become the basis for ten or twelve pilot alternative production committees located around the country.

As all this union activity suggests, education is the crucial component of any attempt at conversion planning. The members of the vast majority of unions are, unfortunately, unfamiliar with the concept and philosophy of economic conversion as well as with the nuts and bolts of conversion planning. Thus, any union attempt at conversion planning must include a two-tiered educational thrust.

The first step in such an educational program involves convincing members that conversion is both a sensible and feasible employment creation stategy. A broad argument for conversion has to help workers understand how uncontrolled military spending affects their economic well-being and gives them less security and less—rather than more—bargaining power. Membership surveys and studies like those commissioned by the Machinists dramatically illustrate this point. So do summaries of a variety of statistics and reports available from any number of organizations. By making economic analyses accessible to lay people, union research and publication departments can explain the impact of declining investment in manufacturing and production techniques that would increase productivity (thus making it unnecessary for employers to seek profits through wage and benefit cuts); of plant closings; of corporate capital flight; of failure to invest in civilian product research and development; and of failure to maintain plant and equipment.

Consider, for example, the following figures revealed in a January 1984 report in *The Wall Street Journal*: "The pool of domestic funds available for new, private investment shrank to 1.8% of the Gross National Product (GNP) in 1983. This compares with about 7% of GNP available for new investment in the 50's, 7.5% in the 60's, and 6.3% in the 70's." When those figures are related to heightened investment in the military sector, such a brief report can speak as eloquently and persuasively as a thousand words.

Any analysis of the broader social impact of military spending also has to point out the dangers of the kind of reverse conversion—abandonment of civilian production in favor of military production—so prevalent in companies today. While workers may feel that increased military production will save their jobs, it in fact jeopardizes them. As more and more American companies abandon civilian production, American industry loses valuable production competence, and American companies are increasingly less diversified.

Because conversion is so intimately connected to larger economic issues and is a vehicle not only for dealing with problems created by the military contracting process but by general economic decline, it is essential to relate conversion to other labor struggles. The fight against plant closings and for plant closing legislation is one. The attempt to create a national industrial policy is another. Similarly, conversion can play a crucial role in the major battle against contract concessions in which every national union is engaged.

For the last four years, concession bargaining has been the rule rather than the exception in a wide range of American industries—from auto, steel, rubber, and trucking to meatpacking, mining, construction, and the airlines. (Military contractors—their soaring profits notwithstanding—have also jumped on the concession bandwagon.) Hundreds of thousands of union members have seen their contracts reopened or renegotiated to freeze or cut wages, defer or divert cost-of-living payments, reduce employer-paid benefits, alter working conditions, and eliminate premium paid time-off. During the first nine months of 1983, give-backs like these have resulted in the poorest contract settlements in the last fifteen years.

At the heart of this strategy is management's attempt to restore wage competition among workers, something unions have traditionally tried to minimize or eliminate through industry-wide organization and pattern bargaining. Now, the growth of nonunion competition and the dismantling or downgrading of national contract standards has enabled employers to pit union members who work for the same or different companies against each other—producing a scramble to undercut other locals— even of the same company-wide union.

Without the kind of concrete and practical employment-creation program conversion represents, unions will never be able to create the kind of unity needed to fight a variety of employer attacks. Conversion planning, then, can do much more than construct concrete production options that can be presented to military contractors or employers about to shut down a plant. It can help resolve the potential and existing conflicts between different unions and different unionized workers. It can begin to connect workers in military industries who are concerned about the vicissitudes of the military procurement cycle and workers in public employee unions that have been decimated by layoffs due to cuts in federal spending. And it can bring together workers in ailing industrial unions and those in thriving military production enterprises.

Conversion can help create such labor unity because it requires cooperation among various locals in an industry on bargaining and job creation programs. It requires interunion cooperation, if workers are to convince management to take conversion proposals seriously. And it will take cooperation between public sector and industrial unions if conversion planning is to involve the community and create a labor-community constituency that will support local, regional, and national conversion planning. Finally, conversion implies international trade-union cooperation if workers are to deal with corporate flight, multinationals, and the highly integrated global arms and international economy.

Conversion and trade-union activists who want to promote conversion, then, must be familiar with labor's problems and agenda. When approaching a local or national union, conversion advocates must find out what issues the union is concerned with, what their trade union agenda is, what their legislative agenda includes, and what coalitions they participate in.

Once initial educational programs have been launched, it is time to move on to the nuts and bolts of conversion planning. First, it is essential to convince workers that conversion can actually work. This means familiarizing them with workable conversion experiments in the United States and in Western Europe. Trade-union exchange between the United States and the United Kingdom, Sweden, West Germany, and Italy—where major, successful conversion experiments are taking place—are invaluable. In the summer of 1983, for example, the National Nuclear Weapons Freeze Campaign, National Jobs With Peace, and SANE brought seven high-ranking trade union officials—all of them involved with conversion in their respective countries—to the United States for a two-week, seventeen-city tour. In their meetings with rank and file union members, they explained how conversion works, and—more importantly—that it can work. Such living proof that conversion is not pie in the sky, and that it can take place in countries where conservative governments make national legislation impossible is invaluable.

Through these and other meetings, seminars, and publications (written for union members by union members), trade unionists can learn how to set up alternative use committees. They can learn how to go about assessing their skills, their plant, and equipment and to poll membership about alternative product ideas. They will need to find out how to enlist the help of technical, engineering, and design experts—perhaps from their own plant, perhaps from local community colleges or universities. And they will need to identify a pool of marketing specialists and legal advisers to help them determine product profitability, and—when necessary—consider how to finance and arrange a worker buy-out. Finally, they will have to make connections with community groups to assess community product and service needs and thus recruit community organizations, churches, peace groups, and environmental groups to the conversion campaign.

The South Shore Conversion Committee operating at General Dynamics' Quincy, Massachusetts, shipyard has, for example, been fairly successful in its efforts to win community support for its conversion activities. To get the community involved, the committee wrote a series of newspaper editorials and gave speeches at local community groups like the Kiwanis Club and the local church parish councils explaining how its attempts to create alternative employment at the city's single largest employer would not only benefit shipyard workers but the entire Quincy community. The committee's advisory included not only shipyard workers but a representative sampling of community groups—public employee leaders, clergy, social service workers, a black labor activist, legal workers, academics, and the director of the local poverty program.

When a controversial court case awarded General Dynamics $28 million in tax overcharges and interest—to be paid back by the city of Quincy—the committee immediately became involved in the city versus company struggle. The committee demanded that the city's repayment be earmarked for conversion planning and prototype development. This unconventional proposal attracted few proponents but did spark a debate among community groups and city councillors.

In order to convince workers that conversion does not jeopardize their immediate livelihood, it may be necessary to set up pilot projects that will establish models of conversion activity, rather than result in immediate plant conversions. Such pilot projects would teach workers that it is possible for them to take part in the production and investment decisionmaking process that goes on at their local plant. In military plants, these projects could concentrate on developing proposals designed to be implemented should their company begin to institute reverse conversion. In nonmilitary plants, they could prepare plans that would be implemented should the company propose layoffs, a plant shutdown, or a plant move.

This planning process would not only produce concrete production options that workers could implement whenever necessary but would also create the kind of producer consciousness that helps rank-and-file workers overcome their feelings of powerlessness. When many workers initially hear about conversion planning, their reaction is, "Sounds good, but how are you going to get the company to do this?" After having heard about successful conversion efforts in other localities, and other nations, after winning over a broad coalition of community groups, and after taking part in concrete conversion planning, workers may begin to be able to answer this question and at least see that conversion activity is possible.

The creation of this kind of producer consciousness is also a prerequisite if national union support for conversion legislation is to translate into grass roots lobbying campaign. There is no question that a mass mobilization of union membership could help generate the kind of political pressure needed to push through conversion legislation. Arms manufacturers clearly depend on union lobbying drives when they want to protect a threatened weapons system or get funding for the newest project on the drawing board. Imagine, then, how the same kind of energy could be used to support legislation mandating innovative planning and production options to replace both ailing civilian product lines and unneeded military product lines.

Any labor-community movement for conversion will ultimately have to include those members of both the labor movement and grass-roots community movements who are active peace campaigners. This means, of course, transforming antipeace movement attitudes within American labor movement, and antilabor attitudes within the American peace movement. While we have discussed how labor can use conversion to connect economic decline and military expansion, it will be equally necessary for peace campaigners to educate their members about the economic ramifications of the arms race and the need to construct a strategy that appeals to America's working people.

Unfortunately, when many peace groups try to introduce the peace issue to working-class audiences, they do it in the most counterproductive, alienating manner conceivable. Without any prior contact with workers or their organizations, peace campaigners will march up to an arms factory gate, and distribute leaflets criticizing those workers who "profit from the war-machine by producing weapons of death." When workers react hostilely to such accusations and refuse to take leaflets distributed by peace protestors, the latter respond with shock and indignation. How, they wonder, can American workers be so narrow-minded, callous, and reactionary?

Even when peace activists do manage to grasp the fact that they should initiate a discussion with a labor union before appearing, en masse, at a local armaments producer's gates, their lack of patience often jeopardizes what could be a strong, working union-peace alliance. When a group of nuns in the midwest began working with an international union committed to conversion work, the latter explained the need to downplay the peace component of the developing campaign and stick to the economic issues that would persuade workers to join the conversion struggle. After months of discussion, the nuns agreed. Several weeks later, however, the union was shocked to learn that the nuns had taken part in a large peace demonstration at the plant gates. Their signs and literature failed to link the peace and economic issues and stressed only a moral appeal that, once again, explicitly or implicitly, blamed workers for choosing employment in weapons production. When questioned by both local and national officials, the nuns said they felt it was more important to "alert the community about the kinds of weapons of death being produced in their backyard" than to build a strong labor-peace alliance. Needless to say, that was the end of their working relationship with the union.

Although the kind of impatience peace campaigners exhibit is understandable, their attitudes, nonetheless, reflect a failure of understanding and sensitivity. Coming as they do from middle- and upper-middle-class families, many members of the American peace movement do not understand that most workers are confronted with an uncomfortable choice—working in a defense plant or standing on the unemployment line. It is not surprising that a man or woman whose family depends on their weekly paycheck and who has no other options in life would choose the former.

Nor do many peace campaigners understand the pressures workers face on the job. When a defense worker refuses to take a protestor's leaflet, he or she may not necessarily be hostile to either the protestor or his message. He or she may simply be afraid. For if a supervisor or plant manager is watching, workers in some plants could jeopardize their jobs by displaying sympathy with peace or conversion activists. (This is particularly true of defense workers who work in nonunionized plants. Such workers can be fired or disciplined without just cause.)

Given the economic conditions prevalent in the country today, peace campaigners must also understand that to define conversion solely as peace conversion is a losing strategy. Getting workers to quit work at an arms factory is not a victory. It is, in fact, a defeat. If one worker quits, first of all, there are 300 out-of-work men and women to take his place. Moreover, when a worker committed to peace leaves a defense plant, the peace movement has lost a valuable, on-the-job ally who could educate his fellow workers and urge them to form the kind of alternative production committees that will really convert a plant to peace—peacetime production, that is. Thirdly, every time a peace activist suggests that "conversion means converting workers and getting them to quit," as one peace conversion advocate recently told a peace meeting, this merely reinforces working peoples' impression that the peace movement is anti-jobs and thus against the millions of Americans whose livelihood depends on stable, industrial employment.

If understanding is to replace the coolness, distance, and frequent hostility that currently characterizes relations between peace and labor activists, peace activists must learn to adopt new strategies that do not threaten but rather support union members. When peace campaigners are planning an antimilitary demonstration, for example, they could consider an innovative form of protest. Instead of heading directly for the factory gates where they are, in effect, confronting workers over production decisions that are totally out of their control, they might do some research to find out who owns the plant, who manages it, and what banks and insurance companies support it. Designing their campaign to target the people who really profit from war production, they could hold their demonstrations outside of these banks and insurance companies, outside corporate headquarters, or in front of the homes of owners and managers. Thus, they would accomplish their goals without alienating working people in the process.

To win workers over to disarmament campaigns, peace activists must also show that they are as concerned about creating employment opportunities as they are about cutting weapons programs. All too often, peace activists express anger because the labor movement has consistently failed to support the peace agenda. Yet, most peace activists consistently fail to support labor's agenda. When President Reagan used the employment equivalent of the neutron bomb against an entire union— the Professional Air Traffic Controllers Organization (PATCO)—where was peace movement protest? During the recent rash of plant closings, enforced contract concessions, and major strikes that are literally decimating American unions, where is peace movement support for workers' demands?

Just as the labor movement could provide the bodies and energy that would create a strong lobby against military weapons appropriations, so too the growing American peace movement could provide an equally strong mobilizing force in favor or workers' demands and needs. If peace campaigners began to demonstrate a willingness to support labor's agenda, this might have an enormous influence both on national union officials and local rank and file members.

One excellent place to begin is the current labor campaign against Litton Industries. One of the nation's top military contractors, Litton also is one of the nation's most aggressively antiunion firms. Because Litton totally disregards the nation's labor laws, the AFL-CIO and ten international unions have launched a campaign against Litton. They are asking the government to withhold military contracts from Litton if it flagrantly continues to defy the law. If the peace movement were seriously to consider joining the anti-Litton campaign—making sure to follow labor's lead and stress economic rather than peace issues—it could patiently build a working alliance that would demonstrate that peace advocates are pro-labor. By generating trust, it could then begin to educate union members about the peace issues that are the movement's primary concern.

Another important step toward building labor/peace alliances is encouraging peace movement support of national conversion legislation. If the American nuclear freeze movement were to lobby as extensively for conversion legislation as for nuclear freeze legislation—if, in fact, the movement would adopt a dual demand that legislators support both—it would succeed in taking the jobs issue out of the national security debate and create a strong basis for a labor/freeze alliance.

In many unions and committees, activists and committed workers are already demonstrating that conversion planning is a sensible "insurance policy" that helps prepare for the eventual outbreak of peace and protect us from the rapid transformations of an uncertain economy. They have demonstrated that conversion is a crucial bridge between the concerns of the predominantly middle-class participants in the peace movement and workers who currently have little choice but to produce the weapons of destruction that threaten us all. The struggle to educate workers and community members about conversion is not an easy one. It will take years of seed work and preparatory planning to convince corporate and government managers to take conversion seriously. But if we are to form the kind of mass movement that will prevent the nuclear and economic holocausts that are devastating and could devastate the planet, the conversion bridge must be built and must be continuously and ceasely strengthened.

Appendix A:
The Lucas Plan

Medical Equipment

We propose that Lucas Aerospace should:

1. increase production of kidney machines at G.E. Bradley's by approximately 40 percent, and look into the development of a portable kidney machine. We regard it as scandalous that people should be dying for the want of a kidney machine when those who could be producing them and working them are facing the prospect of redundancy.

2. in conjunction with the Ministry of Health build up a "design for the disabled" unit to look into, among other things:

    a) artificial limb control systems, which could use Lucas Aerospace control engineering expertise.

    b) sight substituting aids for the blind, drawing on the radar technology involved in blind landing systems.

    c) developing the "Hobcart," the vehicle designed in the early 1960s by an apprentice at Lucas Aerospace at Wolverhampton to give mobility to children suffering from Spina Bifida, which Lucas had refused to develop on the grounds that it was incompatible with their product range.

3. manufacture an improved life-support system for ambulances. An ex-Lucas Aerospace engineer turned doctor has offered to help design and build a prototype of this, using a simple heat exchanger and pumping system.

Alternative Energy Technologies

One of the basic problems facing society is the scarcity of energy resources. The recent energy crisis has brought home to many people the political and economic insecurity of our advanced technological society, resting as it does on fossil fuel energy supplies, access to which is limited. And beyond this there are absolute and finite limits to the resources that are available, and to the capacity of the ecosystem to absorb pollutants and environmental degradation without undergoing irreversible changes.

Consequently there is a need to find not only new sources of energy but also new forms of energy use. New, renewable, sources and more efficient methods of conversion must be developed.

Solutions to the problem based on nuclear power give rise to new problems of health, safety, and even survival. Instead R&D should focus on new sources of energy and new types of energy conversion transmission and storage. Such long-term investment in technological development would, in addition to its intrinsic benefits, help to reflate the economy; and the development of alternative energy systems would relieve the balance of payments problem by reducing oil imports and perhaps also enlarging exports of these systems.

The following are some proposals for energy-related products that could be produced or partially produced with the resources available at Lucas Aerospace.

1. Development and production of heat pump units. Heat pumps are potentially a very efficient and economical form of heating. They operate like a refrigerator in reverse. Instead of pumping out the heat from the air in an insulated cabinet, they absorb heat from a thermal mass (whether air, water, or soil) and provide heat for warming air or water in an insulated space (e.g., a house). Heat pumps do not generate energy, only convert it: They require fuel in order to pump heat from "cold" to "hot". But they can deliver up to three times more heat than would be produced if the fuel was burnt conventionally. Local authorities would be interested in heat pumps to provide cheaper heating for council tenants. Lucas used to produce electric heat pumps itself, but this product line was not developed.

2. Development of existing solar-cell technology (Lucas Marine are marketing solar cells for use in boats and caravans) and flat-plate solar collectors to provide for low-energy housing. Lucas workers' main contribution would be likely to be in the associated electrical and mechanical control equipment; for example, switching circuits and fluid control systems.

3. Development of windmills both for electricity generation and direct (friction) heating, using Lucas Aerospace's expertise in aerodynamics. We suggest ducted-fan windmills and pneumatic power transmission systems as possibilities, together with rotor speed regulation systems.

4. Development of fuel cell technology. Fuel cells, widely used in spacecraft, work like electrolysis in reverse: Hydrogen or natural gas is

fed into a chemical cell that produces electricity. Units for domestic use had already been developed in the United States.

5. A flexible power pack that could provide power for a wide range of purposes (e.g., generating electricity, pumping water, lifting equipment, and providing compressed air for pneumatic tools). It has a basic prime mover that could run on a wide range of fuels including naturally available materials, methane gas, and so on. It also has a specially designed variable-speed gearbox so that it is possible to vary the output speed over a very wide range. This power pack would be especially appropriate for people in many Third World countries. At present there is no such flexible pack available. Instead people have to buy different packs complete with different prime movers for each purpose. The Combine Committee sees the present situation in relation to power packs as an example of the neo-colonialist nature of our trade with Third World countries.

Transport Technologies

1. Road-rail vehicle

We propose the development and production of a complete wheel and axle unit for a lightweight coach that would run on road and rail, combining two important innovations. By using a small guidewheel running on the rail, with servo-mechanism feedback to the running wheels, the wheel can be steered along the track while pneumatic tyres run on the rails. As a result there is not the same problem of shock absorption as there is for traditional trains running on metal rims. And, therefore, it is no longer necessary to have the heavy, costly, rigid superstructure that has always been necessary to absorb shock. Not only does this lightweight vehicle make it easier to follow the natural terrain of a country in laying down tracks, it also makes these tracks cheaper and makes it possible to go easily from the rail to the road. This lays the basis for integrated transport systems and better transport facilities for remote areas. We propose that Lucas make contact with Richard Fletcher of North East London Polytechnic, who has been working on these ideas.

2. A new hybrid power pack for motor vehicles

The Combine sees pollution and toxic emissions from cars as a major ecological problem. It is also concerned at the expense and scarcity of fuel as further disadvantages of the traditional wasteful ways in which cars use fuel. Battery-powered vehicles are often seen as a substitute, but they have their own problems as far as normal car use is concerned. It is necessary to recharge the battery at least every hundred miles. Furthermore, it is necessary to carry a considerable weight of batteries. We propose a solution, drawn from the experience of the Ground Support Equipment

Group of Lucas Aerospace. This group has had considerable experience in the packing of coupled prime movers and generators. It has also developed considerable expertise in the silencing of units of this kind without greatly impairing the inefficiency of the engine. On the basis of this kind of experience we propose that a hybrid system be evolved utilizing the internal-combustion engine connected to a generator that would charge the battery that in turn supplies the power to the electric motor driving the vehicle. Initial calculations suggest a 50 percent fuel saving in such a hybrid. Such a system would greatly reduce atmospheric pollution—the toxic emissions would be reduced by some 70 to 80 percent—and noise pollution would be reduced likewise. Such a power pack could last for fifteen years or so. Maintenance services would have to be developed to repair and maintain them, thus requiring the creation of more skilled jobs. This is completely contrary to the whole ethos of existing automotive design that assumes the desirability of a virtually nonrepairable throwaway product with all the terrible waste of energy and materials that that implies.

3. Airships

In Western Europe the pressure of urbanization and the density of population will mean that transport systems, other than rail and road, will increasingly be sought. There is a growing and understandable public hostility to conventional air traffic systems with the problems of air and noise pollution in the immediate vicinities of airports. These considerations and ones of economy are likely to give rise to a growing interest in airships, especially for cargo. Explosion hazards associated with hydrogen are likely to continue to make that an unsuitable lifting source, and helium is extremely expensive. Docking, loading, and unloading problems are considerable. To release a load of 250 tons would require a release of nearly 9 million cubic feet of helium and cost something in the order of £100,000.

In addition, there is growing concern as to the availability of helium in the future. The present rate of consumption of the resources of crude helium can only be expected to last for a few more decades. Given these problems the plan suggests using a modified version of the vertical and horizontal vectoring power unit used in the Harrier jump-jet to control the loading and unloading position of the airship. This would avoid the costly need to vent some of the helium in the ship before unloading. We suggest that Lucas could make a major contribution to this. It is proposed that direct contact should be made with Dr. Edwin Mowforth and his team at Surrey University, who are working on the problem of a viable airship.

Braking Systems

In Britain public attention has been dramatically focused on the weaknesses of existing braking systems by the Yorkshire Coach disaster, which claimed thirty-two lives in May of this year. The *Sunday Times* of 1 June stated: "Last week's crash might have been avoided if the coach had been equipped with an extra braking device such as an electro-magnetic retarder which is being fitted to an increasing number of coaches in this country." In fact, it would appear that only 10 percent of Britain's 75,000 buses and coaches actually have retarders fitted to them. There is, therefore, clearly a vast market available to Lucas if it adopts an imaginative approach to this problem. It is not suggested that Lucas should simply produce dynamometers; rather what is proposed is that they should analyse the whole nature of braking systems through a wide range of vehicles, including buses, coaches, articulated lorries, underground and overhead trains as used by British Rail. It is proposed that a braking system analysis and development team should be set up to take an overview of this problem.

We propose a combined electro-magnetic eddy current braking system—based on experience gained with dynamometers—coupled directly to a traditional mechanical brake based on a Lucas Girling disc. This could be fitted as a fail-safe auxiliary unit to heavy vehicles, trains, etc. This electro-braking system overcomes the fundamental weakness of normal mechanical brakes, which is that when subjected to long braking periods they overheat and as a result the brake linings tend to temporarily lose their gripping qualities. Such systems also make it possible to store energy that would otherwise be lost during braking; for example, in electric powered vehicles.

Oceanics

We suggest three main purposes for which the ocean bed is likely to be exploited on an increasing scale: the exploration and extraction of oil and natural gas, the collection of mineral-bearing nodules, and submarine agriculture. Lucas Aerospace workers could contribute to these different activities in the following ways:

1. with the use of existing Lucas Aerospace valve technology and ballscrew manufacturing facilities, to provide a complete valve operating and controlling system for North Sea oil work.

2. The generating and actuating systems for the submersible vehicles needed for all three kinds of underwater work. This would require Lucas Aerospace to enter working agreements with submersible manufacturers such as Vickers Oceanics.

3. Telechiric machines

Telechiric means "hands at distance," which would enable workers to carry out underwater operations by remote control. This is preferable to a robotic device that eliminates human improvization completely. The repair work involved in oil rigs clearly requires the kind of intuitive and flexible diagnostic skills to recognize and deal, for instance, with a barnacle on a vital nut, for which no computer can ever be adequately programmed! Telechiric devices have a wide range of applications; for example, in mining and any other work in unsafe or unpleasant conditions.

Our support for such systems is based not only on a concern for safety but also on a desire to develop systems that enhance rather than eliminate human skill. From this point of view the importance of telechiric devices is that they are capable of mimicking in real time the actions of a skilled worker so that when the worker stops the system stops, and the worker is in control all the time. Thus the system does not "absorb" or "objectivize" human knowledge. It merely responds to it. It is therefore possible to link advanced technology with human skill to provide for human-centered equipment rather than equipment that deskills, controls, or even displaces the human being.

Given adequate research and development backing, human-centered systems could be designed for many fields of work. In the case of skilled machining such as turning, it would be possible to design analogic equipment that would enable the worker to "program by doing." As with the telechiric device, the tacit knowledge—the sense of feel for the job—would be retained.

Appendix B:
National and International
Conversion Groups

The United States

Bay State Conversion Project
639 Massachusetts Avenue, Room 316
Cambridge, MA 02139

Bendix Conversion Project
811 East 47th Street
Kansas City, MO 64110

Connecticut Campaign for a U.S.–USSR Nuclear Arms Freeze
R. D. #1, Box 494
Voluntown, CT 06384

Connecticut Economic Conversion Task Force
St. Luke's Parish
Box 3128
Darien, CT 06820

Highlander Research and Education Center
Rte. 3, Box 370
New Market, TN 37820

Mid-Peninsula Conversion Project
222-C View Street
Mountain View, CA 94041

Monsanto Peace Conversion
3211 Silver SE
Albuquerque, NM 87106

National Jobs With Peace
76 Summer Street
Boston, MA 02110

National Nuclear Weapons Freeze Campaign
National Labor Coordinator
303 Massachusetts Avenue NE
Washington, D.C. 20002

Puget Sound Conversion Project
6532 Phinney Avenue
Seattle, WA 98103

SANE
711 G Street, SE
Washington, D.C. 20003

South Shore Conversion Committee
22 Pond Street
Hingham, MA 02043

Unions

International Association of Machinists and Aerospace Workers
1300 Connecticut Avenue, N.W.
Washington, D.C. 20036

United Auto Workers Union
Solidarity House
8000 East Jefferson Street
Detroit, MI 48214

United Electrical, Radio and Machine Workers
1411 K Street N.W., Room 410
Washington, D.C. 20005

International Groups and Unions

Cruise Missile Conversion Project (Litton)
730 Bathurst Street
Toronto, M5S2R4, Canada

Campaign for Nuclear Disarmament
11 Goodwin Street
London N4 3HQ, England

Greater London Conversion Council of the Greater London
    Council Center for International Peacebuilding
South Bank House, Black Prince Road
London SE1 7SJ, England

Greater London Enterprise Board
63–67 Newington Causeway
London SE 6BD, England

Transport and General Workers Union
Transport House
Smith Square
London SW1, England

City of Sheffield Employment Department
Palatine Chambers
22 Pinstone Street
Sheffield S12HN, England

Landskrona Produktion
Box 713
S-261 27 Landskrona, Sweden

Metall–Swedish Metalworkers Union
Tunnelgatan 11
S-10552 Stockholm, Sweden

Projekt Lindholmen AB
Box 8714
402 75 Goteborg, Sweden

Italian Metal Workers Union
Corso Trieste 36
Rome, Italy

Fachberiech Politische Wissenschaft
Institut fur Internationale Politik und Regionalstudien
Freie Universitat Berlin
WE 4, Kiebitzweg 3, 1000 Berlin 33, West Germany

IG Metall
Hauptvorstand
Wilhelm-Leuschnerstrasse 79–85
6000 Frankfurt am Main 1, West Germany

Zentrale wissenschaftliche Einrichtung 'Arbeit und Betrieb'
Universitat Bremen
Universitatsallee
2800 Bremen 33, West Germany

"Aktionsplan Nimwegen"
c/o Industriebond Hauptvorstand
P.O. Box 8107
1005 AC Amsterdam, Holland

Pax Christi
Calabas Straat 60
The Hague, Holland

Bibliography

Adams, Gordon. *The B-1 Bomber: an Analysis of Its Strategic Utility, Cost, Constituency, and Economic Impact.* New York: Council on Economic Priorities, 1976.
————. *The Politics of Defense Contracting: the Iron Triangle.* New Brunswick, N.J.: Transaction Press, 1982.
Anderson, James R. *Bankrupting American Cities: the Tax Burden and Expenditures of the Pentagon by Metropolitan Area.* Lansing, MI: Employment Research Associates, 1982.
Anderson, Marion. *Converting the Work Force: Where the Jobs Would Be.* Lansing, MI: Employment Research Associates, 1980.
————. *The Empty Pork Barrel: Unemployment and the Pentagon Budget.* Lansing, MI: Employment Research Associates, 1982.
————. *The Impact of Military Spending on the Machinists Union.* Lansing, MI: Employment Research Associates, 1979.
————. *The Price of the Pentagon: The Industrial and Commercial Impact of the 1981 Military Budget.* Lansing, MI: Employment Research Associates, 1982.
Armaments Expenditure and Disarmament: Some Consequences for Development. New York: United Nations Trade and Development Report, 1982.
Batson, Wendy, et al. *Shaping Alternatives at Lawrence Livermore Laboratory.* San Francisco: U.C. Nuclear Weapons Labs Conversion Project, 1979.
Bay State Conversion Project. *The Case for Economic Conversion: a Look at Massachusetts.* Watertown, MA, 1979.
Berkowitz, Marvin. *The Conversion of Military-Oriented Research and Development to Civilian Uses.* New York: Praeger, 1970.
Bezdek, Roger H. "The 1980 Economic Impact—Regional and Occupational—of Compensated Shifts in Defense Spending," *Journal of Regional Science* 15:2(1975): 183–98.
Bluestone, Barry, and Bennett Harrison. *The Deindustrialization of America.* New York: Basic Books, 1982.
Bowles, Samuel; David M. Gordon; and Thomas E. Weisskopf. *Beyond the Wasteland: A Democratic Alternative to Economic Decline.* Garden City, NY: Anchor Press, 1983.
California Newsreel. *Planning Work: Resources on Technology and Investment for Labor Education.* San Francisco, 1980.
Choate, Pat and Suan Walter. *America in Ruins: Beyond the Public Works Pork Barrel.* Washington: Council of State Planning Agencies, 1981.

241

Cohn, John and Dan Haifley. *Transition at Lockheed Santa Cruz: a Preliminary Analysis.* Santa Cruz, CA, 1979.

Cooley, Mike. *Architect or Bee.* London, 1980.

———. "Design, Technology, and Production for Social Needs." In Ken Coates, ed., *The Right to Useful Work,* London, 1979, pp. 195–211.

Daniels, Marta. *Jobs, Security and Arms in Connecticut.* Voluntown, CT: 1980.

Defense Dependency and Economic Conversion in California. Hearings before the California Senate Select Committee on Investment Priorities and Objectives, Sacramento, 1978.

DeGrasse, Robert W. Jr., Emerson Street, Alan Bernstein, David McFadden, Randall Schutt, and Natalie Shyras. *Creating Solar Jobs: Options for Military Workers and Communities.* Mountain View, 1978.

———. *Military Expansion, Economic Decline.* New York: M.E. Shapre, Inc., 1983.

Dickson, David. *The Politics of Alternative Technology.* New York: Universe Books, 1975.

Duboff, Richard. "Converting Military Spending to Social Welfare: the Real Obstacles." *The Quarterly Review of Economics and Business* (Spring 1972): 7–22.

Dumas, Lloyd J., ed. *The Political Economy of Arms Reduction: Reversing Economic Decay.* Boulder, CO: Westview Press, 1982.

Edelstein, Michael. *The Economic Impact of Military Spending.* New York: Council on Economic Priorities, 1977.

Elliott, David; Ken Green; and Fred Steward. *Trade Unions, Technology and the Environment.* London: The Open University Press, 1978.

Elliott, David, and Ruth Elliott. *The Control of Technology.* London: Wykeham, 1976.

Fallows, James. *National Defense.* New York: Random House, 1981.

Gansler, Jacques, S. *The Defense Industry.* Cambridge, MA: MIT Press, 1980.

International Association of Machinists and Aerospace Workers. *Let's Rebuild America,* Washington, D.C., 1983.

Kaldor, Mary. *The Baroque Arsenal.* New York: Hill and Wang, 1981.

———. *The Role of Military Technology in Industrial Development.* New York: United Nations, 1980.

Kaufmann, Richard. *The War Profiteers.* Garden City, NY: Anchor Books, 1972.

Lall, B.G. *Prosperity without Guns.* New York: Institute for World Order, 1977.

Leontief, Wassily, and F. Duchin. "Worldwide Economic Implications of a Limitation on Military Spending." New York: New York University, 1980.

Lucas Aerospace Confederation Trade Union Committee. *Lucas Aerospace: Turning Industrial Decline into Expansion.* London, 1979.

Luria, Dan, and Jack Russell. *Rational Reindustrialization: an Economic Development Agenda for Detroit.* Detroit: Widgetripper Press, 1981.

Mack-Forlist, Daniel M., and Arthur Newman. *The Conversion of Shipbuilding from Military to Civilian Markets.* New York: Praeger, 1970.

Melman, Seymour. *Barriers to Conversion in Planned, Market and Developing Economies.* New York: United Nations, 1980.

———. "Beating Swords into Subways," *New York Times Magazine,* 19 November 1978.

———. *Conversion of Industry from Military to Civilian Economy.* New York: Praeger, 1970.

———. *The Defense Economy: Conversion of Industries and Occupations to Civilian Needs.* New York: Praeger, 1970.

————. *The Permanent War Economy.* New York: Simon and Schuster, 1974.

————. *Profits without Production.* New York: Alfred A. Knopf, 1983.

Muller, Ronald E. *Revitalizing America.* New York: Simon and Schuster, 1980.

Musil, Robert K. *The Pentagon in Philadelphia: Economic and Social Effects of Military Spending in Philadelphia, 1968–1977.* Philadelphia: National SANE Education Fund, 1978.

Office of Technology Assessment. *Application of Solar Technology to Today's Energy Needs.* Washington, D.C., 1977.

————. *Energy, the Economy and Mass Transit.* Washington, D.C., 1975.

Palme, Olof, The Palme Independent Commission on International Security and Disarmament. *Common Security: a Program for Disarmament.* Report of the Independent Commission on Disarmament and Security Issues. London: Pan Books, 1982.

Potential Transfer of Industrial Skills from Defense to Nondefense Industry. Sacramento: State of California Department of Labor, 1968.

President's Economic Adjustment Committee. *Twenty Years of Civilian Reuse: Summary of Completed Military Base Economic Adjustment Projects, 1961–1981.* Washington, 1981.

Probstein, Ronald F. "Reconversion and Non-Military Research Opportunities," *Astronautics and Aeronautics* (October, 1969).

Puget Sound Conversion Project. *Economic Conversion in Washington State.* Seattle, 1980.

Ramo, Simon. *America's Technology Slip.* New York: John Wiley and Sons, Inc., 1980.

Rasor, Dina, ed. *More Books, Less Bang: How the Pentagon Buys Ineffective Weapons.* Washington, D.C., 1983.

Rebuilding America. Washington: International Association of Machinists and Aerospace Workers, 1983.

Reuther, Walter P. *Swords into Plowshares: a Proposal to Promote Orderly Conversion from Defense to Civilian Production.* Detroit, United Auto Workers, 1970.

Rittenhouse, Carl. *The Transferability and Retraining of Defense Engineers.* Palo Alto: Stanford Research Institute, 1967.

Russet, Bruce. *What Price Vigilance?* New Haven, CT: Yale University Press, 1970.

Sanaberg, Ake, ed. *Computers Dividing Man and Work: Recent Scandinavian Research on Planning and Computers from a Trade Union Perspective.* Stockholm: Swedish Center for Working Life, 1979.

Sivard, Ruth Leger. *World Military and Social Expenditures.* Leesburg, VA, 1983.

Smith, Dan, ed. *Alternative Work for Military Industries.* London: Richardston Institute, 1977.

————, and Ron Smith. *The Economics of Militarism.* London: Pluto Press, 1983.

Stockholm International Peace Research Institute. *World Armaments and Disarmament, SIPRI Yearbook 1983.* London: Taylor and Francis, Ltd., 1983.

Taylor, Stewart F. *Urban Transportation...Another Alternative: a World-Wide Survey of Light Rail Technology.* Washington, 1975.

Thurow, Lester. "How to Wreck the Economy," *New York Review of Books,* 6 April 1981.

————. *The Zero Sum Society.* New York: Basic Books, 1980.

Ullmann, John E. *Potential Civilian Markets for the Military-Electronics Industry: Strategies for Conversion.* New York: Praeger, 1970.

U.S. Congressional Budget Office. *Economic Conversion: What Should Be the Government's Role?—a Special Study.* Washington, 1980.

U.S. Executive Office of the President, Council on Environmental Quality. *Solar Energy: Progress and Promise.* Washington, D.C., 1978.

Wainwright, Hilary, and Dave Elliott. *The Lucas Plan: A New Trade Unionism in the Making.* London: Allsion and Busby, 1982.

Webre, Philip. *Jobs to People? Planning for Conversion to New Industries.* Washington, D.C.: Exploratory Project for Economic Alternatives, 1979.

Index

About the Contributors

Gordon Adams is Director of the Defense Budget Project of the Center on Budget and Policy Priorities. He is the author of *The Politics of Defense Contracting: The Iron Triangle* (Transition, 1982) and a frequent contributor to *The Nation, The New York Times, The Bulletin of Atomic Scientists,* and *Mother Jones.*

Christopher S. Allen is a research associate at The Center of European Studies, Harvard University, and is coauthor of *Unions and Economic Crisis: Britain, West Germany and Sweden* (Allen and Unwin, 1984).

Gene Carroll is National Labor Coordinator for the National Nuclear Weapons Freeze Campaign. He has worked as an organizer for the Amalgamated Clothing and Textile Workers Union on the J.P. Stevens Campaign and as National Field Coordinator and Disarmament Coordinator for the Coalition for a New Foreign and Military Policy.

Lance Compa has worked for ten years as a staffer for the United Electrical, Radio and Machine Workers Union (UE) and is currently the UE's Washington Representative. He has written extensively on labor topics for *The Nation* and *The Progressive.*

Robert W. DeGrasse, Jr., is the author of *Military Expansion, Economic Decline* (M.E. Sharpe 1982) and is a fellow with the Council on Economic Priorities. He was coordinator of the Mid-Peninsula Conversion Project's 1978 study, *Creating Solar Jobs: Options for Military Workers and Communities.*

Lloyd J. Dumas is Professor of Political Economy and Economics at the University of Texas at Dallas and is editor of *The Political Economy of Arms Reduction* (Westview Press, 1982). He was one of the principal designers of the proposed national legislation, the Defense Economic Adjustment Act.

Kenneth Geiser is Assistant Professor of Urban and Environmental Policy at Tufts University. He is a prominent activist in the environmental move-

255

ment and the movement to curtail the use of toxic substances in the workplace and the community.

David Gold is Director of the Institute on the Military and the Economy. He was formerly Director of Military Research for the Council on Economic Priorities. He is principal author of *Misguided Expenditure* (CEP, 1981) and a frequent contributor to *The New York Times, The Los Angeles Times,* and *The Boston Globe.*

Seymour Melman is Professor of Industrial Engineering at Columbia University. He is the author of *Profits Without Production* (Alfred A. Knopf, 1983) and numerous other works on the economic impact of the arms race. He is Co-Chairman of the National Committee for a Sane Nuclear Policy (SANE) and has been Vice-President of the New York Academy of Sciences.

Clyde Sanger is a Canadian journalist who specializes in international development issues. He has worked on the staff of *The Manchester Guardian* and *The Toronto Globe and Mail* and was Special Assistant to the President of the Canadian International Development Agency. He is the author of *Safe and Sound: Disarmament and Development in the Eighties* (Deneau, 1982), the popular version of the United Nations study on the relationship between disarmament and development for the UN General Assembly 1978–81, from which this chapter was excerpted.

John E. Ullmann is Professor of Management at Hofstra University. He is an industrial engineer and has written widely on industrial and community development, quantitative analysis in business and the interface problems between technology and society. He is also Secretary of SANE and a fellow of the New York Academy of Sciences.

Hilary Wainwright and **Dave Elliott** are the authors of *The Lucas Plan: a New Trade Unionism in the Making* (Allison & Busby, 1982), from which this chapter was excerpted. Wainwright is the Director of the Popular Planning Division of the Department of Industry and Employment, for the Greater London Council. Dave Elliott teaches at the Open University's Technology Faculty and is the author of *The Politics of Nuclear Power* and *The Control of Technology.*

Joel Yudken is Director for Programs at the Mid-Peninsula Conversion Project. A former aerospace engineer who worked in military industry, he has been active in organizing engineers and a variety of conversion efforts in the United States and has lectured and written widely on the problems of economic conversion in both military and civilian industries. He is now creating the National Economic Conversion Clearing House.

About the Editors

Suzanne Gordon is the Director of the International Economic Conversion Conference, and directed the European Labor Tour for Peace in 1983. She is a contributing editor for *Nuclear Times* and the *Boston Review,* an associate of the Center for Investigative Reporting, and an affiliate of Harvard University Center for European Studies. Her books include *Black Mesa: The Angel of Death, Lonely in America,* and *Off-Balance: The Real World of Ballet.* She is presently working on a biography of J. Robert Oppenheimer.

Dave McFadden is Founder and Senior Research Associate of the Mid-Peninsula Conversion Project. He is on the National Executive Committee of SANE, and is presently a Ph.D candidate in U.S.-Soviet relations at the University of California, Berkeley.